The Future of the Welfare State

The Future of the Welfare State

Crisis Myths and Crisis Realities

Francis G. Castles

OXFORD
UNIVERSITY PRESS

OXFORD

UNIVERSITY PRESS

Great Clarendon Street, Oxford OX2 6DP

Oxford University Press is a department of the University of Oxford.
It furthers the University's objective of excellence in research, scholarship,
and education by publishing worldwide in

Oxford New York

Auckland Bangkok Buenos Aires Cape Town Chennai
Dar es Salaam Delhi Hong Kong Istanbul Karachi Kolkata
Kuala Lumpur Madrid Melbourne Mexico City Mumbai Nairobi
São Paulo Shanghai Taipei Tokyo Toronto

Oxford is a registered trade mark of Oxford University Press
in the UK and in certain other countries

Published in the United States
by Oxford University Press Inc., New York

British Library Cataloguing in Publication Data
Data available

Library of Congress Cataloging in Publication Data
Data available

ISBN 0-19-927017-1 (hbk.)
ISBN 0-19-927392-8 (pbk.)

1 3 5 7 9 10 8 6 4 2

Typeset by Newgen Imaging Systems (P) Ltd., Chennai, India
Printed in Great Britain
on acid-free paper by
Biddles Ltd., King's Lynn

To my granddaughters: Hannah, Sophie, and Ellie. For reasons that will become apparent in Chapter 7, I think that there could be social utility—as well, of course, as personal pleasure—in my five children providing me with at least a few more grandchildren in coming years. This is for them also.

Preface and Acknowledgements

This book seeks to bring together, systematize, and update arguments from a series of articles and book chapters I have written in recent years on the broad theme of the future of the welfare state. Whereas the original articles and chapters each focused on somewhat different time periods and different groups of countries, the analysis here is consistently based on an examination of twenty-one OECD countries over the period 1980–98. The idea is to base conclusions about what is likely to happen to the Western welfare state in future on what has been happening to Western welfare states in the recent past. Although something like 70 per cent of what is written here is quite new, it is proper to acknowledge the sources of my borrowings from my own previous work and to thank the respective publishers for permission to use this material. The chapters which follow variously contain passages from the following: Chapter 3 from Castles, Francis G. (2002), 'Developing New Measures of Welfare State Change and Reform', *European Journal of Political Research*, 41: 5, 613–41, published by Blackwell Publishing; Chapter 4 from Castles, Francis G. (2002), 'The European Social Model: Progress Since the Early 1980s', *European Journal of Social Security*, 4: 1, 7–21, published by Intersentia; Chapter 5 from Castles, Francis G. (2001), 'On the Political Economy of Recent Public Sector Development', *Journal of European Social Policy*, 11: 3, 195–211, published by Sage Publications; Chapter 6 from Castles, Francis G. (2001), 'Public Expenditure and Population Ageing: Why Families of Nations are Different'. In Jochen Clasen (ed.), *What Future for Social Security? Debates and Reforms in National and Cross-National Perspective*, published by Kluwer Law International, 143–55; and Chapter 7 from Castles, Francis G. (2003), 'The World Turned Upside Down: Below Replacement Fertility, Changing Preferences and Family-Friendly Public Policy in 21 OECD Countries', *Journal of European Social Policy*, 13: 3, 209–27, published by Sage Publications. The title of this book was also the title of another article of mine, which appeared in the *International Journal of Health Services* published by the Baywood Publishing Company, Inc. in 2002 (32: 2, 255–78), which attempted, for the first time, to bring together the various elements of my thinking about the future of the welfare state. Oddly, my borrowings from this source are more limited than in the case of the previously cited articles. I nevertheless acknowledge the publisher's permission to use this material also.

Apart from these acknowledgements of borrowings from my previous work, I also wish to acknowledge support and assistance from four sources that have made writing this book possible and even at times enjoyable. First, I would like to thank the National Europe Centre at the Australian National University, its Director, Professor Elim Papadakis, and its Administrator, Helen Fairbrother, for providing me with a sabbatical home from home in the five months it took to transform five separate articles into an integrated piece of work. Second, I would like to voice my appreciation to all my colleagues in Social Policy at the University of Edinburgh, who gave me the time and intellectual space to work on the ideas contained in this book. My present colleagues in Edinburgh are without exception the nicest and most supportive bunch of people I have encountered in nearly forty years of professional life. Third, I would like to thank a number of named individuals who helped me in various ways by commenting on drafts or by providing information and data. In particular, I would like to thank Willem Adema, Richard Grant, Richard Parry, Manfred Schmidt, and Duane Swank, all of whom contributed in various ways to making the book or the articles on which it was based better than they otherwise would have been. Finally, I wish to thank my wife Beth, who, as ever, played a major intellectual and emotional role in helping me to bring this project to fruition.

Contents

List of Tables

On Crises, Myths, and Measurement

This book seeks to discern the likely path of future welfare state development in Western nations through an evaluation of a series of accounts of that development over recent years. Influential accounts tell us variously that the entire welfare state project is endangered by global economic trends and that the demands of an ageing population make it impossible to finance the welfare needs of the next generation. They tell us also that policy-makers seeking to accommodate such forces have embarked on a major agenda of welfare state reform, but that the inspiration for this agenda of change is no longer to be found in the programmatic conflicts of Left and Right but rather in the claims and counterclaims of the protagonists of expenditure retrenchment and of a 'new politics of the welfare state'. Accounts are also beginning to come in of another threat to the viability of contemporary societies and the social policy foundations on which they rest: the threat of rapid calamitous population decline brought about rapidly falling fertility rates in many advanced nations. Our aim is to assess the accuracy of these accounts and to speculate on how far the forces they identify are likely to shape the trajectory of social policy development in coming decades. In this introductory chapter, we locate the themes, outline the approach, and identify the topics that will guide our subsequent analysis.

Themes

The three themes, which inform our analysis throughout, are crisis, myth, and measurement. The themes are inextricably linked. For what is now more than three decades—since the time that the First Oil Shock spelled the end of an era of taken-for-granted, continuous economic growth—influential commentators have been arguing that the welfare state project is in dire trouble. As we shall see, the initial crisis warnings of the 1970s and 1980s were falsified by events, their mythical status revealed by measuring the actual experience of social policy development against the predictions of those forecasting doom. The question we pose here is whether the same will prove true today: whether supposed crises of globalization and demographic transformation will lead to social policy disaster or whether they too will turn out to be mythical in character. We begin our discussion with the earlier crisis accounts of the 1970s and 1980s, which have many affinities with the threats we are told we are currently confronting (for a review of this earlier literature, see Moran 1988).

The initial articulation of the crisis theme was in terms of 'democratic over-load' and 'fiscal crisis of the state', the first emanating from commentators seen as being on the Right (see Crozier et al. 1975; Brittan 1977), the second from scholars clearly identified as being on the Left (see O'Connor 1973; Gough 1979; Offe 1984). Although political views might differ, the essential diagnosis does not. The state was in crisis because people demanded more of it than it could possibly deliver in public expenditure terms and, since the mechanisms underlying such demands were the very institutions that underpinned the system of popular representation, any fundamental reform implied the destruction of the modern democratic state. The state—and, obviously, the welfare state, since the source of new expenditure demands was predominantly in the social policy arena—was in crisis because, in the rhetoric of the times, it involved an irreconcilable contradiction: democratic capitalism could not function because democracy created demands that the capitalist mechanism could not fulfil.

This 1970s diagnosis of a public economy out of control was conjoined in the 1980s by an economic analysis, which in less apocalyptic, but no less crisis-ridden tones pointed to the enormous difficulties confronting 'big government' in an era of economic stagnation (see contributions to Hood and Wright 1981). Very early on in the new decade, the Organization for Economic Cooperation and Development (OECD) published a book entitled *The Welfare State in Crisis* (OECD 1981), reporting a conference on 'Social Policies in the 1980s' attended by leading welfare state scholars and various representatives of business, labour, and government. Recurrent themes treated in the volume included the inevitable impact of reduced economic growth rates on the expansion of social security benefits, the potential for high rates of unemployment to create a financial crisis in the social security system, the declining capacity of the state to deliver full employment, and the emergence of a tax backlash which threatened the viability of existing, much less expanded, welfare state funding. The tone of the conference debate was, some times, pessimistic in the extreme, with the President of one session noting 'the strong political pressures on most governments to ease taxes' and 'a general agreement that a limit has been reached' (OECD 1981:

70). In 1985, the OECD returned to the same themes, arguing that 'the exi-
gencies of stagflation demanded the restraint of public expenditure growth
and the reduction of government deficits' and suggesting that '(a)s far as the
Welfare State and its material requirements were concerned what might have
been an evolutionary social process began to assume aspects of an immediate
budgetary crisis' (OECD 1985: 9).

The economic problems confronting further welfare state development
have been a constant theme of informed debate on the future of the welfare
state since the early 1980s, although the notion of immediate and generalized budgetary crisis has receded. Crisis predictions premised on the insati-
ability of democratic demand began to appear exaggerated in the face of
evidence of a general slowdown in OECD public expenditure growth during
the course of the 1980s (for data on the growth of total social expenditure
and total outlays of government from 1960 onwards, see Tables 2.1 and 2.2 in
Chapter 2). Moreover, accounts stressing the peculiar vulnerability of big
welfare states to economic slowdown and unemployment seemed to be con-
tradicted by the experience of the social democratic corporatist states of
Western Europe, including Austria, Finland, Norway, and Sweden, which,
throughout the 1980s, succeeded in combining welfare state expansion with
full employment and reasonable rates of economic growth (see Goldthorpe
1984; Lindberg and Maier 1985). However, just as these older anxieties
were declining in intensity, new ones were emerging, seemingly more
intractable than those they replaced, given that the new sources of threat
were identified as falling wholly outside the sphere of control of domestic
political actors, namely in changes taking place within the international
economy and in the age structure of the population.

Accounts based on changes occurring in the international economy are part
of what is now a huge literature on the political implications and policy
impacts of globalization (for an introduction, see Ohmae 1991; Hirst and
Thompson 1996; Keohane and Milner 1996; Strange 1996). Globalization has
been seen as a major threat to the continued viability of a generous welfare
state for at least two reasons. First, it has been argued that a high level of exposure to international trade creates serious pressures for cutting social expenditure and taxes. Governments, employers, and even trade unions wishing to
see exports compete in world markets must contemplate reducing the expenditures and taxes that translate into higher wage costs and hence higher export
prices (see Pfaller, Gough, and Therborn 1991; Drache 1996). Second, the huge
increase in international capital flows characterizing the transformation of
the international economy since the early 1980s has produced forceful incen-
tives for 'social dumping', a process by which governments terrified of capital

flight by mobile asset holders do everything in their power to cut back imposts supposedly undermining business confidence (see Webb 1995; Aspinwall 1996; Jessop 1996). At their most extreme, both variants of globalization are seen as producing a 'race to the bottom' in which the need to compete in world markets and to attract foreign capital leads to a never-ending series of welfare cutbacks culminating in a minimalist welfare state. Concerns about 'social dumping' within the European Union—with institutions consciously designed to enhance trade and the free flow of capital—imply a similar logic, with the lower 'social wage' costs of some member states seen as a force making for an ultimate downward convergence in standards of social provision (see Leibfried and Pierson 1995: 70–1; Scharpf 1998). In all these accounts, the state is seen as having, to varying degrees, lost its policy-making autonomy. Diverse policy choices in different nations become irrelevant, being overruled by economic forces beyond the control of individual nation-states (see Mishra 1999). The implication is that welfare states become more alike and more miserly as they comply with a set of global imperatives, the constraining impact of which was neatly summed up in Margaret Thatcher's much repeated response to her critics that 'There is no alternative!'

Interestingly, at much the same time that one set of crisis predictions were suggesting that the future of the welfare state involved major downsizing, there were others predicting just the opposite: that there were forces at work making it inevitable that social expenditure would increase very markedly in coming years. The factor making for such an increase in spending was population ageing, described by the World Bank (1994) as having created an 'old-age crisis' and identified by the OECD (1996a) as 'a critical policy challenge' for the welfare state. The logic of the argument is transparent. The two costliest programmes of the welfare state are old-age cash benefits and public health services, the first being the exclusive preserve of those above pensionable age and the second utilized disproportionately by the elderly. In most OECD nations, these programmes amount to around two-thirds of total social spending. At the same time, demographic projections make it quite clear that the proportion of the population aged sixty-five and over is set to increase significantly, by one estimate relied on by the OECD in the latter half of the 1990s from 13.9 per cent of the OECD's population in the year 2000 to 22.5 per cent in the year 2030 (Bos et al. 1994), an increase of more than 60 per cent in just three decades. The implication appears obvious enough: population ageing will give rise to huge and utterly predictable rises in social spending unless national governments can find ways of cutting back existing entitlements.

In fact, in Chapter 6, we shall question both the appropriateness of attributing these expected expenditure increases to population ageing as such and the validity of any generalized notion of an 'old-age crisis'. However, there is little doubt that these are issues with the potential to induce political crises of some magnitude. In 1995, a French conservative government fell as a direct consequence of labour unrest and street protest directed against proposals to curtail pension rights. At the time of writing this chapter in the late spring of 2003, there are again mass demonstrations in France, but also in Austria and Sweden, against government proposals to raise retirement ages or otherwise reduce the eligibility and generosity of existing age pension systems.

The crisis accounts we have so far identified focus directly on the threat posed to the welfare state by changes in its external environment. The final attribution of crisis that we examine is less directly focused on threats to the welfare state, but rather suggests a broad spectrum of adverse social and economic effects stemming from a spectacular decline in advanced country fertility rates over recent decades. Implications for the welfare state are not hard to find, most obviously in a massive impetus to population ageing over the next century, but pale into relative insignificance compared with other potential outcomes, including population implosion, dramatic economic decline, large-scale migration, and changes in the relative geopolitical standing of major players in the international community. Simply to indicate the scale of what is being suggested, it has been estimated that, if current trends remain in place over the next century, both Germany and Japan will have populations—and hence economies—only about a quarter of the size they are today (see McDonald 2000). For countries like Austria, Italy, and Spain, the prognosis is still more extreme. However, if implications for the welfare state are a minor refrain of the literature on below-replacement fertility, an emergent strand in the current debate is the extent to which appropriate welfare state programmes can limit the extent of fertility decline or reverse it where it has already taken place. Here our theme is not so much the crisis of the welfare state, but rather the welfare state's potential to avert a wider societal crisis.

The subtitle of this book distinguishes between 'crisis myths' and 'crisis realities' and separating the two is the purpose of the analysis in this book. We have already noted that the political and economic crises of the 1970s and early 1980s turned out to be much exaggerated, but commentators of the time, speculating on the future development of the welfare state and believing these influential accounts, could scarcely avoid the kind of pessimism imbuing *The Welfare State in Crisis*. The same is true today. If we believe that national policy-makers have no alternative but to embark on a 'race to the bottom' in social spending and that, at the same time, there are ineluctable pressures, hugely, to increase spending on the aged, it would appear that the modern welfare state is caught between a rock and a hard place. Potential scenarios are many and none of them very pretty. A residual welfare state for all but the elderly is one possibility, but that is an invitation to a bitterness about issues of 'intergenerational equity' that is already beginning to be talked about in some countries (see Thomson 1994; Walker 1996; Esping-Andersen and Sarasa 2002 and, for a possible way of defusing generational conflicts about pensions spending, Myles 2002). Another is that governments will seek to make the aged share equally in the pain of swingeing welfare cutbacks, but, as noted above, that appears to be a recipe for large-scale political dissent.

Faced with such alternatives, a further possibility is that governments will do as little as they feel they can get away with, a scenario which some would argue has been characteristic of several of the major continental European welfare states in the 1990s and the early years of the twenty-first century (see Scharpf 2000). In the short term—say the length of a parliament or perhaps two—that may work in the sense of minimizing political conflict, but, if the 'race to the bottom' argument is to be believed, it spells eventual economic disaster, for the message of this account is simply that countries which are unable to reform will be unable to compete. The choice that appears to confront us is between social welfare squalor, political instability, and economic decay.

The question then is whether we should believe accounts that define the future of the welfare state as being 'poor, nasty, brutish, and short'. Previous reports of the demise of the welfare state were much exaggerated and so too may these. Certainly, in terms of the way they are structured and argued, the crisis predictions of the 1990s seem to have much in common with those which preceded them. Their potentially 'mythic' status is underlined by at least three characteristics. First, the predictions are, in a sense, larger than life. A crisis prediction effectively claims that a single factor is so hugely significant that it will overwhelm all contrary tendencies: that the need to compete in world markets will trump democratic demands for social policy spending or that population ageing will totally transform the balance between fiscal parsimony and public spending. A priori, such claims seem improbable—not to mention bad social science—since they implicitly deny the otherwise taken-for-granted complexity of the policy context of advanced, democratic, capitalist societies.

Second, the predictions tend to be invariant, which is to say that the coming crisis is supposed to affect all countries irrespective of their economic, social, and political circumstances and irrespective of their prior social policy development. This too seems highly improbable. Adherents of globalization theory frequently suggest that large-scale welfare retrenchment is likely to be a more or less universal outcome of the greater integration of the world economy, but, in reality, some countries are very much more exposed to the international economy than others and some countries start out with far smaller welfare states than others. Some countries do not need to race to the bottom because they are already there and others do not have the same stimulus to commence such a race in the first instance. Obviously, similar considerations apply to population ageing and the burden of aged spending. As we shall discover in Chapter 6, the advanced countries of the OECD have very different age structures, and have pension systems that differ hugely in their levels of generosity. Some of these countries may, indeed, be facing a crisis in respect of age spending, but it seems extremely unlikely that all of these countries face problems of similar dimensions.

Finally, all these crisis accounts of threats to the viability of the welfare state have in common a mismatch between their supposedly universal applicability and the extreme narrowness of the empirical evidence on which they rely. The issue here is not one of whether the factors identified as threats are real. They are. Public expenditure was growing rapidly in most Western nations in the 1970s and the growth of unemployment and slower economic growth were dilemmas for most of these countries in the 1980s. It is also undoubtedly true that there have been a marked increase in international capital flows from the 1980s onwards and that the demographic structure of Western societies is rapidly changing. Rather, the problem is that virtually all of these accounts tend to extrapolate from societal trends to their implica tions for the welfare state without providing sufficient evidence that the adverse consequences for social policy development they identify are actually taking place in the universe of cases or countries to which they refer. Almost invariably, the evidence that is provided is anecdotal rather than systematic in kind, using instances from one or more countries to demonstrate an argument, which, it is claimed, applies to all. Such accounts are necessarily vulnerable to reality checks of the kind provided by the relative economic success of the social democratic corporatist nations in the 1980s, which made it that much more difficult to persist in the belief that social progress and economic performance were necessarily in conflict.

So ultimately, what distinguishes crisis myth from crisis reality is the quality of the evidence adduced in support of a given account. That evidence is now beginning to emerge, with neither the 'race to the bottom' predicted by the globophobes nor the expenditure blowout predicted by the gerontophobes apparently taking place on anything like the scale assumed by the crisis scenarios. Continued national diversity resting on substantial national autonomy and, in many countries, a real capacity to effect needed reforms, were the keynote findings of surveys of the state of the welfare state at the turn of the twentieth century (see Kuhnle 2000; Bruno, Palier, and Sykes 2001;

Leibfried 2001). Similarly, recent quantitative research has found little support for the notion that social spending, total public expenditure, or the total revenues of government are decisively influenced by either levels of international trade or the extent of international capital movements (see Garrett 1998; Huber and Stephens 2001; Iversen 2001; Swank 2002).

The assessment of evidence highlights issues of measurement. In order to assess the claims made by crisis accounts, we require some kind of a measuring rod that we can use to identify how well the claims stand up in individual cases. Although there is considerable debate amongst social policy scholars about the most appropriate way of measuring the essential characteristics of the modern welfare state and of what it means to say that there has been welfare state retrenchment (see Green-Pedersen 2003), virtually all quantitative studies and much of the qualitative research on welfare reform use social expenditure as their measuring rod. The reason is obvious. Crisis accounts invariably state their implications in expenditure terms even if they sometimes spell out other implications as well. The supposed evidence for democratic overload and a fiscal crisis of the state in the 1970s was precisely a rapidity of expenditure growth that betokened a public economy out of control. Stripped down to basics, the crisis diagnosis of the 1980s was simply that big social expenditure meant poor economic performance. Expenditure is no less salient in current crisis predictions. The whole notion of a 'race to the bottom' is premised on dog-eat-dog cuts in expenditure and taxation. Population ageing is a concern for national governments because it supposedly provides a powerful engine for expenditure growth. Whether social expenditure is ultimately the most appropriate measure of a nation's welfare effort or commitment, it is unquestionably an appropriate measure of the strongest claims of the crisis accounts we are examining here.

It is certainly possible to 'rescue' crisis predictions falsified by comparative evidence of expenditure trends, but only at the cost of admitting that the factors supposedly leading to crisis are less compelling than originally claimed. Perhaps the reason that exposure to the international economy does not always produce expenditure cuts is because it creates new social policy needs like greater unemployment, but, if that is so, it means that globalization is only one among a number of forces shaping the trajectory of public expenditure development and that the 'race to the bottom' may be postponed indefinitely because the state continues to have important welfare responsibilities. Similarly, population ageing may not lead to substantially higher expenditure on the aged if it serves as a stimulus to pension reform, but, even if that is what happens in only a few instances, it highlights the fact that the source of crisis is not population ageing as such, but rather the reform capacity of individual states.

Although we are strongly committed to the view that the crisis predictions we discuss here stand or fall on the truth of their expenditure claims, we have made efforts to use social expenditure measures more creatively than in previous studies. The possibility of doing so is a function of the availability since 1996 of the OECD Social Expenditure Database, otherwise known as SOCX, which provides data on the social expenditure of all OECD member countries from 1980 to 1998 disaggregated by programme type (see OECD 1996*b* and subsequent CD-ROMs). This database permits us to devise a variety of new measures of the extent, structure, and trajectory of welfare state change and reform over the past two decades, and hence new ways of assessing the impact of external factors—globalization and population ageing included—on the dynamics of contemporary welfare state development. We have already argued that measurement is a prerequisite for distinguishing crisis myth from crisis reality. We further argue that new forms of measurement offer the potential for a more nuanced account of likely future social policy development.

Approach

The approach employed throughout this analysis is, perhaps, best described as comparative hypothesis testing. The crisis accounts with which we are concerned make more or less sophisticated and more or less explicit predictions concerning the likely future trajectory of social spending. Different variants of globalization theory argue variously that all advanced welfare states will experience a 'race to the bottom', that there will be strong pressures for downward convergence in social spending or that welfare states will experience pressures for expenditure retrenchment in proportion to their exposure to the international economy. Commentators focussing on the impact of a changing age structure either assume that upward pressure on expenditure will be experienced quite generally across the Western world or that such pressure will be experienced in proportion to change in each individual country's demographic profile. Irrespective of the nature of what is being claimed, the only sensible procedure for assessing the validity of a given account is to match its predictions to the experience of the countries about which those predictions are made.

Indeed, one might assume that hypothesis testing of this kind would normally be a condition of articulating a theoretical account in the first instance. Why, one might ask, would one want to offer an account that might be readily falsified by what is already known—or readily knowable—about the cases under examination? In reality, however, the social sciences are replete with accounts for which little or no prior testing has taken place. There are, at least, three closely related reasons why this is so. First is the very much higher intellectual status of theory generation than of theory testing in the social sciences. A new way of looking at the world is generally seen as a much greater contribution to knowledge than is a demonstration of the appropriateness or otherwise of an existing theory. Second is the fact that there is frequently a clear division of labour between those who generate theory and those who test it, so that theory generation, sometimes amounting to little more than speculation, is often seen as a quite legitimate scholarly activity. Finally, the social sciences systematically under-invest in measurement and hypothesis testing. Only too often, quite limited evidence is seen as providing sufficient evidence to demonstrate a case. Showing that there are politically inspired pressures to cut certain social programmes in just a few countries may be taken as evidence confirming a 'race to the bottom' in all countries. Likewise, the rapidity of the growth of pension expenditure in just a few countries may be taken as evidence of age-related pressures making themselves felt across the board.

This book starts from the premise that theory generation and theory testing are intellectually equivalent activities, both essential to furthering social science understanding and equally worthy of investment in time and effort. Indeed, given the plethora of theories offered to explain the dynamic of postwar social expenditure development—and certainly not just crisis theories, but theories relating to an almost infinite range of aspects of economic, social, and political causation (see Castles 1998)—it is, at least, arguable that theory testing has the immediately prior claim as the activity most likely to generate some clarity in an otherwise hopelessly confusing and contested field. Certainly, as we shall show, where extremely simplistic accounts of the likely consequences of change in the international economy and demographic structure are widely believed, demystification by measurement has an important contribution to make in terms of clearing the intellectual undergrowth obscuring our view of the likely future of social policy development.

The question is whether an approach focused on measurement and hypothesis testing can do more: whether it can provide us with the elements required to fashion a convincing account of the likely future trajectory of welfare state development? Our claim is that it can do this in two ways. The first way is essentially descriptive. Our method of investigating the claims of recent crisis accounts of the welfare state is to develop measures of welfare spending that allow us to paint a more detailed picture of patterns of recent social policy expenditure than has hitherto been available in the literature.

Using the OECD's disaggregated social expenditure database and other data from OECD sources, we can map not only what has been happening to social spending in total, which has been the focus of most previous quantitative treatments of social expenditure, but also how far the spending priorities of welfare states have changed over time and how far social expenditure has accommodated to changing patterns of need. These kinds of measures not only help us to assess the response of the welfare state to external forces such as globalization and population ageing, but also permit us to locate trends and tendencies in welfare state spending that would otherwise not be readily apparent.

The second way that comparative hypothesis testing can take us forward is explanatory. The process of matching up crisis predictions with the experience of the countries about which those predictions are made is not just a matter of locating a simple correspondence between factors signifying the presence of crisis threats on the one hand and expenditure trends on the other, but rather consists of identifying the impact these factors have in the context of a compelling model of social expenditure causation. Once we assume that expenditure development is a multi-causal phenomenon, we cannot simply reject hypotheses because they do not seem obviously to account for everything that is going on. Nor can we accept them simply because an initial glance at the evidence suggests a development broadly in line with the hypothesis under investigation. Our conviction that a hypothesis is supported or rejected by the evidence is a function of whether it has a measurable impact on outcomes in the context of a model that reasonably accounts for the phenomenon in question. Thus, in order to test hypotheses concerning the potential impacts of globalization and demographic structure on social expenditure, we have to generate a model which can reasonably comprehensively account for cross-national differences in expenditure change in the period under investigation. Similarly, to establish whether particular social policy measures influence the trend of fertility change, we need to provide a fuller account of the factors shaping fertility choices in contemporary societies. It is, of course, here—in bringing together the elements making up these accounts—that theory comes back in. However, this does not necessarily mean providing a wholly novel account of what is taking place, but more usually involves using the same hypothesis testing approach in order to establish which of a number of hypotheses most plausibly accounts for observed cross-national variation. A more nuanced description resting on sophisticated measurement and a hypothesis testing strategy focused on elaborating the determinants of key social processes together have the potential to provide us with substantial knowledge relevant to the likely future course of social policy development.

A further symptom of the cavalier way in which the demands of accurate measurement are treated in the social sciences, even by those whose commitment to comparative theory testing is greatest, is the failure of many recent quantitative studies of the determinants of social expenditure to adopt an appropriate sample frame for their analysis. The preferred research design of most of these studies has been pooled time-series analysis—which multiplies cases by counting each country in a given year as a separate instance—and the preferred time period for the analysis has the thirty or so year period commencing in the mid-1960s and terminating in the mid-1990s. The technical attraction of this approach is its apparent ability to generate more cases than a simple cross-sectional design focusing on countries at a given time-point, thus permitting the use of more independent variables in the analysis than would otherwise be possible. Its substantive attraction is that it permits contrasts to be drawn not merely between different countries, but also between time periods in which the phenomenon under investigation is more or less salient.

Despite these attractions, pooled time-series techniques have been criticized on methodological grounds because they violate the key assumption that the cases under investigation are separate from one another (Stimson 1985; Beck and Katz 1995). Rather than increasing the number of cases under investigation, it can be argued that all the technique really does is proliferate observations of those cases (see Kittel 1999). A more practical objection is that the use of pooled time-series methods has actually tended to restrict the range of countries used in social expenditure research. This is because we do not have all the data required to construct complete time series for all the countries that interest us and so have to exclude those countries for which data are incomplete. This is a major problem because the logic of comparative analysis suggests very strongly that we should be seeking to maximize the number of relevant cases under investigation, with unwarranted exclusions on any scale likely to produce biased findings of a kind essentially similar to those resulting from the use of anecdotal evidence. If our theories concern the likely trajectory of expenditure development in advanced welfare states, clearly we should be looking at the experience of the widest possible range of countries that can be classified in this fashion, lest the cases omitted are precisely those which demonstrate that the evidence does not fit.

The countries of Southern Europe have been systematically excluded from time-series analyses of the determinants of social expenditure because of missing data on their trajectories of social policy expansion in the 1960s and 1970s. Because New Zealand and Switzerland did not measure public expenditure in ways fully comparable with other OECD countries prior to the 1980s, they too are generally excluded. For reasons not wholly apparent, the Irish case is also frequently omitted. Yet, for an analysis of the impact of recent changes in the international economy and demographic structure on the trajectory of social expenditure development, this simply will not do. Southern Europe is the region where population ageing (see Table 6.1) and the growth of old-age cash benefits (see Table 6.2) has been most dramatic in the period since 1980, and is, not coincidentally, the region in which fertility decline has been most pronounced (see Table 7.1). New Zealand is a case relevant to arguments both about population ageing and welfare state retrenchment, with generosity to the aged unparalleled elsewhere in the OECD in the early 1980s (see Table 6.2) and experiencing one of the most strenuous attempts to reshape and downsize the socially protective state in the years thereafter (see Castles, Gerritsen, and Vowles 1996). Switzerland is the OECD country that has experienced the most rapid social expenditure growth since 1980 (see Table 2.1). Ireland is one of the three most internationally exposed economies in the OECD, and the OECD country in which, arguably, such exposure has increased most dramatically in recent decades (see Table 5.1). In other words, the cases excluded in recent time-series analyses are precisely those which might be expected on a priori grounds to be amongst those with the greatest theoretical and empirical relevance to the crisis accounts which we seek to interrogate.

Methodological and practical objections to a pooled time-series approach therefore combine to make us prefer a much simpler cross-sectional research design for this study. Our approach is to concentrate our attention on what has happened to the welfare state in the years from 1980 onwards and to examine the experience of as many advanced welfare states as possible. We are fortunate that the OECD Social Expenditure Database provides disaggregated data on social expenditure trends for the years 1980–98 inclusive. We would, of course, have preferred it if our analysis could have been for the full two decades period terminating in 2000, so that we could have been in a position to reflect on the nature of the welfare state at the turn of the millennium, but, sadly, the OECD does not promise publication of such data until 2004 at the latest. We are also fortunate that the Social Expenditure Database includes information for some twenty-four countries for the entire period 1980–98. Although we omit Iceland and Luxembourg on grounds of their small size, and Turkey on the ground that it cannot properly be designated as an advanced welfare state, that still leaves us with twenty-one countries, including all of Southern Europe as well as Ireland, New Zealand, and Switzerland. We would argue that extrapolating from the experience of the recent and relevant past rather than a period of time stretching back to the 1960s makes it that much more likely that the trends we locate will provide an accurate guide to the course of future welfare state development. We would further argue that testing hypotheses in a universe of cases virtually coterminous with the category of advanced welfare states provides grounds for some confidence that trends identified in our analysis are based on a foundation more solid than anecdote alone.

Topics

We conclude this introductory chapter with an outline of the topics treated in the subsequent chapters. In general, the progression is from description to explanation, with earlier chapters seeking to identify the extent and character of the change taking place since 1980 and later ones developing models capable of accounting for that change. With the single exception of Chapter 7, the focus is firmly on what has been happening to social expenditure in the OECD region during this period. Chapter 7 partially turns things around. Because, over the long term, declining fertility really does appear to have some potential to threaten the existing fabric of society in many countries, we look at the factors driving the decline in birth rates across the OECD, with a particular emphasis on the possible role of social policy as a factor with the potential to serve as a brake on that process.

In respect of the majority of chapters focusing on social expenditure trends, an important preliminary point to recognize is that spending is not the be-all and end-all of the welfare state. Social expenditure is deployed by governments to address problems that they and their citizens confront. Even if expenditure remains stationary or rises slightly—and that is the story these chapters tell—this need not mean that the welfare state is getting better at its job of protecting the weak and the helpless in society. That depends on whether social problems are growing or declining. In some of the chapters that follow, we do attempt to take some account of the ratio of spending to social need, but that is not the major emphasis or rationale in what follows. As we have already pointed out, our focus is on spending, because spending has been the primary focus of the literature forecasting the demise of the welfare state in its present form.

We begin in Chapter 2 by asking whether the past two decades of social expenditure development have witnessed *A Race to the Bottom?* Because, in this instance at least, the relevant crisis account is unequivocal in its predictions of a decline in welfare spending and a deterioration in welfare standards, we are in a position to marry a description of aggregate social expenditure trends over the past two decades with a strong test of an important hypothesis concerning the impact of the international economy on the modern welfare state. In Chapter 2, we examine a series of measures of spending, including total social and public expenditure as percentages of GDP, social expenditure as a percentage of total public expenditure, the ratio of social expenditure to need or 'welfare state generosity', and expenditure measured in real money terms. Looking at the experience of the twenty-one OECD nations featuring in this analysis, our conclusion is that there has been no 'race to the bottom' according to any of these criteria and that, while there are real signs of a slowdown in expenditure growth compared with a previous era of welfare state expansion, there are equally no signs of a consistent trend to welfare retrenchment or diminishing welfare standards.

The conclusion that, in aggregate expenditure terms, there has been relatively little change in recent decades sits somewhat uneasily with the notion that this has been a period in which the welfare state has been in flux. Because that is so, we set out in Chapter 3 to look at whether the change that has been occurring has been in *The Structure of Social Provision*, rather than in its extent. Arguably, aggregate expenditure is too crude a measure to capture what has been happening to modern welfare states in recent times, with downward pressures on social expenditure possibly offset by new demands for government intervention and spending. Chapter 3 shows how it is possible to use the disaggregated social spending data provided by the OECD Social Expenditure Database to devise a whole series of new measures, variously tapping the degree to which welfare states have undergone structural change, have downsized existing programmes, and have altered their spending priorities. Although on each of these measures it is possible to identify a small minority of countries that have undergone a real transformation during the period under examination here, the most significant overall conclusion again concerns the relative absence of significant change. Over nearly two decades, in which welfare state crisis has been the leitmotif of informed social commentary, and welfare state reform an ostensibly major concern, many Western governments, welfare state structures, and priorities, at least in so far as these may be revealed by spending patterns, have remained much as they were in the early 1980s.

Having established that the quantum of change occurring in these decades has been less than is often suggested, Chapter 4 examines whether the change that has taken place has made welfare states more or less similar in character and, in particular, whether it has led to *A European Welfare State Convergence?* This is a notion implicit in the strong vein of scholarship that suggests that recent decades have seen the emergence of a distinctive

'European social model' quite different from that of other Western welfare states. One variant of this argument amounts to a regionally specific version of the 'race to the bottom' story, identifying the progressive removal of barriers to the free movement of goods, services, and capital occurring under the auspices of the European Union as precisely the kind of globalizing development likely to lead to a downward convergence in social expenditure.

Chapter 4 seeks to test this hypothesis by assessing the extent of clustering and convergence amongst different groupings of countries both in Europe and the wider OECD area. The analysis shows that aggregate expenditure patterns have become noticeably more similar without any decline in average spending levels. The picture, however, is more mixed when expenditure is adjusted to take account of need. We also look at spending on the two biggest programmes of the welfare state—public health and age pensions—and note that, while patterns of health spending are highly convergent, patterns of pension spending in Europe are, if anything, divergent. Turning to the structure of social provision, the analysis further shows that neither the countries of the OECD as a whole, nor those of Europe, were any more similar in their spending priorities at the end of the period than they had been at the beginning. Seeking to assess the evidence for a 'European social model', we note the emergence of a quite distinct pattern of aggregate spending amongst the countries of Northern Europe, but also the continuity of prior 'family of nations' patterns based on commonalities of history, language, and culture amongst the countries of Scandinavia, continental Western Europe, Southern Europe, and the English-speaking world.

Low average degrees of expenditure change and an uneven picture of expenditure convergence are sufficient to dismiss the more spectacular crisis predictions of globalization theory, but not the more modest—and far more sensible—argument that globalization is one of a number of factors likely to have influenced expenditure development in recent years. To address this argument, it is necessary to develop models accounting for cross-national variation in the various measures of social expenditure elaborated in this book. This is the task of Chapter 5 on *Explaining Expenditure Outcomes*. In this chapter, we look at two aspects of exposure to the international economy—trade and foreign investment flows—and ask whether either has impacted on expenditure patterns, when controlling for other factors widely theorized as influencing the trajectory of welfare state development over recent years. These factors include programme maturation (i.e. the notion that programmes grow faster in their early years than when fully developed), economic growth, deindustrialization, unemployment, and a variety of political factors including corporatism, institutional veto-points, and the short- and long-term impact of parties. The role of political parties is of special interest because it goes straight to the heart of an active scholarly debate on whether the traditional partisan politics of expenditure growth has been replaced by a 'new politics of the welfare state', in which the main force buttressing existing expenditure programmes against retrenchment initiatives is the constituency of support constituted by the clientele of such programmes.

Chapter 5 produces strong evidence for the influence of a range of factors in determining expenditure growth, including, most prominently, the negative impact of programme maturation and economic growth and, to a somewhat lesser degree, the positive influence of deindustrialization and the long-term, ideological legacy of post-war Left incumbency. These findings cast serious doubts on the proposition that, in recent decades, we have been witnessing the birth of a new kind of politics of the welfare state. Although aspects of the international economy are negatively correlated with aggregate expenditure change in an initial bivariate analysis, these relationships become wholly insignificant in a fuller multivariate modelling, which reveals a linkage between programme maturation and the prior openness of the economy to international trade. The only evidence of a significant globalization effect to emerge anywhere in the analysis is an apparent relationship between the growth of foreign direct investment and cutbacks in existing programme spending. However, this is an effect that proves not to be statistically robust. Thus, the supposed threat of globalization is revealed as a 'paper tiger'. It influences neither aggregate spending nor programme priorities and, as shown by further modelling in Chapter 6, its apparent effect on welfare state downsizing disappears once we take account of the effects of cross-national differentials in pension generosity.

Up to and including Chapter 5, this book is largely about the supposed threat to the continued health of the welfare state emanating from the international economy. In Chapters 6 and 7, the focus changes to supposed demographic threats to the financial viability of welfare state funding and to the wider economic, social, and political structures of modern societies. In Chapter 6, *Population Ageing and the Public Purse*, we deal with the question of how an increasingly elderly population is likely to impact on social spending. The supposed crisis resulting from this aspect of demographic change is that it will lead to a substantial increase in aggregate spending, with particular pressure on programmes such as pensions, services to the elderly, and public health. Our analysis is not concerned to contest the time-series implications of this argument, that, assuming a given level of programme generosity, increases in the number or coverage of the aged population will produce a corresponding increase in expenditure, although we do note that this generalization depends crucially on a variety of economic assumptions that may or may not prove to be correct. Rather, our purpose is to assess the extent to which cross-national differences in the proportion of the population over the age of sixty-four have made for differences in national trajectories of social expenditure over the period from 1980 to 1998.

The answer, as previously in the case of globalization, is almost not at all, with, once again, the only discernable impact being on the extent of existing programme cutbacks, although here the effect has been a restraining one, limiting the extent of expenditure downsizing. Our analysis accounts for this seemingly counter-intuitive finding by showing that the major source of expenditure variation on programmes for the elderly is not variation in the age structure of the population as such, but rather the differential generosity of such programmes in different countries. An important implication of this conclusion is that the so-called 'old-age crisis' is not one of general applica-tion, but limited to particular countries. Another is that the frequent claims by policy-makers that their actions are constrained by the brute facts of a 'greying' population are often simply covers for attempts to make expendi-ture cuts or for an incapacity to do so.

Chapter 7—*Birth-rate Blues: A Real Crisis in the Making?*—looks at another aspect of demographic change, the shift to below-replacement levels of fertility in most of the advanced countries of the Western world plus others in Eastern Europe, the former Soviet Union, and north-east Asia. This crisis—if it turns out to be such—has come upon us far more suddenly and dramatically than the trend towards population ageing, which has been confidently predicted by demographers for many decades. The realization that birth rates were falling precipitately in many countries has only been a subject of scholarly attention for the past decade or so. Once again, we use a comparative hypothesis testing approach as a means of locating the determinants of the outcomes with which we are concerned, although in this case the determinants of fertility levels rather than of expenditure change. A possible objection to this shift in focus is that, while fertility decline is a topic of considerable intrinsic interest, it is hardly a proper part of an enquiry into the likely future of the welfare state. That is not our view. An important finding of this chapter is that a key determinant of fertility levels across the OECD is the extent to which countries have adopted family-friendly public policies. This means that, contrary to the general thrust of the crisis literature, certain kinds of social policy initiatives are crucial to the continued vitality of Western societies. Changing welfare needs define the changing tasks of the welfare state. If the argument of this chapter is correct, a major social policy role of the state in coming decades will be to ensure that the forces making for fertility decline do not get out of control.

The final chapter of this book seeks to identify the implications of what has gone before for the likely future trajectory of welfare state development. Its title, *Towards a Steady-state Welfare State?*, implies a very different perspective on future development from that implicit in the crisis-filled accounts from which we started. Part of the argument is simply that, since an examination of the recent past reveals so little change, it would be highly surprising if the immediate future contained any massive disruption of existing spending patterns. Certainly, the fact that programme maturation and economic growth are revealed as the main engines shaping aggregate expenditure growth suggests only moderate change, since the first of these factors implies a further convergence of expenditure patterns, and the second, on the form of the past two decades, is as likely to be a factor promoting expenditure growth as expenditure decline. Indeed, the only serious prospect of any general downward trend in spending as a percentage of GDP on the basis of our modelling would be a substantial and sustained period of economic growth across the OECD on a scale comparable to that of the early post-war period. At present, that does not seem very likely.

The prospects for some, probably rather modest, expenditure growth seem stronger. Absent significant labour market reform and/or a significant hike in economic growth rates, the time-series implications of population ageing will undoubtedly have some upward effect on average expenditure levels. Attempts to reverse fertility decline also seem likely to produce a shift towards a greater emphasis on family policy intervention. These are likely to be general trends, but an important skein in our concluding argument is that welfare states of different types and in different families of nations confront different problems and, hence, face distinctive challenges in coming years. Just as there has been no generalized crisis of the welfare state in recent decades, there will no generalized crisis in coming decades. Diverse welfare state types will face diverse dilemmas. The greatest challenge for policy-makers in future years will be how to resolve these dilemmas within spending parameters that are unlikely to be easy to change.

A Race to the Bottom?

Some Preliminary Considerations

The notion of a 'race to the bottom' in social provision is only a variant of a more general argument: that enhanced international competition is destructive of regulatory standards across the board. The earliest articulation of the argument is to be found in early twentieth-century debates in US corporate law on the difficulty of regulating corporations under circumstances where they were in a position to escape domestic jurisdiction (see Rieger and Leibfried 2003). In the contemporary debate, the threat of welfare cutbacks induced by global competition is, in fact, only a relatively minor theme in a debate focusing largely on wages, labour protection laws, and environmental standards (see Drezner 2000). The logic, however, is just the same. Insofar as the costs of social provision, better wages and conditions, and environmental safeguards fall on business, they lead to high production costs, which, it is argued, will only be endured where business does not have the alternative of removing itself to a more favourable location. Where countries are heavily engaged in international trade and where enterprises cannot be prevented from relocating to countries in which costs are lower, governments are seen as having little option but to accede to the demands of capital for lower taxes, a more flexible labour market, and less 'red tape' around health, safety, and environmental issues.

The main purpose of this chapter is not to contest the logic of these arguments, but to examine the comparative evidence with a view to establishing how well the 'race to the bottom' hypothesis does actually account for the trajectory of recent social expenditure development. Nevertheless, it is worth noting very briefly a few of the reasons why the logic of international competition might turn out not to have the extreme consequences suggested by these accounts. First, there are reasons for believing that these theories exaggerate the extent of the threat resulting from changes in the international economy. Frequently, they neglect consumption considerations in the determination of locational advantage (i.e. being close to one's market may be as important as minimizing production costs) and offer an exaggerated picture of the likely consequences of capital flight (by the mid-1990s, corporate taxes amounted to somewhat less than 10 per cent of total taxation in Organization for Economic Cooperation and Development (OECD) countries—see Ganghof 2000). Second, there are reasons for supposing that the consequences of globalization may be quite different from those presupposed by such accounts. Indeed, rival accounts suggest that exposure to the world economy may actually serve as an incentive for governments to intervene to maintain or even improve regulatory standards in the hope of thereby mitigating some of the adverse consequences of international economic vulnerability (see Cameron 1978; Ruggie 1982; Katzenstein 1985; Rodrik 1997).

Globalization accounts may also be unrealistic in other ways. A third reason that social expenditures may not have declined as much as predicted is that the extent of change in the international economy in recent years is rather less than is sometimes implied in the crisis literature. Table 5.1 in Chapter 5 shows that, in the 1990s, the average level of imports plus exports as a percentage of GDP in OECD countries was only around 5 per cent higher than in the 1980s. Admittedly, over the same period, the average level of foreign direct investment had more than doubled, but this was from a very low base. Table 5.1 further shows that overseas investment flows in OECD countries during the 1980s and 1990s averaged less than 3 per cent of GDP, a figure hardly indicative of overwhelming capital mobility amongst nations. Finally, these accounts appear totally to misjudge the dynamics of social expenditure change. The implication of the 'race to the bottom' analysis is that countries can rapidly adjust their social expenditure levels in a downward direction, but the prevailing imagery of the policy change literature is of a trajectory of social policy reform strongly shaped by an inertia and irreversibility stemming from a logic of 'increasing returns' and 'path dependent' institutional development (see Pierson 2000). In Karl Hinrichs' beautiful simile, social security systems are like 'elephants on the move' (Hinrichs 2001a). When they are young, they may stampede ahead; but, when they are mature, they generally move forward rather slowly. Irrespective of age, turning them around involves much energy and no less persuasive power.

In this chapter, we are looking for signs that such a turn around has occurred during the course of the past two decades. We assess the extent to which this may have occurred by examining trajectories of social expenditure measured in a variety of ways. Our premise is that, a few minor exceptions apart, it simply does not make sense to talk of a 'race to the bottom' in social provision that is not manifested in social expenditure terms. That is because, in most advanced welfare states, the vast bulk of provision takes the form of income-maintenance schemes and social services funded from various forms of taxation. It is this taxation that business regards as a burden and that it blames for its failure to compete in international markets. For governments persuaded of this diagnosis, there are only two available strategies: to cut benefits and services or to increase borrowing. However, given that the debt interest burden resulting from excessive borrowing is also widely regarded as inimical to the viability of a market economy, the only viable option available to 'responsible' governments is social expenditure cuts. If the theory is correct, there really is 'no alternative'. For countries delivering welfare state provision largely through state-funded benefits and services, a 'race to the bottom' without accompanying expenditure cuts is a contradiction in terms.

There are, however, some circumstances under which adverse changes in welfare standards will not be fully captured by the extent of cutbacks in public provision. These distortions affect only a few countries and are unlikely to impact greatly on the overall relativities of expenditure change reported in this chapter. One possible source of distortion is changes in the extent of mandated provision. In just a few countries, a sizeable part of the nation's welfare effort has been funded by mandatory employer provision not included in the public budget, implying the possibility of a cut in welfare standards resulting from a reduction in the mandated obligations of employers, despite unchanged levels of public spending. However, in the two countries that stand out in this respect—Australia and Switzerland—the period under assessment here has been one in which mandated expenditures and public social expenditure have increased in tandem, so that the net impact of changes in mandated programmes in these countries would actually be positive rather than negative in character.

Another possible source of distortion is changes in the incidence of taxes impacting adversely on welfare beneficiaries (see Adema 1999). The partial replacement of income taxes by consumption taxes in Canada, Japan, and New Zealand during the period under review could, in principle, have had such effects, with an increased tax liability for welfare recipients uncompensated by any increase in benefit rates leading to declining welfare standards without any decline in reported spending or, alternatively, increases in benefit rates leading to higher aggregate spending levels without any improvement in standards of provision. However, even assuming the imposition of a 12.5 per cent consumption tax and total benefit spending equivalent to 15 per cent of GDP—and these are the highest possible figures that could have applied in any of the countries concerned—the maximum distortionary effect would have amounted to less than 2 per cent of GDP. That is not a figure likely to have had a major effect on the cross-national relativities in spending reported below. Finally, it should be noted that another highly significant change in the incidence of expenditure and taxation of recent years, the increasing use in English-speaking countries of tax credits as a means of reducing poverty amongst the working poor, does not bias our test procedure against the 'race to the bottom' hypothesis. It is now the accepted practice of national accounts statistics to count such tax credits as social expenditure, but even if this rule is not always consistently applied across categories of tax expenditure and across countries, any omissions would lead to an underestimation rather than an exaggeration of the extent of the real expenditure increase that had taken place during the period.

Patterns of Aggregate Spending

The first measures we examine in this chapter are changes in total public social expenditure and total public expenditure, both measured as percentages of GDP. We have already argued that the trajectory of welfare spending in a given period is the key to establishing the reality or otherwise of a 'race to the bottom'. Aggregate social spending as a percentage of GDP is also the most widely used measure of the 'welfare effort' that governments make on behalf of their citizens, and changes in this measure provide a useful indicator of a nation's continuing commitment to welfare. A focus on total public expenditure provides a context for our discussion of social expenditure trends. It allows us to ask whether trajectories noted as typical of social expenditure development are replicated in other public expenditure arenas and whether expenditures for social policy purposes have become a more or less salient aspect of overall public sector spending over the course of time. Because we seek also to contextualize our discussion in wider historical terms, we provide data not only for the period of our specific analysis from 1980 to 1998, but also for the two preceding decades from 1960 to 1980, allowing us to compare and contrast the trajectory of expenditure change over time as well as between countries.

Table 2.1 provides data for total public social expenditure as a percentage of GDP in 1960, 1980, and 1998, and for expenditure change in the time periods 1960–80 and 1980–98. These data come from the OECD Social Expenditure Database (OECD 2001a). This data source brings together systematic information on thirteen components of social spending for all the long-term

Table 2.1 Total public social expenditure as a percentage of GDP in 21 OECD countries, 1960, 1980, 1998, and change over time

	1960	1980	1998	1960–80[a]	1980–98
Australia	7.4	11.3	17.8	3.9	6.5
Canada	9.1	13.3	18.0	4.2	4.8
Ireland	8.7	18.9	15.8	10.2	−3.1
New Zealand	10.4	19.2	21.0	8.8	1.8
United Kingdom	10.2	18.2	21.4	8.0	3.2
United States	7.3	13.1	14.6	5.8	1.5
Family mean	*8.9*	*15.7*	*18.1*	*6.8*	*2.4*
Denmark	10.6	29.1	29.8	18.5	0.8
Finland	8.8	18.5	26.5	9.7	8.0
Norway	7.8	18.6	27.0	10.8	8.4
Sweden	10.8	29.0	31.0	18.2	2.0
Family mean	*9.5*	*23.8*	*28.6*	*14.3*	*4.8*
Austria	15.9	23.8	26.8	7.9	3.0
Belgium	13.8	24.2	24.5	10.4	0.4
France	13.4	22.7	28.8	9.3	6.1
Germany	18.1	20.3	27.3	2.2	7.0
Netherlands	11.7	27.3	23.9	15.6	−3.4
Family mean	*14.6*	*23.7*	*26.3*	*9.1*	*2.6*
Greece	7.1	11.5	22.7	4.4	11.3
Italy	13.1	18.4	25.1	5.3	6.7
Portugal	—	11.6	18.2	—	6.6
Spain	3.2	15.8	19.7	12.6	3.9
Family mean	*7.8*	*14.3*	*21.4*	*7.4*	*7.1*
Switzerland	4.9	15.2	28.3	10.3	13.1
Japan	4.1	10.1	14.7	6.0	4.6
Overall mean	*10.1*	*18.7*	*22.7*	*9.0*	*4.0*
Coefficient of variation	*38.9*	*31.2*	*22.3*		

Notes and sources: Data for 1960 from OECD (1994), 'New Orientations for Social Policy', *Social Policy Studies*, No. 12, Paris. In the cases of Denmark, Belgium, and Spain, the 1960 figures are the sum of social security transfers plus health spending (data from Castles 1998). Data from 1980 onwards from OECD (2001a), *Social Expenditure Database, 1980–1998*, Paris. Missing data in 1980 for occupational injury spending for Australia and for other contingencies for Denmark, Greece, and Italy. 1980 unemployment cash benefits for Austria, France, and Ireland interpolated from OECD (1985). 1998 UK total expenditure reduced by 3.3 per cent of GDP to take account of a definitional change relating to old age cash benefits.

[a] Because data for 1960 and for 1980 and onwards come from different sources, the figures for change 1960–80 are, at best, approximations. All calculated figures subject to rounding errors.

member countries of the OECD from 1980 onwards. Aggregate spending is simply the total of these components, but the existence of a disaggregated database of this kind permits us to use expenditure data to generate measures that more accurately describe the structure of welfare provision in a given nation. These measures will be elaborated in Chapter 3.

Table 2.1 has a format which is standard in much of the subsequent presentation. The data are for twenty-one OECD countries, classified into four 'family of nations' groupings designed to capture affinities and commonalities arising from history, geography, language, and culture. The four families—in order of their appearance in this and subsequent tables—consist respectively of English-speaking, Scandinavian, continental Western European, and Southern European countries. Two countries, Switzerland and Japan, are difficult to classify in the family of nations terms and data for them are presented separately. These groupings are similar to those found in my earlier work on comparative public policy (see Castles 1998), but with the slight modification that—on the basis of findings from a cluster analysis by Obinger and Wagschal (2001)—Italy is classified here as a member of the Southern European rather than the continental Western European family. In Table 2.1 and in all later basic data tables, we separately present family of nations means and overall means for all the twenty-one cases. This serves as a simple device for assessing the extent of differences amongst groupings of nations. An overall measure of the similarity of cases is given by the coefficient of variation, which is provided for all measures of expenditure levels, but not for changes over time. Lower values of the coefficient imply a reduction in the overall variation of cases and a consistent downward trend in values suggests a move towards greater similarity in spending patterns over time.

Looking initially at the family of nations patterns in respect of levels of aggregate spending, we note changes in the groupings featuring as welfare state leaders and laggards. Table 2.1 shows that, in 1960, continental Western Europe was the area making much the greatest welfare effort, with little to choose between the English-speaking and Scandinavian countries in the middle of the distribution, and with Southern Europe, Italy excepted, in the rearguard. By 1980, however, this clear hierarchy of spending had collapsed into two broader groupings, with the Scandinavian and continental Western European countries spending around a quarter of GDP for social policy purposes and the English-speaking and Southern European countries around 15 per cent. Finally, during the course of the period that concerns us here, hierarchy was restored, but along lines rather different to those of the early post-war era. By 1998, the Scandinavian countries had become outright welfare state leaders, with average spending levels of just below 30 per cent of

GDP. The countries of continental Western Europe followed close behind, with Southern Europe now somewhat ahead of an English speaking rearguard. Changes in the welfare state ranking of individual countries were no less dramatic than those of country groupings, with Switzerland moving from the position of being OECD's second lowest spender in 1960 to its fourth highest in 1998, and with Ireland moving from a position marginally above the OECD mean in 1980 to the third lowest level of spending in 1998. The diversity of expenditure patterns demonstrated in Table 2.1, and the relatively tight bunching of nations sharing close historical, cultural, and linguistic affinities, does not seem readily compatible with hypotheses of the kind offered by the crisis literature, suggesting that welfare states everywhere were responding to the same powerful external forces.

Turning now to patterns of expenditure growth, the initial point to note is the substantial contrast between periods. The 1960–80 period was one of consistent and strong social expenditure growth. All the OECD member countries featuring in Table 2.1 experienced increases in spending measured as a percentage of GDP, with Denmark and Sweden leading the way with increases in spending of 18.5 and 18.2 per cent of GDP, respectively. For OECD countries in general, expenditure grew by 9 per cent of GDP, which meant a virtual doubling in size of the average OECD welfare state in just two decades. The 1980–98 period was, in comparison, an era of more inconsistent and much reduced spending growth. In the earlier period, there were eight countries which increased their spending by more than 10 per cent of GDP; in the later period, there were just two: Switzerland and Portugal, both of them catching-up from the rear of the distribution. In the earlier period, the smallest increase in spending was Germany's 2.2 per cent of GDP; in the later period, there were no less than seven countries with expenditure growth of less than 2.2 per cent. Finally, in the second period, the average rate of expenditure growth was more than halved, dropping from 9 to 4 percentage points of GDP. Whether as a consequence of globalization or some other concatenation of factors, there can be no question at all that the pace of welfare state growth had slowed dramatically after 1980.

However, it declined on nothing like the scale hypothesized by the crisis literature. Three sets of figures in Table 2.1 make this abundantly plain. A 'race to the bottom' implies an across-the-board contraction in social spending. However, as the final column of Table 2.1 shows, there were, in fact, only two countries—Ireland and the Netherlands—that experienced any overall cutback in aggregate social expenditure during these years. The second relevant figure is the average 4 per cent increase in spending as a percentage of GDP between 1980 and 1998. Translated into a percentage rise in spending, this means that the average OECD country increased its welfare effort by slightly more than 20 per cent—from 18.7 to 22.7 per cent of GDP—in precisely that period in which the prevailing crisis accounts suggest that expenditure should have been dropping like a stone. The salience of this finding is highlighted by a third set of figures, the consistent downward trend in the coefficients of variation appearing in the final row of Table 2.1, demonstrating a growing similarity of social expenditure levels over a period of almost four decades. The 'race to the bottom' argument implies a sharp break in trend, with a general movement towards higher expenditures in the early post-war years replaced, more recently, by a process of downwards convergence. What Table 2.1 demonstrates is that, throughout the post-war period, increased similarity has been conjoint with increased spending.

We now turn to corresponding patterns of overall public expenditure development. Table 2.2 presents data on total outlays of general government as a percentage of GDP from OECD *Economic Outlook* (various years) for the same time points and periods as Table 2.1. In fact, Table 2.2, in most respects, tells much the same story as Table 2.1. Total expenditure magnitudes are, of course, much greater than for social spending, with mean levels of total expenditure starting out at a level nearly three times higher than social expenditure and ending up at a level marginally less than twice as high. By 1998, the OECD mean for total outlays was 43 per cent of GDP, with a high of 55.5 per cent of GDP in Sweden and a low of 30.5 per cent of GDP in the United States. However, despite differences in magnitudes, family of nations patterns were similar, with the single exception that the countries of Southern Europe remained well below the level of public spending of the English-speaking countries in 1980. By 1998, the hierarchy of families of nations in respect of social spending is almost exactly replicated for total outlays. Also, as in the case of aggregate social expenditure, there was a very substantial contrast in growth trajectories in the two periods. In the 1960s and 1970s, average total outlays growth of 15 per cent of GDP was about 60 per cent greater than social expenditure growth in the same period. However, in the period from 1980 to 1998, overall total outlays in the OECD were effectively becalmed—according to the figures in Table 2.2, ending up only 0.7 of a percentage point of GDP higher at the end of the period than at its beginning.

This is where the one really significant contrast between total outlays and aggregate social expenditure trends is to be found. Only two out of twenty-one countries experienced social expenditure cutbacks between 1980 and 1998, but no less than eight of the nineteen countries for which we have total outlays data experienced overall public expenditure cuts in the same period. It is also possible to surmise the expenditure trajectories of the countries for

Table 2.2 Total outlays of general government as a percentage of GDP in 21 OECD countries, 1960, 1980, 1998, and change over time

	1960	1980	1998	1960–80	1980–98
Australia	21.6	31.4	33.2	9.8	1.8
Canada	28.6	38.8	40.2	10.2	1.4
Ireland	28.0	49.3	32.2	21.3	−17.1
New Zealand[a]	—	—	39.5	—	—
United Kingdom	32.2	43.0	37.7	10.8	−5.3
United States	27.2	31.4	30.5	4.2	−0.9
Family mean	*27.5*	*38.8*	*34.8*	*11.3*	*−4.0*
Denmark	24.8	56.2	54.0	31.4	−2.2
Finland	26.6	38.1	48.1	11.5	10.0
Norway	29.9	43.3	46.3	13.4	3.0
Sweden	31.0	60.1	55.5	29.1	4.6
Family mean	*28.1*	*49.4*	*51.0*	*21.3*	*1.6*
Austria	35.7	48.1	50.3	12.4	2.2
Belgium	34.6	58.3	48.0	23.7	−10.3
France	34.6	46.1	49.9	11.5	3.8
Germany	32.4	47.9	46.0	15.5	−1.9
Netherlands	33.7	55.8	43.4	22.1	−12.4
Family mean	*34.2*	*51.1*	*47.5*	*16.9*	*−3.6*
Greece[b]	17.4	30.4	42.7	13.0	12.3
Italy	30.1	41.9	47.6	11.8	5.7
Portugal	17.0	23.8	39.8	6.8	16.0
Spain	—	32.2	40.6	—	8.4
Family mean	*21.5*	*30.1*	*42.7*	*10.5*	*12.6*
Switzerland[a]	—	—	—	—	—
Japan	17.5	32.0	34.8	14.5	2.8
Overall mean	*27.9*	*42.6*	*43.0*	*15.2*	*0.7*
Coefficient of variation	*21.8*	*25.0*	*16.6*		

Notes and sources: Data for 1960 from OECD (1991) *Historical Statistics, 1960–1989*, Paris. Data for 1980 from OECD (1997), *Economic Outlook*, Paris, Vol. 61. Outlays data for 1998 from OECD (2001) *Economic Outlook*, Paris, Vol. 71.

[a] Data for New Zealand and Switzerland are not available. All calculated figures subject to rounding errors.

[b] The Greek figure for 1960 is for current disbursements of general government rather than total outlays. For that reason, the figure for change in Greek total outlays for the period 1960–80 should be regarded as an approximation.

which data is missing. Given the very substantial expansion of Swiss social spending in this period shown in Table 2.1 and documented in a number of studies (see Kriesi 1999; Lane 1999; Armingeon 2001), it seems reasonable to assume that total outlays in Switzerland increased markedly between 1980 and 1998. By the same token, the relatively small increase in New Zealand's social expenditure shown in Table 2.1 combined with a public sector which, by all accounts, was cut to ribbons in this period (see Kelsey 1993; Boston and Uhr 1996; Stephens 1999), seems likely to have contributed to an overall decline in total outlays in the period after 1980. Given the probability of diverse spending trends in these two countries, it may be concluded that there was some degree of expenditure reduction in nearly half the countries of the OECD. There was also extreme diversity in spending trajectories. Belgium, Ireland, and the Netherlands all experienced expenditure cutbacks in excess of 10 per cent of GDP. The public sectors of Finland, Greece, and Portugal, on the other hand, grew by the similar amounts.

This discrepancy between trends in aggregate social spending and in total public expenditure is extremely interesting. The items of spending included in total outlays which are not also included under the social expenditure head are general public services, public order and safety, defence, education, housing and community services, economic affairs, recreation and culture, and a residual other category which includes debt interest payments (see United Nations 1999). Reading Tables 2.2 and 2.1 in conjunction suggests that, over the past two decades, these non-social components of public spending have, in aggregate, been subject to greater attrition and downward pressure than has aggregate social spending. Whether these cutbacks are of sufficient magnitude to suggest a possible 'race to the bottom' in respect of total outlays is quite another matter. It certainly seems probable that commentators on the lookout for the influence of globalizing trends on public sector spending would see it as significant that Belgium, Ireland, and the Netherlands, the three countries experiencing the greatest cutbacks in total outlays, were simultaneously the three countries which, on most counts, can be seen as the most internationally exposed economies of the 1980–98 period (see Table 5.1 and Chapter 5 for more analysis). However, the facts, nevertheless, remain that the number of countries increasing their overall public spending in this period outweighed the number reducing their public spending and that the average trend of outlays in this period was, however marginally, in an upward direction. Although total spending may have been under greater pressure than aggregate social spending, and although individual country fluctuations in total spending were considerably greater, the evidence for a 'race to the bottom' is simply not there.

However, the possibility that changes in the international economy may be implicated in the broader public expenditure trends we have been examining cannot be so simply dismissed. The globalization literature does not have anything to say about non-social expenditure as such, but it certainly seems quite possible that many commentators in this genre would be quite happy to adopt a broader measure of social spending than that used by the OECD and underlying the figures appearing in Table 2.1. Probable inclusions might be spending on housing and community services, education, and economic affairs, the last two of which have been declining in the majority of OECD countries during the period under examination here (see IMF, *Financial Statistics*, various years). Moreover, while debt interest payments are not part of the welfare state by any definition, the higher levels of public indebtedness giving rise to such expenditures are often regarded by these same commentators as a consequence of welfare state profligacy. Given that so much of what is classified as non-social spending may properly be seen as aspects of a more widely conceived socially protective state or as consequences of its growth, it seems sensible to avoid premature conclusions and to include total public spending as well as aggregate social expenditure in the more comprehensive modelling of sources of expenditure variation that is the subject of Chapter 5.

Welfare Salience and Welfare Standards

While data on patterns of aggregate spending clearly contradict the 'race to the bottom' hypothesis, it is perfectly possible that other ways of thinking about recent trajectories of spending might yield findings that provide clues as to the nature of the malaise underlying crisis predictions. In this section, we address two questions with a bearing on such issues. First, we ask whether public spending on welfare has become a more or less salient part of the public budget in recent decades. Greater salience might itself be a reason magnifying the sense of possible threat. Second, we ask whether increases in aggregate expenditure in these years might actually mask a decline in welfare standards. If governments in Western nations no longer view social protection as a major priority, and if, in consequence, standards of provision are dropping, the notion of a threat to the future of the welfare state becomes rather more comprehensible.

Göran Therborn (1983) has argued that in order to qualify as a welfare state, a nation's spending for welfare purposes must exceed its spending for other purposes and Gøsta Esping-Andersen (1990) has noted that, by this criterion, there were few welfare states in the world until the 1970s. An interesting implication of the 'race to the bottom' hypothesis is that it suggests that any increase in the number of countries qualifying as welfare states as a consequence of expenditure growth in the 'golden age' of welfare state expansion is likely to have been reversed in recent decades. In the 'golden age', captured in our data by the huge increases in social spending occurring in the period between 1960 and 1980, spending on health, pensions, sickness, unemployment, and other benefits gradually came to rival the older priorities of state spending for general public services, defence, public order, and community services. However, had the 1980s and 1990s really been a period in which cutbacks were concentrated on social programmes, as implied by the 'race to the bottom' hypothesis, the status of welfare as the dominant concern of the modern state would clearly have been in some jeopardy.

In fact, we already know that, in broad terms, such a reversal of the growing salience of the welfare state cannot have occurred. Tables 2.1 and 2.2 show that the average rate of growth of social expenditure exceeded that of total outlays in the period after 1980, which can only mean that, on average, the salience of the welfare state in OECD countries was continuing to increase. What we do not know, however, is how individual countries were affected by the expenditure changes taking place in this period. It would, for instance, be quite compatible with the evidence of our analysis so far, if we were to discover that some of those countries experiencing cutbacks or relatively small increases in social spending had simultaneously experienced a decline in the ratio of social to non-social spending. While that might not be the same thing as a 'race to the bottom', it could very well explain why welfare elites and welfare recipients in certain countries felt themselves to be under pressure. Table 2.3, which measures aggregate social expenditure as a proportion of total outlays, provides us with a means of mapping the balance between social and non-social priorities in state spending. It allows us to compare the relative salience of the welfare state in different countries, amongst different families of nations and at different time points.

An initial point to notice about the figures in Table 2.3 is the massive convergence they demonstrate. In the 1960s, there were very substantial differences in the extent to which individual nations and families of nations prioritized welfare state spending. In 1960, Germany was devoting more than 55 per cent of its total spending to welfare, but Japan, Norway, and the United States only around 25 per cent. Although not as pronounced as these individual country differences, the gaps between families of nations were also considerable. Initially, patterns were somewhat different from those

Table 2.3 Total public social expenditure as a
proportion of total outlays of general government in
21 OECD countries, 1960, 1980, and 1998

	1960	1980	1998
Australia	34.3	36.1	53.6
Canada	31.8	34.2	44.9
Ireland	31.1	38.4	49.0
New Zealand	—	—	53.1
United Kingdom	31.7	42.3	56.7
United States	27.1	41.8	47.8
Family mean	*31.1*	*38.6*	*50.8*
Denmark	42.7	51.7	55.2
Finland	33.1	48.6	55.2
Norway	26.1	42.8	58.3
Sweden	34.8	48.3	55.8
Family mean	*34.2*	*47.8*	*56.1*
Austria	44.5	49.4	53.3
Belgium	39.9	41.5	51.1
France	38.7	49.2	57.8
Germany	55.9	42.3	59.3
Netherlands	34.7	48.9	55.1
Family mean	*42.7*	*46.3*	*55.3*
Greece	40.8	37.8	53.2
Italy	43.5	44.0	52.7
Portugal	—	48.9	45.8
Spain	—	49.0	48.5
Family mean	*42.1*	*44.9*	*50.0*
Switzerland	—	—	—
Japan	23.4	31.6	42.1
Overall mean	*36.1*	*43.5*	*52.4*
Coefficient of variation	*22.2*	*13.5*	*9.0*

Notes and sources: Social expenditure data from Table 2.1 expressed as
percentages of the total outlays of general government. Sources for
total outlays as indicated in Table 2.2. All calculated figures subject to
rounding errors.

characterizing aggregate spending. Table 2.1 reveals that, with the exception of Italy, the countries of Southern Europe were the expenditure laggards of the 1960s, but Table 2.3 suggests, despite incomplete data, that the priority these countries accorded welfare was akin to that of the countries of continental Western Europe, the expenditure leaders of the time. Both in 1960 and 1980, the countries according welfare the lowest priority were to be found largely within the English-speaking family of nations. By the end of the period, individual country differences had diminished appreciably. Germany and Japan remained poles apart in terms of welfare salience, but the gap had decreased from 32.5 to 17.2 percentage points. Gaps between family of nations groups had also diminished and the ordering of family groupings had changed. The salience of welfare spending in the Scandinavian countries had increased hugely over nearly four decades, and these countries' high levels of spending were now matched by the high priority they attached to spending of this nature. In 1960, the gap in salience between the top and bottom family groups—continental Western Europe and the English-speaking nations—was 11.6 percentage points. In 1998, the gap between top and bottom—Scandinavia and Southern Europe—was just 6.1 percentage points. Summary statistics tell the same story, with a strongly declining coefficient of variation over time.

The next important point to note is that this process of convergence had occurred as a consequence of more and more countries becoming welfare states according to Therborn's criterion. In 1960, Germany was the only OECD country to devote more resources to welfare than to other purposes. In 1980, Denmark had replaced Germany as the OECD's only welfare state. By 1998, however, fourteen of the twenty countries featuring in Table 2.3 were welfare states by this criterion and Switzerland, the country for which there are missing data, would also undoubtedly qualify if the data were available. Finally, and most significantly, this mass shift across the threshold of welfare statehood occurred, not in the golden years between 1960 and 1980, but in the supposedly crisis-ridden years after 1980. In 1980, the average level of welfare salience was 43.5 per cent; by 1998, it 52.4 per cent. By one reckoning, the OECD area had itself become a giant welfare state, insofar as it was constituted largely by nations spending more on welfare than for all other purposes. By another, there was still some way to go, given that two of the countries yet to become welfare states according to this criterion were the OECD's most populous nations, the United States and Japan.

This analysis has important implications. Over the past two decades, most OECD countries have committed themselves to social policy as their first priority and Table 2.3 provides absolutely no sign that this is a trajectory of change which has exhausted its potential. As we have seen, part of what happened in the 1980s and 1990s was an increase in real spending on welfare, but just as important was a decline in non-social spending. Admittedly, as already noted, the barriers between the categories of spending are far from watertight, but, accepting the distinction as given, what appears to have been happening is that, in a period in which overall expenditure increases have been constrained, policy-makers have been privileging welfare priorities at the margin. This is not what the 'race to the bottom' theorists would have us believe, but clearly finding out why this kind of trade-off is occurring is vital for an understanding of contemporary welfare state dynamics.

A possible explanation that might simultaneously account for a generalized malaise about the future of the welfare state and for an enhanced priority for welfare over other purposes would be if demands or needs for welfare had been increasing over time. This is, in essence, the basis of the account offered in Paul Pierson's *The New Politics of the Welfare State* (Pierson 2001). The argument is that expenditure retrenchment is a difficult project for modern governments because they are expected to tackle a wide range of problems from deindustrialization to population ageing and to provide a whole range of new services from drug rehabilitation to services enabling women to combine labour force participation and maternity. Under these circumstances, it is easy to see why commentators interpret what is happening in terms of increased pressure on the welfare state or even of crisis. If governments feel that there are economic and/or political constraints on higher taxing and spending, and if, at the same time, there is an increased demand for welfare services, one of two things must happen: either other expenditure must be cut or existing standards of provision must decline.

We have already seen that there has been some decline in non-social expenditure. In what follows, we discuss briefly what has been happening to standards of welfare provision. Although the 'race to the bottom' argument is essentially a hypothesis about the likely future trajectory of welfare spending, an analogous argument is sometimes encountered about effects on welfare standards. Indeed, for many left-of-centre commentators that is the main concern. Their worry is that capital will press governments to reduce existing standards in order for business to compete in an era of global competition. The arguments are familiar. Enterprises are not competitive when employers must pay huge social security contributions, when generous sickness benefits create mass absenteeism, and when unemployment benefits are so high that they diminish the incentive to work. Reducing standards of protection—'social dumping'—can be presented as the only way for a country to attract new capital or to retain the capital it already has. In effect, this argument concedes that globalization is not the sole factor determining expenditure growth, with increased welfare demand and welfare dependency countering the 'race to the bottom'. The impact of globalization under these circumstances is not to reduce aggregate welfare spending, but rather to reduce individual welfare generosity.

Table 2.4 provides an admittedly simplistic measuring rod for assessing how well contemporary welfare states have been coping with the increased demands made of them. The two categories of increased welfare need most generally noted in the literature are the impact of population ageing and increasing levels of unemployment. The latter has been highlighted by many commentators as a snare and delusion for those measuring welfare states in purely monetary terms, since increased spending on this count is simply seen as a measure of the welfare state's incapacity to control unemployment (see Esping-Andersen 1990; Mishra 1990; Clayton and Pontusson 1998). All that we do in Table 2.4 is to divide the aggregates of expenditure appearing in Table 2.1 by the percentage of the dependent population, that is, the population aged sixty-five and over plus the percentage of the civilian population registered as unemployed. The resulting ratio gives a crude measure of welfare generosity, theoretically to be interpreted as the percentage of GDP received in welfare spending for every 1 per cent of the population in need.

There are two obvious deficiencies with this measure. First, it presents an average figure for each country, when we know that benefits to different sections of the population in need in a given country often vary quite markedly. In some countries, and particularly in Southern Europe (see Ferrera 1996), a marked insider/outsider differentiation in the labour market is translated directly into the sphere of social security provision, with pension provision for core workers being much more generous than for peripheral workers and the unemployed. Second, it implies that all expenditure is delivered to just two categories of welfare recipient. Ideally, apart from these traditional sources of welfare need, we would have liked to include a proxy for the new kinds of need emerging from a changing family structure (see Orloff 1993; Daly 1997; Esping-Andersen 1999). The percentage of the population constituted by children living in single-parent families might have served this purpose, but the information required to calculate such a measure is simply unavailable for the time period covered by this study. The best data available are for eighteen of our twenty-one OECD countries for the period 1986–96 (see Beaujot and Liu 2002). On the basis of these data, we calculate that the percentage of the population constituted by children living in single-parent families increased from an average of 1.8 to 2.4 per cent

Table 2.4 Welfare state generosity ratio in 21 OECD
countries, 1980, 1998, and change over time

	1980	1998	Change
Australia	0.73	0.89	0.16
Canada	0.78	0.88	0.09
Ireland	0.93	0.83	−0.11
New Zealand	1.61	1.10	−0.51
United Kingdom	0.88	0.98	0.10
United States	0.71	0.85	0.13
Family mean	*0.94*	*0.92*	*−0.02*
Denmark	1.36	1.46	0.10
Finland	1.11	1.02	−0.09
Norway	1.12	1.43	0.31
Sweden	1.57	1.20	−0.37
Family mean	*1.29*	*1.28*	*−0.01*
Austria	1.35	1.36	0.01
Belgium	1.07	0.87	−0.20
France	1.04	1.04	0.00
Germany	1.08	1.05	−0.03
Netherlands	1.54	1.34	−0.20
Family mean	*1.21*	*1.13*	*−0.08*
Greece	0.72	0.81	0.08
Italy	0.89	0.86	−0.03
Portugal	0.61	0.92	0.31
Spain	0.70	0.56	−0.14
Family mean	*0.73*	*0.79*	*0.06*
Switzerland	1.09	1.52	0.43
Japan	0.91	0.72	−0.19
Overall mean	*1.04*	*1.03*	*−0.01*
Coefficient of variation	*29.0*	*25.5*	

Notes and sources: Welfare state generosity ratio calculated by dividing
social expenditure data from Table 2.1 by the sum of the percentage of
the population aged sixty-five years and over and the percentage of the
civilian population unemployed. Data on both aged population and
unemployment from OECD (2001*b*), *Labour Force Statistics 1980–2000*,
Paris. All calculated figures subject to rounding errors.

over this period of ten years. Only in five of these countries—Germany, New Zealand, Sweden, the United Kingdom, and the United States—did this lead to an increase in the population in need of more than 1 per cent. In these countries, the trend in welfare generosity is likely to have been somewhat— although not hugely—more adverse than indicated by the figures in the final column of Table 2.4.

Looking at Table 2.4 in conjunction with Table 2.1 shows that taking dependency levels into account really can make a big difference to our comprehension of the relative performance of welfare states. This can be seen by looking at the cases of New Zealand and Switzerland in 1980 and of Greece and Italy in 1998. In the earlier period, New Zealand is close to the expenditure average and Switzerland a complete laggard, but in ratio terms New Zealand turns out to be the OECD's most generous welfare provider of the early 1980s and Switzerland close to the average. This is because, in this period, these countries had much lower levels of dependency than most other OECD countries. The Greek and Italian cases tell the reverse story. In 1998, Greece and Italy were at or around OECD average spending levels, but both were very much below the OECD average in terms of the generosity of provision, because both experienced relatively high levels of dependency. Spain is, undoubtedly, the country in which high and increasing dependency led to the most serious outcomes, with an extraordinarily high level of unemployment producing a level of generosity markedly lower than in any other OECD country.

Where generosity is the criterion, there seems to be a three-tier hierarchy of welfare performance. In both 1980 and 1998, the hierarchy is quite distinct as demonstrated by a relatively high coefficient of variation that does not decline markedly over time. In both periods, there was a small group of countries with levels of generosity considerably higher than the mean. In 1980, it consisted of New Zealand, Sweden, the Netherlands, Denmark, and Austria. By 1998, New Zealand and Sweden had dropped out of this elite group to be replaced by Switzerland and Norway. In both periods, there is a second middling rank of countries constituted almost entirely by Scandinavian and continental Western European countries, but with New Zealand joining in 1998. At the other end of the distribution, with generosity ratios well below the OECD mean, are a group of Southern European and English-speaking countries together with Japan and, by the end of the period, also Belgium. These countries' relative lack of generosity stems from different causes. The Southern European countries other than Portugal, but plus Belgium, are around the middle of the distribution in spending terms, but have high levels of dependency. The English-speaking nations, other than New Zealand and the United Kingdom, together with Japan are, by contrast, extremely low spenders, despite quite moderate levels of dependency. These latter are countries which, one might conclude, are ungenerous by policy choice.

The most important conclusion, however, relates to what was happening to OECD levels of generosity across the board during this period. Between 1980 and 1998, the average level of dependency in OECD countries increased from 17.8 to 22.8 per cent of the population or by just over 25 per cent. What Table 2.4 tells us is that this very substantial increase in need was accommodated with virtually no alteration in the average OECD level of welfare state generosity. Admittedly, standards declined in about half the countries featuring in Table 2.4, but, interestingly, most of the really large cuts in generosity—in New Zealand, Sweden, and the Netherlands—occurred in those countries where generosity was highest in 1980. Only four countries— Belgium, Ireland, Japan, and Spain—experienced sizeable reductions in generosity leaving them well adrift of average OECD standards of provision. That is simply not enough to sustain an argument that increasing exposure to the international economy has fuelled a general trend towards declining welfare standards. The fact, however, that an average 4 percentage point increase in social expenditure led to essentially unchanged standards of provision might well be argued as evidence for the proposition that the countries of the OECD have now probably reached the outer limits of welfare state generosity measured in these terms.

Patterns of Real Expenditure

We complete our survey of what has been happening to social expenditure over the past two decades with an examination of trends in real spending: not how much countries spend as a percentage of GDP, but how much they spend in real dollars and cents adjusted for the impact of inflation. This discussion can afford to be quite brief because real spending patterns cannot possibly have had the downward trajectory suggested by the 'race to the bottom' hypothesis, since, for average expenditure as a percentage of GDP to have been increasing as we know it did, average real spending on welfare must have been increasing by an amount equivalent to GDP growth over the period as a whole. Real expenditure levels are of genuine interest, however. Although offering only the most approximate of yardsticks, they do tell us something about changes in absolute standards of provision. While it is extremely difficult to get a handle on exactly how much expenditure is required to prevent destitution, or what Rowntree, the great pioneer of poverty research, described as 'primary poverty', it is perfectly reasonable to argue that substantial increases in real spending are likely to reduce poverty levels in this sense. Similarly, while a precise measure of what is required to achieve adequacy of provision is not available, it again seems clear that the more generous the welfare state is in real terms, the more likely it is that such standards will be met.

The difference between social spending as a percentage of GDP and social spending in real terms is that the latter figure is not merely influenced by the priority a country puts on welfare vis-à-vis other goals, but also by its level of economic development and rate of economic growth. For a given level of welfare effort, a country's real per capita spending as shown in Table 2.5 is a function of how affluent that country is. Thus, while Table 2.1 shows us that, in 1980, Portugal and the United States were spending quite similar proportions of GDP on welfare state purposes, Table 2.5 shows us that, in terms of real expenditure measured in 1985 US dollars per capita, the hugely richer United States was outspending Portugal by a ratio of around four to one. The same applies to economic growth, with higher growth leading to higher increases in real social expenditure. Between 1980 and 1998, Table 2.1 tells us that Ireland's social spending as a percentage of GDP actually declined by 3.1 per cent. However, as a consequence of almost two decades of economic growth averaging 4.3 per cent per annum, Ireland's spending on welfare increased by more than a $1,000 per capita. Greece provides a contrasting story. Greece was another poor OECD country which increased real spending by around a $1,000 per capita, but with average economic growth of only 1.6 per cent per annum, this could only be achieved by a vast increase in the share of national expenditure going to welfare.

One effect of measuring expenditure in real terms is to modify the relativities between the Southern European and English-speaking families of nations noted in previous tables. Table 2.1 shows that, by 1998, Southern Europe, in general, was committing more resources to social purposes than the English-speaking world and Table 2.3 shows that, already by 1980, the welfare state was more salient in Southern Europe than in the English-speaking world. Table 2.4, however, indicates that, New Zealand apart, the two regions were throughout remarkably similar in generosity levels. What Table 2.5 tells us is that, with the exception of Italy, this level of generosity translated into far higher levels of real spending in the English-speaking world than in Southern Europe because the English-speaking countries were so much richer than those of Southern Europe. A further effect is to magnify differences

Table 2.5 Real social expenditure per capita in 21 OECD
countries, 1980, 1998, and change over time in 1985 US dollars

	1980	1998	Change
Australia	1,417	3,108	1,690
Canada	1,874	3,331	1,457
Ireland	1,154	2,251	1,097
New Zealand	1,984	2,686	701
United Kingdom	1,849	3,179	1,330
United States	2,008	3,066	1,057
Family mean	*1,714*	*2,936*	*1,222*
Denmark	3,296	4,806	1,510
Finland	2,009	3,875	1,866
Norway	2,252	5,098	2,846
Sweden	3,612	4,787	1,175
Family mean	*2,792*	*4,641*	*1,849*
Austria	2,452	3,799	1,347
Belgium	2,686	3,633	947
France	2,485	4,290	1,805
Germany	2,417	4,303	1,886
Netherlands	3,076	3,612	536
Family mean	*2,623*	*3,927*	*1,304*
Greece	677	1,693	1,015
Italy	1,901	3,428	1,526
Portugal	579	1,642	1,062
Spain	1,166	2,208	1,042
Family mean	*1,081*	*2,243*	*1,162*
Switzerland	2,169	4,559	2,389
Japan	1,019	2,319	1,300
Overall mean	*2,004*	*3,413*	*1,409*
Coefficient of variation	*40.4*	*29.9*	

Notes and sources: Real social expenditure per capita calculated by multiplying
social expenditure data from Table 2.1 by real GDP per capita and dividing by 100.
Real GDP per capita in 1985 US dollars from Summers and Heston (1991), 'The Penn
World Table (Mark 5)', *Quarterly Journal of Economics*, 106: 2, 327–68, updated to
1998 with data from OECD (2001), *Historical Statistics 1970–1999*, Paris. All
calculated figures subject to rounding errors.

between the Scandinavian countries and those of continental Western Europe, again because, on average, Scandinavia is richer than continental Western Europe. Although claims for the Scandinavian countries' welfare state superiority are often made on the grounds of these countries' high spending as a percentage of GDP, by the end of the period, their claims in terms of real expenditure levels were, if anything, greater.

Focusing on change in the period 1980–98, the story of Table 2.5 is of real expenditure growth on a dramatic scale. In this period, when the welfare state was supposedly in continuous crisis and under continuous attack from its political enemies, per capita real social expenditure in the OECD countries increased by no less than 83 per cent or by around 4.5 per cent per annum. In the laggard Southern European and English-speaking nations, the increases were, respectively, 107 and 71 per cent. In the leading Scandinavian and continental Western European countries, the increases were respectively 66 and 43 per cent. Insofar as real spending tells us anything about the probable success of countries in coping with absolute poverty, we note that, in 1980, there were ten countries with per capita spending of less than $2,000 per annum and that, in 1998, there were only two. Insofar as real spending levels tell us anything about the capacity of welfare states to deliver the highest standards of care and benefit adequacy, we further note that what, in 1980, was the highest level of real spending in the OECD—Sweden's expenditure of $3,612 per capita—was an expenditure level achieved by no less than ten OECD countries in 1998.

These figures tell us how much real spending went up in particular countries, not how much it went up for those who were actually dependent on the welfare state in those countries. This difference is important, since some commentators, arguing against the proposition that Western welfare states have been resilient in the face of crisis, have claimed that increases in real social expenditure per poor person were failing to keep up with GDP during the 1980s and early 1990s (see Clayton and Pontusson 1998). Table 2.6, the final table in this chapter, seeks to give a more accurate indication of what was actually happening to absolute standards of provision in this period by providing data on real spending per dependent, with dependency calculated as previously in Table 2.4. We have already noted that, on average, there was a roughly 25 per cent increase in dependency over these years and this necessarily somewhat modifies the impression of massive real expenditure growth given by Table 2.5. Taking into account the growth in dependency, the expenditure increase per beneficiary in real terms was 36.8 per cent as compared with a 41 per cent increase in real GDP per capita during the same

Table 2.6 Real social expenditure per dependent in 21 OECD countries, 1980, 1998, and change over time in 1985 US dollars

	1980	1998	Change
Australia	9,144	15,538	6,394
Canada	11,089	16,169	5,080
Ireland	6,378	11,787	5,409
New Zealand	16,675	14,061	−2,614
United Kingdom	8,934	14,517	5,583
United States	10,914	17,823	6,908
Family mean	*10,522*	*14,982*	*4,460*
Denmark	15,474	23,560	8,086
Finland	12,027	14,845	2,818
Norway	13,649	27,116	13,467
Sweden	19,526	18,483	−1,043
Family mean	*15,169*	*21,001*	*5,832*
Austria	14,172	19,283	5,111
Belgium	11,938	12,883	944
France	12,182	15,431	3,249
Germany	12,927	16,616	3,688
Netherlands	17,379	20,293	2,914
Family mean	*13,720*	*16,901*	*3,181*
Greece	4,261	6,002	1,741
Italy	9,231	11,779	2,548
Portugal	3,018	8,291	5,273
Spain	5,137	6,290	1,153
Family mean	*5,412*	*8,090*	*2,678*
Switzerland	15,608	24,510	8,902
Japan	9,183	11,426	2,243
Overall mean	*11,374*	*15,557*	*4,183*
Coefficient of variation	*38.7*	*35.7*	

Notes and sources: Real social expenditure per dependent calculated by multiplying the welfare state generosity ratio from Table 2.4 by real GDP per capita in 1985 US dollars from sources cited in notes to Table 2.5. All calculated figures subject to rounding errors.

period, the difference between the two accounting for the minuscule decline in the average OECD generosity ratio shown in Table 2.4.

Table 2.6, also like Table 2.4, shows a very distinct hierarchy of provision, indeed one more pronounced than in any other table in this chapter. The coefficient of variation for real spending per beneficiary started out very high and stayed very high. Conspicuous amongst the reasons was the persistence of low per capita GDP levels in the countries of Southern Europe. These were countries which were catching-up in terms of welfare effort as shown in Table 2.1, but which still had a very long way to go in real expenditure terms because of their relatively lower levels of economic development than other countries in the OECD. The impact of Ireland's dramatic economic growth during this period is again apparent from the figures in Table 2.6, with an improvement in real spending per beneficiary above the OECD mean, despite a marked decline in welfare effort. The continuity of a distinct hierarchy of provision when levels of dependency are taken into account contrasts strongly with the marked tendency to convergence shown in aggregate spending patterns. Levels of welfare effort may have been becoming more similar over time; welfare standards were not.

Table 2.6 also shows clearly that there were, indeed, countries in which the growth of dependency had marked effects on real standards of provision. New Zealand and Sweden stand out as the only two countries in the OECD in which real expenditure per beneficiary actually declined. They were, however, countries with exceptionally high levels of real spending at the beginning of the period, and, arguably, the experience of a country like Belgium, which, despite a small increase in real spending, had, by 1998, fallen well behind the OECD average, may have been as traumatic. Interestingly, the Netherlands, which experienced a much larger decline in spending as a percentage of GDP than either Belgium or Sweden, did not suffer the same fate in real GDP terms because its economy was growing much faster. However, although some countries experienced a decline in standards, there were many others in which real spending per beneficiary increased considerably, with Norway, Switzerland, and Denmark the most conspicuous in absolute terms and Portugal and Ireland in growth rate terms. In 1980, there were eight countries in which expenditure per beneficiary was less than $10,000 per annum; in 1998, there were only three. In 1980, there were five countries spending in excess of $15,000 per beneficiary; in 1998, there were eleven. Any claim that, overall, this was a period of decline in real spending per beneficiary or that it was one in which there was a marked tendency for real expenditure levels to fall behind the growth of GDP is quite unsustainable.

Conclusion

This chapter's main objective has been to use cross-national analysis to establish the validity or otherwise of the 'race to the bottom' hypothesis. If that hypothesis is to have any meaning above and beyond the fact that a minority of countries suffered adverse trends in this period, it must point to some generalized trend towards cutbacks in spending or, in what is, essentially, an extremely watered-down variant of the argument, that there has been some generalized decline in standards of provision. Despite an extensive examination of a wide range of expenditure indicators, no evidence of such trends has been forthcoming and we can only conclude that the 'race to the bottom' is a crisis myth rather than a crisis reality. Despite cutbacks in a number of countries, our analysis demonstrates unequivocally that OECD *average levels* of social expenditure, whether measured as percentages of GDP, as generosity ratios, or in real terms, either increased or remained constant between 1980 and 1998. Indeed, given that, during this period, social expenditure was increasing as a percentage of GDP and that non-social categories of expenditure were declining, expenditure for welfare purposes was becoming appreciably more salient with the passing of time.

This enhanced salience combined with a general slowdown in the rate of expenditure growth may, in itself, be part of the explanation for increasing anxiety about the future of the welfare state at a time when all the objective indicators suggest that expenditure levels and standards of provision were being maintained at roughly existing levels. In the 'golden age' of the welfare state, high levels of economic growth made it possible for governments to increase the scope of social spending without cutting back real levels of private consumption and without holding back other public projects. However, in the 1980s and 1990s, new welfare demands could only be satisfied by cutting private consumption or by making trade-offs against other public spending programmes. The welfare state had become simultaneously more salient and more vulnerable on several fronts. Clearly, this has meant that those fighting to extend its frontiers have had to fight harder in recent decades than they did in the years of plenty. Clearly, too, some battles have been lost, making it extremely tempting for those involved to seek compelling explanations of why the forces of 'social progress' are now apparently on the back foot.

This is one of the reasons crisis myths are born. Such accounts generalize from particular reverses and from adverse developments in particular countries in a way that makes such defeats more comprehensible and less blameworthy. When political actors are confronted by forces 'beyond their control', they no longer need excuses for failure. But alibis for failure are only part of the story. Myths also provide excuses for new attacks on the welfare state by its enemies (see Drezner 2000). Globalization or declining economic growth or whatever the currently supposed cause of crisis provides a cloak of legitimacy for those seeking to advance plans to cut taxes and spending. Once they have convinced policy-makers that 'there is no alternative' and that the state has no capacity to stand against the economic forces arrayed against it, they have won half the battle. If a 'race to the bottom' is on the cards, it clearly makes sense to be in it and in it with a vengeance! Crisis myths flourish when opposing sides find that the same abdication of responsibility serves both of their purposes and when neither side seeks to question anecdotal evidence of supposedly general trends. As this chapter demonstrates, the best antidote to myth-making is systematic comparative analysis.

3

The Structure of Social Provision

Using Disaggregated Data

The kinds of aggregate expenditure measures relied on as evidence in the previous chapter are averages seeking to summarize the extent of a nation's welfare effort in a single number and, as such, are at best only broad-gauge indicators of general trends. It is only possible to use such measures as tests for the crisis hypotheses we are examining because those hypotheses are themselves so broad-gauge and sweeping in character. When average expenditures have been rising, it is not difficult to use this fact as convincing evidence that there has been no wholesale 'race to the bottom' in social spending. More subtle hypotheses require more subtle measures. In this chapter, we make use of the disaggregated data available in the Organization for Economic Cooperation and Development (OECD) Social Expenditure Database (SOCX) to develop a whole series of new measures that allow us to explore the possibility that, beneath the surface of relatively unchanged aggregate expenditure, there have been changes in the structure of provision justifying at least some of the anxieties of those who see the welfare state as being under threat.

Disaggregated expenditure data allow us to do a number of things that would otherwise be impossible. First, they make it possible to improve existing aggregate measures by making them more consistent and more theoretically relevant. Consistency is a crucial issue because sometimes reported spending totals exclude items routinely included for other countries. Unless we know that aggregates are identically constituted both across time and countries, the conclusions we arrive at on the basis of comparison will be anything but secure. Theoretical relevance is an issue because not all items of spending included under the social expenditure heading are necessarily indicative of higher welfare. This is a point famously made by Gøsta Esping-Andersen (1990: 19–20), when he argues that 'expenditures are epiphenomenal to the theoretical substance of welfare states', noting that high spending on civil service pensions may not be indicative of a 'commitment to social citizenship and solidarity' and that high spending on unemployment benefits is not necessarily a sign of a society 'seriously committed to full employment'. Esping-Andersen's rejection of expenditure as an adequate measure of citizen welfare is the starting point for his elaboration of a typology of welfare regime types based on the extent and character of welfare entitlements. In principle, the use of disaggregated spending data also allows us to develop aggregate spending measures in which the criterion of inclusion for each separate spending component is its theoretical relevance to the concept of welfare under investigation.

Second, disaggregated data permit us to devise measures of how the structure of the welfare state has changed over time. These measures of the shape and direction of change make it possible to address the question of whether the apparent stability of aggregate spending patterns revealed in Chapter 2 disguise a much greater volatility at programme level. Volatility of this kind is potentially implicit in some variants of crisis theory. A possible explanation of constant levels of aggregate spending despite strong global pressures could be that increased unemployment spending had crowded out welfare programmes for the active population. Similarly, unchanged expenditure aggregates could coexist with an 'ageing crisis' if the response of governments to demographic pressure was to reduce spending on programmes for younger citizens. Hence, an understanding of how much the structure of social provision has changed over recent decades is a necessary element in any comprehensive assessment of the validity of these theories.

Third, disaggregated data permit us to distinguish welfare state structures in terms of the kinds of social provision they offer. This makes it possible to develop empirically based typologies and to use them to test hypotheses. In this chapter, we elaborate a typology of the structure of social provision that distinguishes between 'social security', 'poverty alleviation', and 'state services' states, which closely mirrors the distinction between 'conservative', 'liberal', and 'social democratic' welfare regime types that has become standard in the literature since its introduction by Esping-Andersen in 1990. Because the 'race to the bottom' literature clearly implies a dramatic shift in the structure of provision, we can use this typology to assess further the implications of that account. Social security provides citizen entitlements. State services involve a major diminution of the role of the market. In Esping-Andersen's terms, both serve to decommodify market relationships. Poverty alleviation, however, is about mopping up after market forces have had their say. If a 'race to the bottom' has been occurring at the level of welfare state structuring, the trajectory of change one would expect to encounter would involve a reduction in the share of welfare state expenditure devoted to social security and state services and an increased salience of the poverty alleviation functions of the state. Or, to put it in Esping-Andersen's terms, one would expect an across-the-board decline in the extent in welfare state decommodification and a shift to a 'liberal', more market-conforming welfare state.

Finally, an important advantage of using the SOCX is that it provides disaggregated information on spending patterns for a large number of countries on an annual basis that is readily available for scholarly usage. In this, it contrasts radically with the database from which Esping-Andersen derived his regime typology. Although this programme-specific database on citizenship entitlements in eighteen Western welfare states collected at the Swedish Institute of Social Research (SOFI) has been updated to the 1990s, and has been extensively used in welfare state research by those attached to the Institute (see, for instance, Korpi 1989, 2001; Palme 1990; Kangas 1991; Korpi and Palme 2003), it has not yet been published and is unavailable for wider use. Thus, while the majority of scholars concede the broad applicability of Esping-Andersen's types, they have had no systematic means of assessing the extent of change in nations' regime characteristics in the years since 1980, the data point for Esping-Andersen's original analysis. There have, of course, been many studies that have attempted to assess the trajectory of recent welfare state change (see Bonoli, George, and Taylor-Gooby 2000 and Green-Pedersen 2002 as well as studies in Ferrera and Rhodes 2000; Kuhnle 2000; Scharpf and Schmidt 2000b; Clasen 2001; Liebfried 2001). However, these studies have necessarily relied on whatever scattered data on programme characteristics happen to be available and which appear to give some leverage on trajectories of programme reform in the countries in which they are interested. Because the disaggregated data provided by the SOCX is available on an annual basis for many countries, it makes it possible to examine recent trajectories of change on a more comprehensive basis than has hitherto been possible.

Building Better Aggregates

The thirteen categories or components of social expenditure reported in the OECD SOCX cover spending on public and mandatory private programmes in the following social policy areas (OECD 2001a):

- Old age cash benefits
- Disability cash benefits
- Occupational injury and disease
- Sickness benefits
- Services for the elderly and disabled

- Survivors' benefits
- Family cash benefits
- Family services
- Active labour market programmes
- Unemployment
- Public expenditure on health
- Housing
- Other contingencies.

Apart from these categories, the database reports sub-components of expenditure. For instance, old-age cash benefits are broken down into five sub-components: old-age pensions, old-age civil servant pensions, veteran's old-age pensions, other old-age cash benefits, and early retirement pensions. At its greatest level of specificity, the database reports spending on individual national programmes: for instance, for countries with occupationally based social security schemes, spending under each occupational category. Education is the only programme of spending widely regarded as part of the welfare state which is not included in SOCX. Table 2.3 in the previous chapter shows that social spending according to the standard OECD definition already takes up more than half of total public spending. Including educational expenditure as part of the welfare state would further underline the dominance of spending for social purposes in contemporary societies.

Data at the level of specificity provided by the SOCX allow us to develop more consistent measures of aggregate spending than have hitherto been available and ones that are more relevant to the theoretical concerns of the researcher. The problem of consistency is one that has only become apparent in retrospect. Earlier reporting of aggregate social expenditure figures by the OECD has not contained anything like full information on the components and sub-components constituting that expenditure. But missing data for any of the larger categories of spending make cross-national comparison inaccurate and misleading and this is compounded in research with a time-series dimension. The Irish expenditure series provides what is, almost certainly, the most dramatic instance. For the period 1980–4, this series does not contain data on spending on active labour market programmes or on unemployment benefits. This information is reported from 1985 onward and these two components are together shown to involve spending in excess of 5 per cent of GDP in that year. This means that early 1980s OECD reported figures for aggregate social spending substantially underestimate Irish welfare effort and that estimations of total Irish social expenditure growth from dates prior to 1985 based on those figures will markedly exaggerate the extent of welfare state expansion in that country for this period. From 1991 onward, for the

18–21 countries featuring in most welfare state expenditure comparisons, the SOCX offers full coverage of all thirteen expenditure components, although detailed information at sub-component and individual programme level is sometimes unavailable. For comparisons using data from that time onward, there should no longer be a problem of inconsistently constituted aggregates. For comparisons of total spending for earlier periods or for change over time commencing in the 1980s, gaps in the data remain a problem.

There are a variety of strategies for coping with missing data in comparative research of this kind. Dropping cases is commonplace, but should really only be a strategy of last resort in an area where the small-n problem is the foremost methodological obstacle to more firmly based comparative findings (see Przeworski 1987). Often using data from immediately preceding or succeeding time points is a quite legitimate procedure for avoiding the need to drop cases. Sometimes, too, we know enough about the development of expenditure categories over time to be quite certain that missing data could not conceivably lead to any major distortion of aggregate statistics. In the comparisons that follow, we ignore missing data for spending on occupational injury in Australia in 1980 and for other contingencies in Denmark, Greece, and Italy in the same year because in none of these cases could this omission make a difference of as much as one percentage point of GDP to the relevant spending totals. Sometimes, too, we know of information from other sources that can make good serious gaps in the data. Thus, in Table 2.1 in the previous chapter, the figures for total public social expenditure reported for Austria, France, and Ireland for 1980 contain unemployment cash benefit expenditure interpolated from another OECD source. In the Irish case, this makes a difference of almost exactly two percentage points of GDP to the total of aggregate spending.

On some occasions, however, gaps in the data cannot be overcome in these ways. A case in point is spending on active labour market programmes, where SOCX coverage is extremely patchy for earlier years and where the omission of single cases through until the early 1990s could lead to distortions in cross-national and cross-time comparisons of well over one percentage point of GDP. Here, however, the fact that we possess disaggregated data provides us with an alternative strategy. Rather than sacrificing cases, we can sacrifice components of expenditure. This is the technique we use in the first three columns of Table 3.1 to create a 12-component measure of public social expenditure for 1980, 1998, and change over time, excluding spending on labour market programmes. This involves a trade-off between information and accuracy. We lose information on an important aspect of welfare state functioning (the effort some countries make to avoid high levels of unemployment through

Table 3.1 12-component, 11-component, and modified 11-component measures of public social expenditure in 21 OECD countries, 1980, 1998, and change over time

	12-component measure			11-component measure			Modified 11-component measure		
	1980	1998	Change	1980	1998	Change	1980	1998	Change
Australia	11.3	17.4	6.1	10.6	16.3	5.6	10.6	14.8	4.1
Canada	13.0	17.5	4.6	11.7	16.5	4.8	11.7	15.7	4.0
Ireland	18.9	14.6	−4.3	16.9	12.9	−4.0	15.8	12.1	−3.7
New Zealand	19.1	20.3	1.2	18.6	18.8	0.2	18.6	18.8	0.2
United Kingdom	17.8	21.1	3.3	16.7	20.7	4.0	13.8	n.a.	n.a.
United States	12.9	14.4	1.5	12.2	14.2	2.0	11.4	12.3	0.9
Family mean	*15.5*	*17.5*	*2.0*	*14.5*	*16.6*	*2.1*	*13.6*	*14.7*	*0.9*
Denmark	28.6	28.2	−0.5	23.8	24.8	1.0	22.7	23.7	0.9
Finland	17.5	25.1	7.6	16.9	22.6	5.7	16.9	22.6	5.7
Norway	17.7	26.1	8.4	17.3	25.6	8.3	17.3	25.6	8.3
Sweden	26.6	29.0	2.4	26.2	27.1	0.8	26.2	27.1	0.8
Family mean	*22.6*	*27.1*	*4.5*	*21.0*	*25.0*	*4.0*	*20.8*	*24.7*	*3.9*
Austria	23.8	26.4	2.6	23.3	25.5	2.1	20.5	22.5	2.0
Belgium	24.2	23.2	−1.0	21.7	20.7	−1.0	20.1	18.3	−1.9

France	22.6	27.5	4.9	21.1	25.7	4.6	18.7	22.9	4.2
Germany	20.3	26.0	5.8	19.8	24.7	4.9	17.9	23.0	5.1
Netherlands	26.6	22.6	-4.0	24.9	20.0	-4.9	23.8	19.2	-4.6
Family mean	*23.5*	*25.1*	*1.7*	*22.2*	*23.3*	*1.1*	*20.2*	*21.1*	*0.9*
Greece	11.5	22.6	11.1	11.2	22.1	10.8	9.3	20.3	11.1
Italy	18.4	24.4	6.0	17.8	23.7	5.9	16.8	n.a.	n.a.
Portugal	11.4	17.5	6.1	11.1	16.7	5.6	10.2	14.0	3.9
Spain	15.7	19.1	3.4	13.7	17.5	3.8	12.7	16.8	4.1
Family mean	*14.2*	*20.9*	*6.7*	*13.4*	*20.0*	*6.6*	*12.2*	*17.0*	*6.4*
Switzerland	15.0	27.5	12.5	15.0	26.5	11.6	15.0	26.5	11.6
Japan	10.1	14.4	4.3	9.7	13.9	4.2	8.8	12.9	4.1
Overall mean	*18.2*	*22.1*	*3.9*	*17.2*	*20.8*	*3.6*	*16.1*	*19.4*	*3.2*
Coefficient of variation	*30.5*	*21.7*		*29.5*	*21.8*		*30.5*	*25.2*	

Notes and sources: 12-component measure includes: old-age cash benefits, disability cash benefits, spending on occupational injury and disease, sickness benefits, services for the elderly, survivors benefits, family cash benefits, family services, unemployment benefits, housing expenditure, health expenditure, housing benefits, and spending on other contingencies (including low income assistance programmes). 11-component measure is the 12-component measure minus unemployment benefit spending. Modified 11-component measure is the 11-component measure minus expenditure on pension and disability schemes for civil servants. All components measured as percentages of GDP. All data calculated from OECD (2001*a*), *Social Expenditure Database, 1980–1998*, Paris. Missing data in 1980 for occupational injury spending for Australia and for other contingencies for Denmark, Greece, and Italy. 1980 unemployment cash benefits for Austria, France, and Ireland interpolated from OECD (1985). 1998 UK total expenditure reduced by 3.3 per cent of GDP to take account of a definitional change relating to old-age cash benefits. All calculated figures subject to rounding errors.

active labour market policies) in return for obtaining a measure of total social spending that is more consistent and, hence, more comparable across time and space.

This enhanced capacity to generate consistent aggregate measures may be seen as a relatively trivial analytical gain, given that the very completeness of the OECD SOCX from the early 1990s means that the problem of inconsistently constituted aggregates will soon be a thing of the past. However, precisely the same technique of stripping aggregates of particular components or sub-components of expenditure provides a means of constructing aggregate measures with potentially greater relevance to researchers' theoretical concerns than has been previously possible. The remaining columns of Table 3.1 contain instances of what is possible in this respect. As noted in Chapter 2, many commentators have questioned the theoretical appropriateness of including unemployment spending as part of the welfare state effort, when increases in such expenditure may be seen as demonstrating the failure of the welfare state to protect employees from the consequences of economic downturn. From some theoretical and measurement viewpoints, there are also problems in including spending which reflects the cyclical functioning of the economy rather than the intentions of welfare state policy-makers. Using SOCX data, our aggregate expenditure measure can readily be reduced from a 12-component to an 11-component measure excluding spending on unemployment benefits. In principle, it is possible to use the disaggregated data from the SOCX to create an infinity of consistent expenditure aggregates. Because Esping-Andersen's plea for more theory-based measures of welfare explicitly identifies the inegalitarian impact of high spending on public service pensions, the final three columns of Table 3.1 remove spending on civil service pensions, civil service early retirement pensions, and civil servant disability pensions to create a modified 11-component measure.

We make no big claims about the value of the particular measures presented in Table 3.1 beyond the fact that it is possible to use the SOCX to generate them and that, ultimately, consistent measures must be preferred to inconsistent ones. A preference for consistent measures is the reason that, throughout the remainder of the book, all further analysis of aggregate expenditures is based on the 12-component measure, the most comprehensive and comparable measure of total public social expenditure that is available to us. However, in reality, the choice of one of these indicators in preference to another is not really a matter of any great moment, since a statistical analysis of the relationships between the various measures in Tables 2.1 and 3.1 suggests extremely high correlations of an order of 0.96 and higher in both 1980 and 1998 and of 0.98 and higher in respect of change over time. This finding in itself demonstrates the theoretical value of using disaggregated data to develop novel measures of welfare effort. The extremely close relationships between these different measures of aggregate expenditure suggests that, at least for the period under investigation here, unemployment expenditure does not mask underlying patterns of spending and that, whatever else may make a difference to national welfare state performance, generosity to public service pensioners is not amongst the bigger ticket items. The availability of disaggregated data allows us not only to improve our theoretical measures, but also to assess the validity of speculations concerning the role of particular expenditure components, such as unemployment benefits and public service pensions, in influencing cross-national variation in welfare effort.

All our comments so far have been on issues involved in constructing better aggregate measures. We turn now to the substantive question of whether the use of more consistent measures of aggregate spending reveals a pattern substantially different from that identified in Table 2.1 in the previous chapter, and, in particular, whether it reveals a pattern more readily interpretable in terms of a 'race to the bottom' in social spending. The answer is that, irrespective of the measure we look at, the differences are minor and the evidence for a generalized downward trend in expenditure no greater. Table 2.1 suggests that OECD average aggregate expenditure for social purposes increased by 4 per cent of GDP between 1980 and 1998. Table 3.1 gives figures of 3.9 per cent for the 12-component measure, 3.6 per cent for the 11-component measure, and 3.2 per cent for the nineteen cases for which we have data for the modified 11-component measure. Table 2.1 locates strong patterns of similarity within different families of nations and these patterns are closely duplicated by the measures presented in Table 3.1. Admittedly, Table 2.1 identifies only two countries—Ireland and the Netherlands—in which aggregate spending as a percentage of GDP actually declined, whereas Table 3.1 identifies four—Ireland and the Netherlands plus Belgium and Denmark—in respect of the 12-component measure, and three—Ireland and the Netherlands plus Belgium in respect of the 11- and modified 11-component measure. We accept that the measures in Table 3.1 are more consistent in their inclusion of expenditure components both between countries and across time, but expenditure cuts in four countries, all but one of which left the countries concerned above the 1998 OECD expenditure mean, hardly qualify as a 'race to the bottom'. We conclude—as we concluded in Chapter 2—that no sensible reading of the available aggregate data could possibly support such a contention.

The Shape and Direction of Change

We now turn to the question of whether the same conclusion holds in respect of the structure of social provision. A prerequisite for systematic research on whether welfare states are undergoing structural transformation is to have cross-nationally commensurable measures of the shape and direction of change which are sensitive to the kinds of activities constituting social policy effort in different nations. Expenditure aggregates, however consistent and modified, are incapable of performing such a function because major changes in spending priorities may be disguised by compensatory movements in other categories of expenditure. Although we have just demonstrated that increases in unemployment spending did not mask cross-national spending relativities *in the particular period we are investigating here*, it is perfectly possible that countervailing expenditure trends could have such effects. Because this is so, aggregated measures provide us with only very limited information about the shape and direction of change. Programme-specific spending data of the kind provided by the SOCX clearly allow us to address this problem. We are now able to compare countries at component, sub-component, and programme levels and, for each individual nation, we can uncover the specifics of growth and decline in social policy areas and programmes in minute detail. However, these gains may come at a real cost in our capacity to analyse and compare welfare states at a general level. If we cannot measure differences between nations at system level, we cannot assess or contrast system-level performance. Indeed, strictly speaking, if we cannot measure what welfare states do, we cannot intelligently discuss welfare states at all. The big question, then, is whether the programme-specific data provided by the SOCX can be harnessed to provide new measures, which, more adequately than the old aggregates, summarily capture the shape and direction of welfare state change as a whole.

Debates about welfare state reform and retrenchment are often as much about the shape of the welfare state and how that shape is changing as about changes in the extent of its aggregate spending (cf. Green-Pedersen 2004). Can we, then, devise a summary measure of change in the welfare state over time which captures change in the size of social policy expenditure components relative to each other, a measure capturing whether unemployment benefits are growing at the expense of health and housing or whether pensions for the aged are crowding out more expenditure on families? The answer is that such a measure of the overall structural transformation can be quite easily constructed now that we possess the information contained in the SOCX. Since the SOCX makes it possible to describe national cases by the size distribution of the thirteen expenditure categories into which social expenditure is disaggregated, we can simply assess the degree of statistical association between these distributions at different times. It is appropriate to use the measure of adjusted R^2 as the statistical basis for calculating our measure of association, since Pearson's R, from which it derives, is a pure measure of the shape of distributions, 'insensitive to differences in the magnitude of the variables used to compute the coefficient' (Aldenderfer and Blashfield 1984: 23). This means that if all components of expenditure go up or down in the same proportions, it will have no effect on the measure. Only changes in the shape of the welfare state, that is, changes in the relative size of specified expenditure components, will register as changes in our measure of structural transformation.

Two variants of this measure are presented in the first two columns of Table 3.2, based on our earlier calculations of 12- and 11-component aggregate expenditure measures. If our purpose is to capture the fullest extent of structural change, the 12-component variant is the most appropriate one on which to focus. If our concern is with changes in the shape of the welfare state brought about by purposive reform activity, the 11-component variant may be of more interest, since it excludes the often cyclical effects of unemployment. Examining the two variants in conjunction allows us to examine how far the changing face of social policy is attributable to labour market changes beyond the short-term control of welfare state policy-makers.

A number of interesting points emerge from the figures in Table 3.2. First, both variants of the structural transformation measure confirm two of the more significant findings of Chapter 2. They demonstrate that there is no more evidence of massive overall change in the shape of the welfare state than there was of massive cutbacks in aggregate spending during this period. On the contrary, an average level of structural transformation of 8.5 percentage points over eighteen years for the 12-component measure, and 7.6 for its 11-component equivalent, is suggestive of a trajectory of change that is more evolutionary than explosive. They also demonstrate considerable cross-national variation in the extent of structural transformation, with a small minority of countries experiencing a substantial shift in spending priorities and some very little indeed. There is no sign here that Western welfare states are marching in tune to the beat of a single drummer. Indeed, even less so than in the case of aggregate expenditure, since the structural transformation measure demonstrates no obvious family of nations patterning.

Second, it is clear that this measure picks up on dimensions of change hidden by aggregate expenditure totals. Table 3.1 shows that the United Kingdom and Sweden are close to the mean in respect of 12-component expenditure

Table 3.2 Structural transformation of the welfare state and welfare state downsizing in 21 OECD countries, 1980 to 1998

	Degree of structural transformation		Extent of downsizing	
	12-component	11-component	12-component	11-component
Australia	6.2	6.3	−5.6	−6.0
Canada	5.3	4.3	−2.8	−0.9
Ireland	7.4	7.5	−26.4	−27.9
New Zealand	5.8	4.6	−11.8	−12.1
United Kingdom	17.6	16.1	−12.7	−9.0
United States	6.3	6.0	−7.8	−4.7
Family mean	*8.1*	*9.0*	*−11.2*	*−10.1*
Denmark	12.8	10.5	−14.8	−11.5
Finland	9.8	5.3	0.0	0.0
Norway	8.7	9.1	−2.3	−2.4
Sweden	18.1	15.8	−13.7	−10.6
Family mean	*12.3*	*10.2*	*−7.7*	*−6.1*
Austria	3.5	3.4	−5.7	−5.8
Belgium	5.2	5.3	−11.3	−12.4
France	4.5	4.6	−7.8	−8.3
Germany	1.3	0.8	−2.2	−2.3
Netherlands	19.1	16.0	−23.6	−30.0
Family mean	*6.7*	*6.0*	*−10.1*	*−11.8*
Greece	6.3	6.5	−0.2	−0.2
Italy	9.8	10.0	−6.7	−6.9
Portugal	9.3	9.1	−3.7	−3.8
Spain	9.8	7.8	−12.1	−10.6
Family mean	*8.8*	*8.4*	*−5.7*	*−5.4*
Switzerland	3.6	3.0	−2.6	−2.7
Japan	7.1	7.2	−1.0	−1.0
Overall mean	*8.5*	*7.6*	*−8.3*	*−8.2*

Notes and sources: Degree of structural transformation is calculated as 100 minus (100 times the adjusted R^2 obtained by regressing the values of the components of social expenditure for a given country in 1998 measured as percentages of GDP on the values for that country in 1980). Extent of downsizing is calculated as the sum of cutbacks in the components making up a given aggregate social expenditure measure as a percentage of spending on that measure in 1980.

change, but according to Table 3.2, both feature amongst the countries manifesting the highest levels of structural transformation. An opposite reversal occurs in the Irish case. Ireland is the country in which aggregate expenditure declines most sharply over the period, but, in structural transformation terms, its experience is very close to the OECD norm. In the cases of both the United Kingdom and Sweden, there are reasons for believing that the structural transformation measure is more sensitive to reform initiatives than are measures of aggregate expenditure. The Thatcherite attempt to dismantle the welfare state may not have shown up in a reduced budget, but it did show up in changed spending priorities (Pierson 1994). In Sweden, the onset of economic crisis and mass unemployment in the early 1990s reinforced a reprioritization of welfare goals that some commentators see as 'steps toward recommodification of the Swedish welfare state' (Huber and Stephens 2001: 249). The Irish case also makes sense, given that Ireland was the country which, during this period, had much the highest economic growth rate in the OECD, automatically shrinking spending as a percentage of GDP across all programmes without the necessity for any massive change in spending priorities.

The sensitivity of the structural transformation measure is also apparent at the other end of the distribution. The absence of a family of nations pattern in the case of continental Western Europe is simply a function of the fact that the Netherlands manifests the highest level of 12-component structural transformation of any country in the OECD. However, the four remaining continental Western European countries—Austria, Belgium, France, and Germany—despite exhibiting quite diverse aggregate expenditure change profiles, manifest the four lowest transformation scores of any countries in the sample. This is a finding that fits neatly with the many analyses of these countries as exemplars of reform inertia or Eurosclerosis (see e.g. Esping-Andersen 1996b; Scharpf 2000).

Finally, it is worth noting that the contrast between the 12- and 11-component measures in Table 3.2 reveals no cases where the inclusion of unemployment benefit expenditure makes much of a difference to how we view the extent of structural transformation occurring during the period, once again demonstrating that, for the particular period under investigation

The programmes making up the 11- and 12-component measures of social expenditure are as listed in Table 2.1. All data calculated from OECD (2001a), *Social Expenditure Database, 1980–1998*, Paris. Missing data in 1980 for occupational injury spending for Australia and for other contingencies for Greece and Italy. 1998 UK total expenditure reduced by 3.3 per cent of GDP to take account of a definitional change relating to old-age cash benefits. All calculated figures subject to rounding errors.

here, the expenditure impact of unemployment was not masking other adverse programmatic changes. It should be noted, however, that this is a conclusion that does not hold irrespective of period. Between 1990 and 1993, Finnish unemployment expenditure went up from just over 1 per cent of GDP to around 5 per cent of GDP and remained above 4 per cent for the next two years. For measurements of change terminating in this period, it is clear that there would have been a considerable disparity between Finland's ranking in terms of 12-component structural transformation, which would have been well above average, and its ranking in terms of the 11-component measure, which would have been much lower.

The measures of the structural transformation of the welfare state appearing in Table 3.2 derive from an attempt to provide a summary indicator of the full range of changes taking place in the relative size of the components of social policy spending over a given period of time. An interesting alternative for some purposes may be to concentrate on changes of a particular type. In the final columns of Table 3.2, we provide a measure of the direction of welfare state change that is particularly well suited for assessing the extent to which expenditure retrenchment pressures have been dominant in recent years and which, therefore, serves as a further test of the 'race to the bottom' hypothesis. The theoretical premise on which this downsizing measure rests is the possibility that the relationship between global economic forces and expenditure cutbacks may have been inaccurately specified in the earlier globalization literature. If, as implied in a number of recent studies (Scharpf and Schmidt 2000a, b; Huber and Stephens 2001), the real situation is that major globalization-induced pressures to cut back spending are contending with no less significant structural and demographic forces promoting higher spending, we would expect to discover a world in which cuts in some welfare components are accompanied by expansion in others.

Hence, it can be argued that, if we are interested in the extent to which retrenchment pressures have influenced social policy over recent decades, we should be looking neither at aggregate spending totals nor at degrees of structural transformation (if all components are cut proportionately, no measured structural transformation will occur), but at the aggregate of cuts in existing programme expenditure. The two variants of the downsizing measure appearing in the final columns of Table 3.2 are simply the sum of cuts in programme components for the period 1980–98 expressed as percentages of the initial levels of 12- and 11-component aggregate spending in 1980. The measure may be interpreted as an indicator of the extent to which policy-makers have been willing or have been forced to downsize existing welfare provision either to reduce overall aggregates of taxing and spending or to make way for other, higher priority items of social spending.

The figures in the final columns of Table 3.2 need to be interpreted carefully. The fact that all bar one of the figures are negative is simply a consequence of the fact that we are measuring the extent of cuts to existing programmes, which, as we have already established, are more than outweighed by increased expenditures to other programmes. What is required is a criterion of cutbacks with a serious potential impact on existing programme performance. Here, we, somewhat arbitrarily, take that demarcation line as being equivalent to a reduction in overall programme expenditure of 10 per cent or more. By this criterion, eight countries made serious programme cutbacks in 12-component expenditure and seven in 11-component expenditure, with the percentage cutbacks in Ireland and the Netherlands markedly greater than in any other of the countries. The 10 per cent criterion identifies all the countries shown as making an overall reduction in aggregate expenditure in Table 3.1 as major downsizers. It also picks up on New Zealand, the country with the fifth lowest expenditure growth on the 12-component measure and the fourth lowest according to the other measures in that table. No one, remembering New Zealand's role as an exemplar of neo-liberal policies from the mid-1980s to the mid-1990s, will find the inclusion of New Zealand in our list of major downsizers in the least surprising (see Kelsey 1993; Huber and Stephens 2001). In addition to the countries of low expenditure growth, both downsizing measures also identify the major countries of structural transformation as leading instances of welfare downsizing, with the United Kingdom in respect of the 11-component measure the only exception. Seemingly, then, the downsizing measure is one that picks up on both aggregate and structural aspects of recent social expenditure change. Because that is so, it will be among the measures we seek to model in Chapter 5, where we seek to establish which of a wide range of economic, social, and political factors has had the greatest impact in shaping expenditure outcomes.

Our findings in respect of welfare state downsizing do lend some support to the notion that, under the surface of relatively unchanging aggregate spending, there are currents and counter-currents of cutbacks and new programme growth. Clearly, there are a number of countries in which significant programme growth was accompanied by significant programme attrition in other areas. However, even if there is some link between cuts to existing programmes and exposure to the international economy, there is no evidence of any mass retreat from the welfare state. Just as many countries experienced cutbacks of less than 4 per cent as experienced cutbacks of more than 10 per cent, and 4 per cent over nearly two decades is not a race to anywhere. Even the average cut in existing programmes of around 8 per cent implies that a reduction in overall spending of 25 per cent would take just over fifty years. Finally, it should be noted that the difference between the countries making big cuts and those making small ones is clearly patterned. Many of countries making the largest proportional cutbacks—including Belgium, Denmark, the Netherlands, and Sweden—were amongst the biggest aggregate spenders in 1980, and many of those making negligible cuts— including Finland, Greece, Portugal, Switzerland, and Japan—were among the smallest welfare states in 1980. Here, as in respect of many of the measures of aggregate expenditure discussed in Chapter 2, the dominant trend is one of catch-up and convergence.

Types and Trajectories of Social Provision

The measures devised in the previous section seek to assess the extent to which the shape of the welfare state has changed in recent years and the extent to which components of social spending have been downsized without specifying the precise nature of existing social provision. Ideally, we would also like to possess measures of the character of social provision and of change in these characteristics over time. To proceed along these lines requires that we classify the kinds of things welfare states do, creating a typology of welfare states which can then be operationalized for use in comparative research. As it turns out, the literature is big on the classification of welfare states and the development of typologies (see Abrahamson 1999; Castles 2001a), but extremely weak on their operationalization and measurement.

There is also a fair amount of consensus about the most important kinds of differences between types of welfare state. The classic formulation is Richard Titmuss's (1974: 30–1) distinction between 'residual', 'industrial achievement-performance', and 'institutional redistributive' types of social policy, with the 'residual' type identified with an unreformed poor law tradition, the 'industrial achievement' type with social security in the Bismarckian mould, and 'the institutional redistributive' type with a social services state along Beveridgean lines. Later analyses have highlighted similar distinctions. Rimlinger (1971) distinguishes between the 'patriarchal' or conservative character of the continental social security systems and the 'liberal' character of the system of provision in the United States, with the latter hugely reluctant to offer to anyone but the old, income guarantees that might deter recipients from gainful employment. Furniss and Tilton (1977: 18–20) describe the United States as a 'positive state', seeking to protect the interests of the owners of property, and contrast it with Sweden's 'social welfare state', which seeks to promote 'equality and solidarity'. Esping-Andersen's distinction between 'liberal', 'conservative', and 'social democratic' welfare regimes–refurbishes

Titmuss's typology, providing it with a more clearly articulated theoretical rationale and much stronger linkages to factors seen as shaping the historical and political development of contemporary welfare states.

Esping-Andersen is also the first scholar in the typologizing tradition to provide clear-cut empirical criteria for assigning particular social policy systems to particular types. However, as noted previously, the database from which he derives those assignments is not available to the scholarly community at large. The challenge, then, is to use the data available in the SOCX to locate a set of distinctions broadly analogous to those found in the classificatory literature, which can be used on a routine basis to characterize the nature of social policy provision and measure its trajectory of change over time. There is no self-evident strategy for doing this. Since any given programme of spending can be designed along residual, contributory, or redistributive lines, and since the SOCX does not tell us which is which, we cannot assign, say, residual pension spending to one category of provision, contributory pension spending to a second, and redistributive pension spending to a third.

Hence, in order to proceed at all, we must assign whole programmes or social expenditure components to different categories of provision, and this can only be done on the basis of prior assumptions, ideally ones tying in with the consensus of the existing literature. The assumptions underlying the analysis we present here are as follows:

1. That where programmes and components are potentially income replacing (are, in most instances, used by recipients as their primary source of income), they are more likely to involve substantial expenditure—and a proportionately larger share of total expenditure—when designed along Bismarckean, contributory, and conservative lines.
2. That where programmes and components are predominantly contingency based (i.e. provide income and services on the basis of need), liberal welfare states are likely to be distinguished from social democratic ones by their stronger emphasis and proportionately greater spending on traditional sources of need (poverty and ill-health) than on newer, essentially demographic categories of need (for personal care for the aged and disabled and for support in child-rearing by women in employment).

If the first assumption is a reasonable one, proportionately greater spending on age pensions, disability benefits, occupational injury, sickness benefits, and survivors benefits are likely to be the marks of the social security state. If the second assumption is reasonable, and it is explicit in much recent writing on welfare state responses to changing labour market conditions

Table 3.3 Percentage shares of different types of social expenditure in 21 OECD countries, 1980 and 1998

| | Income-replacing expenditure share — social security | | Contingency-based expenditure share | | | |
| | | | Poverty alleviation and health care | | State services | |
	1980	1998	1980	1998	1980	1998
Australia	44.4	40.9	54.0	51.9	1.6	7.2
Canada	32.3	39.4	66.8	60.6	0.9	0.0
Ireland	45.0	36.6	51.7	59.5	3.3	3.8
New Zealand	47.6	45.7	52.0	53.7	0.3	0.5
United Kingdom	48.5	49.1	45.1	44.7	6.4	6.2
United States	57.4	50.7	38.9	46.9	3.7	2.4
Family mean	*45.9*	*43.7*	*51.4*	*52.9*	*2.7*	*3.3*
Denmark	41.5	38.2	39.9	40.8	18.7	20.9
Finland	51.5	49.8	38.4	37.3	10.2	13.0
Norway	46.8	41.6	43.8	39.8	9.5	18.5
Sweden	43.0	43.2	42.4	36.9	14.6	19.9
Family mean	*45.7*	*43.2*	*41.1*	*38.7*	*13.2*	*18.1*
Austria	58.6	60.3	35.8	31.8	5.6	8.0
Belgium	59.2	57.5	39.5	41.1	1.3	1.4
France	56.0	53.2	39.8	39.5	4.2	7.3
Germany	56.2	50.9	40.2	42.9	3.6	6.2

Netherlands	51.4	52.3	43.5	39.2	5.1	8.5
Family mean	*56.3*	*54.8*	*39.8*	*38.9*	*4.0*	*6.3*
Greece	63.6	64.0	36.3	31.5	0.1	4.5
Italy	61.0	72.8	37.2	25.2	2.0	2.0
Portugal	60.2	60.1	38.7	36.3	3.6	3.6
Spain	64.1	63.2	35.2	34.6	2.2	2.2
Family mean	*62.2*	*65.0*	*36.8*	*31.9*	*2.0*	*3.1*
Switzerland	56.0	60.4	40.3	36.5	0.1	4.5
Japan	46.1	52.7	51.0	43.2	2.9	4.1
Overall mean	*51.9*	*51.6*	*43.5*	*41.6*	*4.4*	*6.5*
Coefficient of variation	*16.0*	*18.8*	*17.8*	*21.5*	*107.0*	*91.1*

Notes and sources: Income-replacing expenditure share is the sum of old-age cash benefits, disability cash benefits, spending on occupational injury and disease, sickness benefits, and survivors benefits as a percentage of GDP divided by the 11-component expenditure measure multiplied by 100. Poverty alleviation and health care expenditure share is the sum of family cash benefits, health expenditure, housing benefits, and spending on other contingencies as a percentage of GDP divided by the 11-component expenditure measure multiplied by 100. State services expenditure share is the sum of expenditures on services for the elderly and family services as a percentage of GDP divided by the 11-component expenditure measure multiplied by 100. All data calculated from OECD (2001a), *Social Expenditure Database, 1980–1998*, Paris. Missing data in 1980 for occupational injury spending for Australia and for other contingencies for Greece and Italy. 1998 UK income-replacing share reduced to take account of definitional change relating to old age cash benefits. All calculated figures subject to rounding errors.

(see Esping-Andersen 1990, 1999; Anttonen and Sipilä 1996; Castles 1998; Daly 2000), we have a means of distinguishing between liberal and social democratic welfare states. Both will exhibit proportionately greater contingency-based spending as compared with conservative welfare states. However, the former will be primarily focused on poverty alleviation measures, such as family cash benefits, housing, and other contingencies, together with health care, while the latter will devote an increasingly large proportion of spending to services catering to the old and to families (for a similar set of distinctions as to the purposes of different welfare state types, see Palier 2001).

Obviously, these assumptions cannot be empirically tested in the strict sense of the word. Apart from the decommodification index that features in Esping-Andersen's original study, we do not have empirically based classifications against which to match our findings. Nevertheless, we can examine the degree of correspondence between the expenditure share measures appearing in Table 3.3 and conventional attributions appearing in the literature. Continental Western European countries are generally seen as characterized by Bismarckian institutional designs. Table 3.3 shows that, in both 1980 and 1998, all of these countries had an income-replacing share of social expenditure in excess of 50 per cent. Southern Europe is more controversially located as 'conservative' (Esping-Andersen 1993 and Castles 1995 argue in favour; Liebfried 1993 and Ferrera 1996, against; Guillén and Álvarez (2001) offer a more recent and nuanced conclusion). The data here suggest that the Southern European pattern of provision is even more biased towards income replacement than that of continental Western Europe proper. In the English-speaking nations and Scandinavia, the share of income-replacing expenditure is much lower, with only a couple of deviations from the pattern that might be expected on the basis of most standard classifications. In 1980, the United States and Finland devoted more than 50 per cent of their spending to income replacement and this remained true for the United States until the end of the period. Only in the case of the United States in 1980 is the deviation from the family of nations pattern of any magnitude. Unlike earlier measures of aggregate spending, the income-replacing expenditure share is not convergent over time, with the coefficient of variation actually increasing slightly between 1980 and 1998.

Turning now to the patterns exhibited by the contingency-based expenditure share, it is clear that there is a sharp distinction between the English-speaking liberal nations and the Scandinavian social democratic ones, with the former spending an average 50 per cent or more of the social policy budget on poverty alleviation and health care and very little indeed on state services, and the latter devoting only about 40 per cent of spending to poverty alleviation and health, but almost 20 per cent to services for the aged, disabled, and families. Neither the continental Western European nor the Southern European welfare states spend as much as 40 per cent of their social policy budgets on poverty alleviation and health and their share of state service spending is similar to that of the English-speaking nations. As in the case of social security spending, the coefficients of variation for poverty alleviation and health are indicative of divergence rather than convergence over time. State services do converge but from an extraordinarily high level of cross-national variation, with the Scandinavian countries, in this respect, manifesting a wholly different set of priorities from all other OECD nations.

Looking at the patterns revealed by Table 3.3 as a whole, one can clearly distinguish three distinct welfare state types, corresponding closely with the previously identified types in the literature and characterized by quite distinct expenditure profiles. They are:

1. A continental Western European *social security state* with more than 50 per cent of expenditure devoted to income replacement and around 40 per cent to poverty alleviation and health. In structural terms, if not initially in respect of the extent of aggregate spending, Switzerland should, arguably, also be included in this grouping (see the discussion of this matter in the concluding section of Chapter 4). The Southern European countries seem to be a variant on this type, with a somewhat greater income-replacing share (mainly constituted by expenditure on age pensions) and a somewhat lesser share on poverty alleviation and health. The justification for counting Italy as part of the Southern European rather than the continental Western European family of nations is apparent, with Italy in 1998 manifesting the most lopsided balance between income-replacing and poverty-alleviation programmes in the OECD.

2. An English-speaking *poverty alleviation state* in which the share constituted by contingency-based expenditure is 50 per cent or more, but in which state services are only of minor importance. The clear instances of this pattern are Australia, Canada, Ireland, and New Zealand. Although, in 1998, neither the United States nor the United Kingdom came close to the 50 per cent level, they too had poverty alleviation and health care shares higher than elsewhere in the OECD, thus confirming the standard designation of the English-speaking countries' welfare states as 'residual' or 'liberal' in character. In 1980, Japan also qualified as a member of this grouping, but has now, apparently, shifted towards a stronger social security profile (cf. Esping-Andersen 1997).

3. A Scandinavian *state services state*, in which contingency-based spending exceeds income-replacing expenditure, but in which state services make up between 10 and 20 per cent of total spending and between

25 and 33 per cent of contingency-based spending. The Finnish case appears suspended between types 1 and 3 (a finding which confirms a similar point made by Esping-Andersen 1990: 52), while the United Kingdom combines elements of types 2 and 3, although the level of state service provision remains markedly lower than in the social democratic north.

Finally, before moving on to discuss trajectories of change and reform, it is worth re-emphasizing that all of the characterizations here are based on expenditure shares rather than on expenditure aggregates measured as percentages of GDP. Countries with lower expenditure shares on particular social policy programmes may be spending far more as a share of GDP than countries with a higher share, a point that is relevant to any overall comparison of British and Scandinavian models of social provision. A still more dramatic instance is the contrast between Sweden and Australia at the beginning of the period. Table 3.3 shows that, in 1980, Sweden had a poverty alleviation and health care expenditure share of 42.4 per cent, while the corresponding figure for Australia was 54 per cent. However, in that year, SOCX shows that Swedish spending on family cash benefits, housing, other contingencies, and health care was 11.8 per cent of GDP, somewhat more than Australia's entire 11-component spending as shown in Table 3.1. Clearly, how much countries spend and what they spend it on are quite different matters; this, of course, being the justification for presenting separate measures of the extent and structure of social provision.

The capacity to classify welfare states in expenditure share terms allows us to measure changes in the extent to which given countries conform to given welfare state types. Systematic cross-national comparisons of the consequences of welfare state reform efforts require measures of this kind in order to characterize resulting trajectories of change. Without common metrics of the nature of the change that is occurring, we cannot say which countries have gone farthest along the paths of reform or in what directions. Such measures are also required for comparative hypothesis testing, with our focus here on whether there has been a shift in priorities towards the poverty alleviation functions of government in the manner implied by the 'race to the bottom' literature. Table 3.4 presents data on changes in the size of the expenditure shares in Table 3.3. These data make it possible to compare and contrast trajectories of change in welfare state structuring between 1980–98 and to consider what they tell us about the forces shaping social policy development in recent years.

Examining the overall means in Table 3.4 demonstrates that changes in types of social provision were no more dramatic than any of the other kinds of expenditure change surveyed in Chapters 2 and 3. The income-replacing

Table 3.4 Change in percentage shares of different types of social expenditure in 21 OECD countries, 1980–98

	Income-replacing expenditure share	Poverty alleviation and health care	State services expenditure share
Australia	−3.4	−2.2	5.6
Canada	7.1	−6.2	−0.9
Ireland	−8.4	7.8	0.5
New Zealand	−1.9	1.7	0.2
United Kingdom	0.6	−0.4	−0.2
United States	−6.7	8.0	−1.3
Family Mean	*−2.1*	*1.5*	*0.5*
Denmark	−3.2	1.0	2.3
Finland	1.7	−1.1	2.8
Norway	−5.1	−4.0	9.1
Sweden	0.2	−5.5	5.3
Family Mean	*−2.4*	*−2.5*	*4.9*
Austria	1.7	−4.1	2.4
Belgium	−1.7	1.6	0.1
France	−2.8	−0.3	3.1
Germany	−5.3	2.7	2.6
Netherlands	0.9	−4.3	3.4
Family Mean	*−1.4*	*−0.9*	*2.3*
Greece	0.3	−4.7	4.4
Italy	11.8	−12.1	0.3
Portugal	−0.1	−2.4	2.5
Spain	−1.0	−0.6	1.6
Family Mean	*2.7*	*−4.9*	*2.2*
Switzerland	4.4	−6.5	2.1
Japan	6.5	−7.7	1.2
Overall mean	*−0.4*	*−1.9*	*2.3*

Notes and sources: All data calculated from OECD (2001a), *Social Expenditure Database, 1980–1998*, Paris. Missing data in 1980 for occupational injury spending for Australia and for other contingencies for Greece and Italy. 1998 UK income-replacing share reduced to take account of definitional change relating to old-age cash benefits. All calculated figures subject to rounding errors.

share of social expenditure declined by just 0.4 of a percentage point and the poverty alleviation share by just 1.9 percentage points, contributing to a 2.3 percentage point increase in the state services expenditure share. This is hardly the pattern of change that would be expected on the basis of a 'race to the bottom'. Rather than a shift towards a market conforming, poverty alleviation stance, the general tendency was in the opposite direction, with this share of spending declining in no less than fifteen of these twenty-one OECD countries. Moreover, given that this was a period in which there was a strong increase in health spending across the OECD, the decline in the purely poverty-alleviating components of expenditure was, in fact, considerably greater than indicated here. More convincing than an account based on globalization might be one premised on a very gradual, but quite general, shift to forms of welfare provision accommodating demographic trends—in particular, the increase in female employment and the proportion of the population in the age group above seventy-five years of age and in need of intensive care—with eighteen out of these twenty-one OECD nations experiencing an increase in the state services expenditure share during these years. Although average change was modest, there are distinct family of nations patterns. Indeed, the story is one of a slight accentuation of existing welfare regime biases. Southern European welfare states become somewhat more social security biased and the decline in the income-replacing share is less in continental Western Europe than in Scandinavia or the English-speaking world. At the same time, the English-speaking nations are the only grouping to experience an increase in the poverty alleviation and health care share, while Scandinavia manifests the greatest average increase in the size of the state services share.

Although overall trends were modest, there were a number of countries that experienced change of a more substantial nature. Six countries, in particular, stand out. Two—Ireland and the United States—experienced major increases in the poverty alleviation and health care expenditure share at the expense of the income-replacing expenditure share. However, calculations from SOCX suggest that the increasing salience of the poverty alleviation and health expenditure share in the United States was entirely accounted for by increased spending on public health. This is the trajectory of change that we argued was likely to be most characteristic of a 'race to the bottom', and that only one case unequivocally fits the crisis scenario speaks for itself. Three other countries, Canada, Italy, and Japan, made the reverse shift from a poverty alleviation to a social security stance. In the case of the last two countries named, this was almost certainly, in some part, due to the pressures of an ageing population (see Table 6.1). Finally, Norway experienced a decline in both the income-replacing and poverty-alleviation shares and a marked increase in the salience of state services spending. This change can be seen as part of a pattern of convergence within the Scandinavian family of nations, with Norway moving from laggard status in respect of state services provision to a stance similar to that of other members of the family grouping.

Conclusion

This chapter has had interlinked objectives. We have sought to use the disaggregated data made available in the OECD Social Expenditure Database to develop more consistent and theory-relevant aggregates as well as new measures of the structure of welfare provision, partly with the aim of showing that the development of such measures is feasible and partly further to test the implications of the 'race to the bottom' hypothesis. In respect of the latter, our conclusion can be unequivocal. All our measures tell the same story. Whether we look at improved aggregates, measures of structural change, downsizing, or changing trajectories of provision, what we discover is that welfare state change has been relatively modest, has taken place unevenly, with only a minority of nations experiencing substantial upheaval on any given measure, and with more evidence for idiosyncratic or family of nations-specific patterns of change than for shifts in a particular direction. At least as revealed by the changing patterns of disaggregated spending examined here, there is no evidence that Western welfare states have turned their backs on the structures of provision established in the 'golden age'. The overall shape of Western welfare states has changed very little, downsizing has been counterbalanced by upsizing in other areas, and welfare state priorities have manifested little sign of convergence, with the only trend of note being a slight overall shift towards state service provision.

Our remaining conclusions are methodological. We would argue that the measures of the structure of social provision elaborated here go some way towards resolving a difficulty that has bedevilled comparative social policy research in recent years. Until now, researchers have been faced with a difficult trade-off: between the use of data on citizenship entitlements, which, in principle, offer direct measures of welfare outcomes for individuals, but which are hugely expensive and time consuming to generate, and total expenditure data that is too highly aggregated to offer more than tangential clues as to what is happening to individuals, but which is routinely produced by national governments on an annual basis. Except where the ideas under investigation were extremely sweeping, as in the case of the 'race to the bottom' hypothesis, the use of aggregate expenditure data under these circumstances, could, uncharitably, be likened to looking for a lost coin under a lamppost, not because it was there that the coin had been lost, but because it was there that the light existed to find it.

The availability of disaggregated data has transformed this trade-off. Because we can now look at the separate components and even sub-components of expenditure, we can get a lot closer to the point at which particular programmes impact on particular classes of welfare recipients and we can design expenditure-based instruments, like our expenditure share measures, which have some purchase on the 'theoretical substance of welfare states'. It remains the case that we would often prefer more directly, outcomes-related data—for individuals, the immediate test of whether welfare retrenchment is taking place is whether their own benefits are cut—but, in the absence of such data, we no longer have to be concerned that we are seeking evidence in the wrong place, only that the resolution of the lens through which we are looking may not always be the optimum one for our purposes.

We would also argue that the capacity to measure change in new ways allows us to test hypotheses in more sophisticated ways than previously. For at least three decades, trends in aggregate welfare state spending have been the primary empirical test-bed for theories concerning the forces shaping the role of the state in modern society. Accounts have highlighted the contributions of many factors, of which demography, industrialization, culture, democratization, partisanship, and institutional differences are only subheads for the aggregation of particular kinds of explanation (for more on the variety of such accounts, see Castles 1998 and the later discussion in Chapter 5). Our small-n problem in this area of research is not that we have 'too many cases and not enough variables', but that we actually have more variables than we have cases. New measures may be one way out of this methodological dilemma. Instead of using a single variable, aggregate expenditure, as a test-bed, we may examine a variety of measures hypothesized as responding to imputed causal factors in different ways. If a hypothesis fails in one context, we can test to see if it works in others, precisely as we have here checked out whether the absence of an imputed 'race to the bottom' effect on aggregate expenditure change amongst OECD countries during this period was replicated in these countries' experience of structural transformation, downsizing, and expenditure share change. Positive findings on some measures and not others are likely to facilitate a more subtle understanding of the causal relationships in question. Reiterated negative findings, of the kind demonstrated here, should give us additional confidence in rejecting the theoretical assumptions underlying such hypotheses.

4

A European Welfare State Convergence?

On Convergence and Clusters

Chapters 2 and 3 have established that welfare states in the OECD have not been subject to change on anything like the scale implied by the 'race to the bottom' hypothesis. This chapter examines whether the change that has taken place has made welfare states more or less similar to each other and, in particular, whether it has led to greater social policy convergence amongst the countries of the European Union (EU). The notion of welfare state convergence has had a chequered career. Early functionalist analyses of the welfare state saw the widespread growth of social expenditure during the 'golden age' as offering strong evidence for the thesis that, as nations industrialize, their levels of provision become more similar (see Wilensky and Lebeaux 1958; Wilensky 1975; cf. Flora and Heidenheimer 1981). In the 1970s and 1980s, however, the notion of growing similarity in levels of welfare provision was challenged as more and more studies emerged showing that cross-national differences in the party composition of government had led to quite different trajectories of welfare state development across the OECD (see Stephens 1979; Castles 1982; Hicks and Swank 1992; Schmidt 1996). More recently, the idea of welfare state convergence has reappeared in a new form, with an active debate on the potential of EU institutions to bring about a 'harmonization' of social policy in Europe and the emergence of a 'European social model' providing social protection in a manner distinctively different from that elsewhere in the Western world (see Emerson 1988; Leibfried 1993; Leibfried and Pierson 1995; Beck et al. 1997; Grahl and Teague 1997; Falkner 1998; Ferrera, Hemerijck, and Rhodes 2001).

The literature on the 'European social model' is becoming extensive, but is anything but consensual. Sometimes, the usage is descriptive, arguing that there already is a common European or EU cluster or pattern of provision that can be contrasted with that of other countries. Such descriptive uses generally point to massive differences in spending, welfare state structuring, and social rights in Europe on the one hand and in Anglo-American or Asian countries on the other (see Ebbinghaus, 1990). More often, the emphasis is on trajectories of development, with the focus on the directions in which European social policy has been moving over recent decades. Even here there is widespread disagreement. Integration within the EU may be leading to social policy harmonization, but commentators are divided as to whether that integration is 'negative' or 'positive' and whether the harmonization is 'downward' or 'upward' (for these usages, see Pinder 1968; Scharpf 1998). Those identifying a potential for downward harmonization suggest that the evolution of EU institutions is likely to lead to pressures on Europe's leading welfare states to cut back their levels of provision. Commentators emphasizing the potential for upward harmonization focus on aspirations for the EU to become a vehicle of enhanced social protection in those countries in which standards of provision are currently lowest.

The downward harmonization thesis has much in common with the notion of a 'race to the bottom' except that its ambit is restricted to European welfare state development rather than to developments in the OECD as a whole. The argument is essentially that the moves towards a single market, tax harmonization, monetary union, and the like have set in train developments likely to impact negatively on the high standards of social provision characterizing many European nations (see Hodges and Woolcock 1993; Grahl and Teague 1997; Tsoukalis and Rhodes 1997; Rhodes 1998). Each successive move away from national sovereignty restricts 'the policy options of member states', leaving them less able to cope with external competition (Leibfried and Pierson 1995: 3). Greater competition amongst nations has made it necessary for big spenders to reconsider the generosity of their social provision, now seen as imposing serious costs in terms of economic efficiency, and to move towards reforms designed to make their welfare systems leaner, meaner, and more residual in character (see Chassard and Quentin 1993; Teeple 1995; Rhodes 1998).

The focus of the thesis is European, but the 'shape of things to come' that it predicts is not. As in the 'race to the bottom' literature, the fate of Europe's advanced welfare states is that they will become progressively more Americanized, 'liberal', and market conforming as a result of the progressive removal of barriers to trade and commerce. Assessing whether the trajectory of recent European welfare state development has been in line with such predictions is, therefore, an important part of the task of determining how far globalization really constitutes a threat to the levels and structures of provision established in the 'golden age'. The core of the downward harmonization argument is that European welfare states built up behind protective economic barriers are extremely vulnerable now that those barriers have been deliberately dismantled.

Most scholarly writing on European welfare state trajectories has shared, to a greater or lesser degree, the kinds of anxieties sketched above (however, see Ferrera, Hemerijck, and Rhodes 2001, for a more balanced treatment of recent developments). By contrast, the upward harmonization thesis is largely an in-house product of EU institutions. From the late 1980s onwards, the European Commission headed by Jacques Delors took a series of initiatives, including the Social Charter and EU-wide anti-poverty initiatives, aimed at ensuring that the advent of the single market did not lead to social dumping on an increasing scale (see Delors 1992). The premise for such policy innovations involved no contradiction of the view that enhanced economic integration could have adverse social consequences. Rather the argument was that adverse trends could only be addressed if integration was accompanied by a strengthening of social policy institutions.

Europe will be a Europe for everyone, for all its citizens, or it will be nothing. It will not tackle the new challenges now facing it—competitiveness, the demographic situation, enlargement and globalization—if it does not strengthen its social dimension and demonstrate its ability to ensure that fundamental social rights are respected and applied (Comité des Sages 1996: 23).

Although Delors' departure from the Commission was a setback to such aspirations, 'the social democratic moment' at the turn of the millennium gave another fillip to EU social policy institution building. The Dutch Presidency took the initiative in launching a common employment policy in 1997, the Lisbon Summit in March 2000 prioritized the social protection agenda, and the Nice European Council in December 2000 was told that 'the European social model, with its developed systems of social protection, must underpin the transformation to the knowledge economy' (Council of the European Union 2000). In October 2001, a report submitted to the Belgian Presidency of the EU, while conceding the existing variety of social policy provision in Western Europe, set out to elaborate the reforms needed to provide 'a new social policy architecture for Europe' (see Esping-Andersen with Gallie, Hemerijck, and Myles 2002, a group of leading social policy scholars commissioned to speculate on the most desirable characteristics of such an architecture).

The notion of a 'European social model', whether as a consequence of downward or upward convergence or merely as a description of supposed differences between the character of social provision in Europe and elsewhere, effectively runs counter to the thrust of much of the recent comparative social policy literature, which has devoted considerable energy to establishing the existence of distinctive models of provision *within* Europe and the OECD. Over the past decade, there has been a substantial intellectual investment in developing empirically based typologies of Western welfare states (Abrahamson 1999), of which the best known is Esping-Andersen's (1990) regimes typology. Most recently, the diversity of types of social policy system in Europe has been explored in the monumental studies edited by Scharpf and Schmidt (2000*a*, *b*), which provide an account of the evolving economic context of Esping-Andersen's 'liberal', 'conservative', and 'social democratic' worlds of welfare capitalism. There have, in addition, been more narrowly focused studies of the commonalities of provision in countries argued to constitute a particular type (e.g. on the countries of Christian Democratic 'social capitalism', see Van Kersbergen 1995; on the Southern European type, see Leibfried 1993; Castles 1995; Ferrera 1996; and on the Nordic model, see Kautto et al. 2001). In this literature, the emphasis is on major differences among types of welfare provision within Europe and the OECD, suggesting that a major challenge for an emergent 'European social model' will be to merge differences between pre-existing policy regimes (Leibfried 1993).

A minimum condition for establishing the existence of a 'European social model' is to show that Western European countries in general or some major subset of such countries manifest social policy characteristics that differentiate them from a wider grouping of nations. Putting it another way, we need to demonstrate that such countries are more similar to each other than is the whole universe of cases that we count as advanced welfare states. A simple statistic for assessing the degree of dispersion of an array of cases is the *coefficient of variation*, which is arrived at by dividing the standard deviation of the distribution by the sample mean and expressing it as a percentage (Miller and Wilson 1983). We have already made use of this statistic in earlier chapters as a measure of cross-time convergence in the OECD as a whole. Here we use it, not only to establish whether countries are converging over time, but also to identify whether groupings of nations form clusters and how distinctive those clusters are (for an alternative methodological approach to establishing the degree of social policy convergence in the EU, which comes to remarkably similar conclusions to this study, see Corrado et al. 2003). In what follows, our criterion for whether a subset of nations is distinctive is whether it manifests a coefficient of variation of half or less than that of the wider OECD sample. It should, however, be noted that, since we cannot assume that the data we are examining are normally distributed, differences between coefficients should be regarded only as approximate guides to the extent of clustering and convergence that is occurring.

The groupings of countries which feature in our analysis of this chapter are as follows:

1. *OECD*. These countries constitute the twenty-one long-term members of the OECD with populations over one million that are widely classified as advanced welfare states. They are the countries that have featured in all our previous analyses and for which data appear in Tables 2.1–2.6 and Tables 3.1–3.4.

2. *Outside Europe*. Of the OECD countries analysed here, five are outside Europe. Four are former British colonies in North America and Oceania: Canada, the United States, Australia, and New Zealand. The other is Japan, the only advanced nation in the OECD whose population is of non-European origin.

3. *Europe*. The remaining sixteen countries in our OECD sample are inside Europe. They are Austria, Belgium, Denmark, Finland, France, Germany, Greece, Ireland, Italy, the Netherlands, Norway, Portugal, Spain, Sweden, Switzerland, and the United Kingdom.

4. *Northern Europe*. Following Grahl and Teague (1997), who argue that the emergent 'European social model' does not include the Southern European or English-speaking countries of Europe, we identify a Northern European grouping of ten countries consisting of Austria, Belgium, Denmark, Finland, France, Germany, the Netherlands, Norway, Sweden, and Switzerland.

5. *Europe of fourteen*. Present EU members minus Luxembourg, for which data are unavailable. The only Western European nations not included in this grouping are Norway and Switzerland, the populations of which have so far decided to stay outside the EU.

6. *Europe of eleven*. Pre-1996 EU members. Europe of fourteen minus Austria, Finland, and Sweden.

7. *Europe of eight*. Pre-1981 European Community members. Europe of eleven minus Greece, Portugal, and Spain.

8. *Europe of five*. European Economic Community founder members. Belgium, France, Germany, Italy, and the Netherlands.

In addition, we also look at the degree of variation manifested by the four OECD sub-groupings we have located as distinct families of nations in previous chapters.

1. *English-speaking*. Australia, Canada, Ireland, New Zealand, the United Kingdom, and the United States.

2. *Scandinavia*. Denmark, Finland, Norway, and Sweden.

3. *Continental Western Europe*. Austria, Belgium, France, Germany, and the Netherlands.

4. *Southern Europe*. Greece, Italy, Portugal, and Spain.

Most of the measures of social provision examined here are drawn from Chapters 2 and 3, including total social expenditure and total outlays, social expenditure adjusted for need, and differential priorities for spending on social security, poverty alleviation and health, and state services. In addition, we also look at spending on age pensions and public health, the two biggest programmes of the welfare state. Because an important objective is to compare degrees of cross-national variation in 1980 and in 1998, measures of change, such as the extent of structural transformation or of welfare state downsizing, are not included in the analysis. Examining the extent to which the groupings and sub-groupings identified above cluster in respect of a variety of measures of the extent and structure of the welfare state permits us to assess the distinctiveness of different groupings. It also makes it possible to identify emergent patterns of similarity and difference over time and to contrast wider European aggregations with the distinct families of nations sub-groups constituting them. To demonstrate the existence of a distinct 'European social model', it would be necessary to show that the degree of variation in the Europe of fourteen or the wider European grouping was markedly less than that in the OECD as a whole. To demonstrate European convergence, we would need to show that variation in patterns of social provision in the Europe of fourteen or the wider European grouping had declined appreciably over time. Finally, to demonstrate that such developments had been 'negative' rather than 'positive' in kind would require that we demonstrate than European expenditure levels and/or standards of provision had been falling rather than manifesting a stationary or upward trend.

Aggregate Spending

We commence our analysis in Table 4.1 by presenting coefficients of variation relating to the two big aggregates of spending: total public social expenditure and total outlays of general government. The former corresponds broadly with our normal understanding of welfare state expenditure. The latter includes additional items, like educational spending, housing and community services, and economic affairs, which many commentators see as having broadly similar social policy objectives. Total outlays are frequently taken as an approximate measure of the reach of the modern interventionist state. The social expenditure measure used in the analysis is the 12-component measure featuring in Table 3.1 of Chapter 3. The total outlays data come from Table 2.2 in Chapter 2. Both are from or are calculated from OECD sources.

Table 4.1 Coefficients of variation for 12-component measure of total social expenditure and for total outlays of general government in 21 OECD countries, 1980 and 1998

Country grouping	12-component measure as a percentage of GDP		Total outlays of general government as a percentage of GDP	
	1980	1998	1980	1998
OECD	30.5	21.7	25.0	16.6
Outside Europe	26.1	14.8	10.8	11.6
Europe	26.4	17.2	23.6	13.6
Northern Europe	20.3	7.9	14.9	7.9
Europe of 14	26.7	18.0	24.4	14.2
Europe of 11	28.6	18.7	25.6	14.0
Europe of 8	18.1	18.6	12.6	15.6
Europe of 5	14.3	8.3	13.7	5.2
Families of nations				
English-speaking	24.8	15.8	19.9	11.5
Scandinavian	25.9	6.6	21.1	8.8
Continental Western Europe	9.8	8.6	10.6	6.0
Southern Europe	24.2	15.2	23.3	8.2

Notes and sources: The figures appearing in the table are coefficients of variation (standard deviation divided by the mean and multiplied by 100). Data on the 12-component total social expenditure are from Table 3.1. Data for total outlays of general government are from Table 2.2. Country groupings are as described in the text.

Looking down the first column of coefficients of variation relating to the 12-component measure, the immediate thing to strike one is the relatively small gain in similarity in moving from the wider OECD grouping to the wider European aggregates. In 1980, the coefficient of variation for the OECD as a whole was 30.5, while for Europe as a whole it was 26.4 and for the Europe of fourteen it was 26.7. Such small differences do not suggest the presence of a distinctive 'European social model' at this time. However, the Europe of eight, which at that time was coincident with European Community membership bar Luxembourg, does manifest a somewhat stronger profile based on the core similarity of the countries of the Europe of five and of continental Western Europe, which do form distinct clusters according to our criterion. Turning now to 1998, and examining the second column in Table 4.1, there is again relatively little difference in the size of the coefficients for the larger European aggregates and of the OECD as a whole. Indeed, as a result of the two waves of enlargement that had taken place in the 1980s and 1990s, the EU was itself now one of the larger aggregates and the case for a distinctive model of social protection at European Community level is actually appreciably weaker than it was two decades previously.

If looking down the first two columns of Table 4.1 casts doubts on the notion of a distinctive 'European social model', comparing across the columns does suggest very strongly that processes of convergence were at work. With the single exception of the Europe of eight, where cuts in Irish social expenditure have left this grouping's profile virtually unchanged, all other coefficients have declined, some of them very appreciably indeed. The countries making up the larger European aggregates—Europe as a whole and the Europe of fourteen—were markedly more similar in 1998 than in 1980. That this did not lead to the appearance of distinct clusters at the European or EU levels was due to the fact that the countries outside Europe were converging just as fast as those within. Moreover, during this period, the distinctiveness of the families of nations within Europe was actually increasing more rapidly than the distinctiveness of Europe as a whole, with the Scandinavian and continental Western European groupings now exhibiting coefficients of variation around half those of the wider European groupings. Perhaps, most interestingly, because the number of countries involved is relatively large, the Northern European grouping, containing all the countries in both of these families of nations as well as Switzerland, had by 1998 become as distinctive as the families constituting them.

Social expenditure is, of course, a large part of government outlays, so it is, perhaps, hardly surprising that, when we turn to variation in total spending, as shown in the third and fourth columns of Table 4.1, many of the same trends are replicated. Once again, there is little difference between the degree of variation in the larger European aggregates and in the OECD as a whole and, hence, no support for a distinct European model. Again, in 1980, the countries of the then European Community manifest strong commonalities in their overall public spending levels and, again, by 1998, the EU member states had ceased to have a distinctive profile. Also, just as in the case of the 12-component measure of spending, most groupings, including the wider European aggregates, manifest a marked convergence, with several families of nations and Northern Europe experiencing a decline in variation of the order of 50 per cent or more. It is worth remembering, however, that these coefficients provide only an approximate guide to the extent of variation amongst groupings, and generally speaking, one which becomes less accurate as groupings get smaller.

Only a few differences between social expenditure and total outlays require mention. Total outlays start out and finish with lower coefficients of variation than was apparent in the case of social expenditure, suggesting that social spending levels are more cross-nationally variable than non-social spending levels. At the beginning of the period, total outlays have a much more distinct profile outside Europe than inside, making the notion of Europe as a model for the rest of the world even more fanciful than in the case of social expenditure. At the end of the period, family of nations patterns are even more distinct than in respect of social spending, with the Southern European countries clustering as tightly as those of Scandinavia and continental Western Europe. Finally, the Northern Europe total outlays profile is as pronounced as it was in the case of social expenditure, with the distinctiveness of this grouping appearing to provide support for Grahl and Teague's (1997) surmise that the boundaries of European policy similarity do not extend beyond the Alps or Europe's continental seaboard.

So our analysis of social expenditure and total outlays in this period tells the same story of strong convergence combined with the emergence of distinct sub-groupings of nations, but not at a Europe-wide or EU level. That leaves the question of whether the convergence that was taking place was upward or downward in character. Part of the answer to that question can be found in earlier chapters. Table 3.1 in Chapter 3 shows that, in the case of the 12-component measure, neither the OECD as a whole nor any of the families of nations constituting it experienced any reduction in social spending as a percentage of GDP in the period under consideration here. Calculations for the larger European aggregations confirm these findings. In Europe as a whole during this period, 12-component spending went up from an average of 19.8 to 23.8 per cent of GDP. In the Europe of fourteen, it went up from 20.3 to 23.4 per cent of GDP. Table 2.2 in Chapter 2 suggests more diverse trajectories in respect of total outlays, with moderate expenditure cutbacks in the English-speaking and continental Western European families of nations being almost exactly counterbalanced by a modest increase in Scandinavia and a very much larger one in Southern Europe. Figures for Europe as a whole and for the Europe of fourteen also suggest a cancelling out of effects and a virtually stationary trend, with average expenditure in the former grouping going up by only 0.5 of a per cent of GDP and the latter by just 0.3 per cent of GDP. These expenditure trends are identical to those identified in Chapter 2 as applying in the wider OECD grouping. They provide absolutely no evidence of a negative harmonization of European aggregate expenditure patterns.

Adjusting for Need

It is possible to argue that trends in aggregate spending are a misleading guide to standards of welfare provision because they take no account of changing patterns of need. In Chapter 2, we also calculated two measures of aggregate spending adjusted to reflect levels of welfare dependency. One was a welfare state generosity ratio obtained by dividing total social spending by the percentage of the population aged sixty-five years and over plus the percentage of the civilian population who were unemployed (see Table 2.4). The other was a measure of real social expenditure per dependent obtained by multiplying the welfare state generosity ratio from Table 2.4 by real GDP per capita (see Table 2.6). In this section, we address the question of whether these adjusted measures lead to any modification of the conclusions arrived at on the basis of aggregate spending data.

The first two columns of Table 4.2 report variation in the welfare state generosity ratio. Contrasting the figures with the equivalent columns of Table 4.1, it is clear that the case for a 'European social model' based on evidence regarding generosity ratios is no stronger than it was in respect of total social expenditure. Indeed, it is apparent that needs adjustment makes for somewhat less distinct cross-national profiles, especially towards the end of the period. 12-component social expenditure in 1980 manifests two distinct clusters; the welfare generosity ratio measure manifests none. 12-component spending in 1998 manifests no less than five clusters; the generosity ratio measure only one. The absence of similarity at the beginning of the period is, arguably, deceptive. In 1980, all three exclusively European families of nations as well as the Northern Europe grouping are characterized by coefficients of variation only marginally above the distinctiveness criterion, while the extreme variation of the Outside Europe and English-speaking groupings is simply a function of New Zealand's outstandingly high level of welfare generosity. By 1998, after more than a decade of neo-liberal restructuring, New Zealand had ceased to be so generous, explaining the emergence of an English-speaking grouping distinguished by the relative meanness of its standards of provision. However, developments in the exclusively European families of nations and in Northern Europe were anything but convergent, with coefficients of variation which remained stationary or even increased somewhat.

There were, however, groupings in which a convergence of standards accompanied a convergence of aggregate spending. One, of course, was the English-speaking family of nations, which we have already noted had become a distinct cluster by 1998. The others were the Outside Europe grouping and,

Table 4.2 Coefficients of variation for welfare state generosity ratio and real social expenditure per dependent in 21 OECD countries, 1980 and 1998

Country grouping	Welfare state generosity ratio		Real social expenditure per dependent	
	1980	1998	1980	1998
OECD	29.0	25.5	38.7	35.7
Outside Europe	39.7	15.3	27.1	16.1
Europe	26.5	25.9	42.4	39.9
Northern Europe	16.4	18.3	17.4	23.9
Europe of 14	28.6	20.2	45.7	36.6
Europe of 11	28.6	25.8	48.4	41.1
Europe of 8	21.4	22.1	30.4	26.5
Europe of 5	21.6	18.9	23.2	21.7
Families of nations				
English-speaking	35.9	11.1	32.9	13.7
Scandinavian	16.9	16.5	21.3	25.8
Continental Western Europe	18.0	18.7	16.2	17.6
Southern Europe	16.6	20.0	49.7	32.9

Notes and sources: The figures appearing in the table are coefficients of variation (standard deviation divided by the mean and multiplied by 100). Data on welfare state generosity ratio are from Table 2.4 and data on real social expenditure per dependent are from Table 2.6. Country groupings are as described in the text.

interestingly, in light of the downward harmonization thesis, the Europe of fourteen. In our Chapter 2 discussion, we noted that average generosity ratios in the OECD had remained virtually unchanged over nearly two decades. Further calculations show that, between 1980 and 1998, the Outside Europe grouping's generosity ratio declined from 0.95 to 0.87, that of the English-speaking family of nations from 0.94 to 0.92, and that of the Europe of fourteen from 1.06 to 1.02. In the first two instances, cutbacks in average standards of provision are not a result of trends widely affecting the countries making up these groupings, but simply reflect the severity of what was happening to New Zealand's welfare state during this period. However, the fact that standards of provision declined in no less than eight of the countries constituting the Europe of fourteen could, possibly, be interpreted as evidence of a more general process and, possibly, one in some way linked to the process of

European integration (for such an interpretation, see Korpi 2003). On balance, the argument is not persuasive. Most of the EU cutbacks were relatively small, and the decline in average generosity ratios was driven largely by major reductions in standards of provision in just two countries: the Netherlands and Sweden. Since these countries, along with New Zealand, had much the highest generosity ratios in the OECD in 1980, it seems more reasonable to suppose that what we are seeing here is part of a process of wider OECD convergence to the centre rather than a downward harmonization peculiar to the member states of the EU.

Turning now to the columns reporting variation in real social expenditure per dependent, it is immediately evident that marked differences in per capita income levels within the OECD magnify some aspects of cross-country variation. The chief consequence is that all the larger groupings—the OECD, Europe, and the Europe of fourteen—are characterized by extremely high coefficients of variation at both the beginning and the end of the period. There can, therefore, be no question of the emergence of a 'European social model' in respect of this measure. Once again, however, the picture concerning convergence is mixed, with many groupings maintaining or marginally increasing their levels of variation, but the English-speaking, Outside Europe, Southern Europe, and Europe of fourteen groupings becoming noticeably more similar. Again there is evidence that the level of real provision in the Europe of fourteen has been growing more slowly than the OECD norm— US$3,391 as compared to US$4,183—but this downward convergence is again substantially attributable to below average increases in the Netherlands and Sweden and to the fact that the Europe of fourteen contains all of the poorest countries in the OECD, now exclusively to be found in Southern Europe.

The only groupings to have distinct real expenditure profiles are those that do not contain countries at markedly varying income levels. In 1980, the poorer countries were Ireland and the countries of Southern Europe, leaving only continental Western Europe and Northern Europe with distinct profiles at the time. Between 1980 and 1998, the countries experiencing the largest increases in per capita incomes were Ireland and Norway, with Ireland moving closer to the European income norm and Norway moving away. This made groupings containing Ireland more similar and groupings containing Norway less similar. In 1998, the countries outside Europe, the English-speaking nations, and continental Western Europe all qualify as distinctive by the half OECD variation criterion. Europe and the Europe of fourteen remain extremely diverse because they are constituted by rich continental Western European and Scandinavian countries as well as by much poorer Southern European ones. This is a diversity that will undoubtedly continue as the 2004 EU enlargement brings in a large number of new and poorer member states. The EU's extension to the east is a guarantee that, for many decades to come, the only groupings likely to maintain anything like a distinct profile of real spending per dependent will be at a family of nations and, possibly, a Northern Europe level.

Individual Programmes

If there is little evidence for Europe-wide clustering in respect of aggregate spending, there is still less sign of any distinct European model in respect of the separate programmes constituting the welfare state. Table 4.3 presents data on coefficients of variation for old-age cash benefits and public health expenditure, the two largest programmes of the welfare state, with the data drawn from the OECD Social Expenditure Database (SOCX) and expressed as percentages of GDP (see OECD 2001a). Throughout the period examined here, these two programmes together constituted around 60 per cent of total OECD social expenditure. Both programmes were growing in the vast majority of countries, albeit age cash spending at a much faster average rate than health spending. In the OECD as a whole, pension spending went up from 5.5 per cent of GDP in 1980 to 7.4 per cent of GDP in 1998, representing an average expenditure increase of just over a third. Comparable figures for Europe as a whole were 5.9 and 8.0 per cent; for the Europe of fourteen, 6.0 and 8.0 per cent; and for Northern Europe, 6.5 and 8.3 per cent. Health spending is a marginally smaller programme than age pensions, but it too was increasing steadily, with the OECD average increasing from 5.4 to 6.1 per cent of GDP or by about one-eighth. Comparable figures for Europe as a whole were 5.6–6.1 per cent; for the Europe of fourteen, 5.6–5.9 per cent; and for Northern Europe, 6.0–6.6 per cent.

Table 4.3 shows that, in 1980, there was somewhat more variation in old-age cash spending patterns than was the case in respect of total social expenditure and that the age spending profiles of the larger European group-ings were only slightly more similar than those of the OECD as a whole. Moreover, in complete contrast to total spending patterns, dissimilarity in the larger European groupings has increased quite markedly over time. In 1980, the coefficient of variation for Europe as a whole was 26.3; in 1998, it was 32.0. The corresponding figures for the Europe of fourteen were 26.9 and 32.1. As already noted, pensions were growing extremely fast and the only three countries experiencing cutbacks in expenditure in this period were New Zealand, Ireland, and the Netherlands (see Table 6.2). Controlling

Table 4.3 Coefficients of variation for old-age cash benefits and public health spending as percentages of GDP in 21 OECD countries, 1980 and 1998

Country grouping	Old-age cash benefits as a percentage of GDP		Public health spending as a percentage of GDP	
	1980	1998	1980	1998
OECD	31.7	35.1	24.3	14.6
Outside Europe	43.1	10.2	24.7	6.3
Europe	26.3	32.0	24.1	16.5
Northern Europe	22.1	24.1	20.7	12.6
Europe of 14	26.9	32.1	25.2	15.8
Europe of 11	27.3	35.7	24.1	17.3
Europe of 8	23.1	40.9	16.2	16.4
Europe of 5	13.7	28.2	4.3	14.7
Families of nations				
English-speaking	33.7	27.3	24.6	11.7
Scandinavian	18.3	9.2	23.8	12.4
Continental Western Europe	15.3	22.4	5.6	13.7
Southern Europe	32.3	30.0	22.0	6.7

Notes and sources: The figures appearing in the table are coefficients of variation (standard deviation divided by the mean and multiplied by 100). Data on old-age cash benefits and public health spending as percentages of GDP are from OECD (2001a), *Social Expenditure Database, 1980–1998*, Paris. Country groupings are as described in the text.

pension expenditure by the proportion of the population aged sixty-five and over provides a measure of pension generosity, which we call the AGE ratio. Only the three countries just mentioned plus the United States experienced any reduction in the AGE ratio between 1980 and 1998 (AGE ratio data is to be found in Table 6.2).

In 1980, the only groupings formally qualifying as distinctive in their pension expenditure profiles were the Europe of five and continental Western Europe. However, the Scandinavian grouping fails to match up to the criterion by only a relatively small margin. The pension systems of continental Western Europe tend to be designed along Bismarckian social insurance lines, while those of Scandinavia seek to combine modest earnings-related relativities with a flat-rate citizenship principle. In 1980, these different design principles appear to have had major implications for expenditure levels, with continental Western Europe consistently outspending the countries of Scandinavia. However, by 1998, the former grouping had become much more diverse in its spending patterns, while the Scandinavian pattern had become more distinct, with all these nations clustered tightly around the OECD age cash expenditure mean. The countries in the Outside Europe grouping also clustered, but very close to the bottom of the OECD distribution.

Patterns of public health spending are far more compressed than those of pensions, a coefficient of variation for the former of 14.6 in 1998 contrasting with one of 35.1 for the latter at the same date. However, variation in spending within the larger European groupings matches or exceeds that within the OECD as a whole, arguing against any notion of a separate European health model. This is despite the fact that, in contrast to age spending developments, European health spending profiles have tended to become markedly more similar over time, with the obvious cause a marked catch-up in expenditure levels by the countries of the new Southern Europe. The only countries to reduce their spending during this period were Denmark, Ireland, New Zealand, and Sweden. Except for Ireland, this too was part of the wider convergence pattern, with these 1980 big spenders making cutbacks, but still remaining above the OECD expenditure norm. In 1980, the only really distinctive grouping in respect of public health spending was the continental Western European family of nations, with expenditure levels all very close to the OECD mean. By 1998, this grouping was more dispersed with both France and Germany in the OECD public health expenditure vanguard. Distinctive groupings were now to be found in the Outside Europe and Southern Europe groupings. The former were distinctive in all clustering near the OECD spending mean. The latter, despite the catch-up trajectory of expenditure change in these years, still clustered towards the bottom of the OECD public health spending distribution.

Expenditure Shares

Having looked at patterns of total social expenditure, expenditure adjusted for need, and spending on individual programmes, the final step in our assessment of claims for a 'European social model' and a downward convergence in levels of provision is to examine the extent of cross-national variation in types of spending. In Chapter 3, we distinguished between expenditures devoted to social security, to poverty alleviation and health care, and to state services. We further argued that the differential emphasis accorded to these priorities by different countries corresponds rather closely to the categorization of welfare types in the mainstream comparative literature. Table 3.3 in Chapter 3 provided measures of national expenditure priorities obtained by calculating the shares of social security, poverty alleviation and health, and state services spending as proportions of total (12-component) social expenditure. The coefficients of variation appearing in Table 4.3 permit us to assess the extent of clustering and convergence in the various groupings covered by this analysis as well as providing a further test of the argument that there is strong correspondence between families of nations and types of welfare state provision.

Table 4.4 shows that, in 1980, variation in the social security share of social expenditure was only marginally lower in the wider European aggregations than in the OECD as a whole. In 1998, the European aggregations manifest a degree of variation almost identical to that of the wider OECD grouping.

Table 4.4 Coefficients of variation of social expenditure shares in 21 OECD countries, 1980 and 1998

Country grouping	Social security share		Poverty alleviation and health care share		State services share	
	1980	1998	1980	1998	1980	1998
OECD	16.0	18.8	17.8	21.5	107.0	91.1
Outside Europe	19.7	12.7	18.9	12.6	73.2	102.6
Europe	13.5	19.0	10.3	19.1	98.2	80.6
Northern Europe	12.3	15.2	6.3	8.1	70.2	65.7
Europe of 14	13.9	19.1	10.8	20.4	100.5	80.7
Europe of 11	13.8	20.0	11.5	21.9	123.5	89.5
Europe of 8	13.3	22.0	10.9	22.5	100.3	87.1
Europe of 5	6.5	15.7	5.7	18.9	50.8	62.9
Families of nations						
English-speaking	17.7	12.9	18.2	12.2	82.4	87.5
Scandinavian	9.8	11.2	6.0	5.0	32.4	19.6
Continental Western Europe	5.5	7.1	6.9	10.9	40.1	45.5
Southern Europe	3.1	8.4	3.9	15.3	77.2	38.2

Notes and sources: The figures appearing in the table are coefficients of variation (standard deviation divided by the mean and multiplied by 100). Data on social expenditure shares are from Table 3.3 and details of the components making up each share are as in the notes and sources to that table. Country groupings are as described in the text.

Moreover, with the exception of the Outside Europe grouping and the English-speaking nations, the degree of variation increases somewhat over time. There is, therefore, no European social security model and no European social security convergence. In both 1980 and in 1998, continental Western Europe and Southern Europe appear as distinct clusters, confirming the contention of Chapter 3 that an emphasis on this type of spending is a defining characteristic of both of these families of nations. In 1980, the Europe of five has a distinct profile, but this disappears in 1998 largely as a consequence of the extreme lopsidedness of Italy's spending priorities, with an extremely high level of pension spending (see Table 6.2) contributing to a social security share of around 75 per cent (see Table 3.3).

Table 4.4 shows that variation in the poverty alleviation and health care share of expenditure is of a rather similar order of magnitude to that displayed by the social security share. In 1980, patterns of variation are extraordinarily distinct, with the Scandinavian, continental Western European, and Southern European families each clearly apparent and the commonalities of Northern Europe and the Europe of five no less clearly pronounced. Coefficients of variation are also substantially lower in the European aggregations than in the OECD as a whole, although not qualifying as distinct by the half OECD variation criterion. Interestingly, however, the only reason that they do not do so is because of the inclusion in these wider groupings of Ireland, a country in which a 'residual' or 'liberal' institutional design and a relatively youthful age structure combine to weight spending priorities heavily in favour of poverty alleviation and health rather than social security.

Excluding the Irish outlier, both Europe and the EU have profiles distinct from that of the wider OECD. Nowhere else in this analysis do groupings as large as these meet the distinctiveness criterion and it is here, if anywhere, that we can identify the commonality of a 'European social model', resting on structures of provision giving a lower priority to poverty alleviation and health than to other welfare state objectives. However, if this was the core European commonality in 1980, it was not to last very long, with the majority of European groupings becoming markedly more diverse over the next two decades. Partly this was because Italy, as we have just seen, had become an outlier at the opposite end the distribution from Ireland. However, even excluding both outliers does not qualify the wider aggregations as distinct clusters in 1998. By that year, the only distinct profiles are to be found in Scandinavia, Northern Europe, and continental Western Europe. These, of course, are the only exclusively European groupings in which neither Ireland nor Italy have a place. Given that Table 3.3 shows that the six English-speaking countries manifested the highest poverty alleviation and health care expenditure shares in the OECD, it is, perhaps, surprising that our clustering criterion does not single out this grouping as distinctive in character.

Turning finally to the state services share of social expenditure, we note hugely more variation in both 1980 and 1998 than elsewhere in the analysis of this chapter. Clearly, wider European and OECD commonalities were extremely weak in 1980, and despite some marginal convergence, remain extremely weak nearly two decades later. Despite this, several countries meet the half OECD variation criterion both at the beginning and end of the period. In 1980, Scandinavia stands out as the area of much the highest spending, with continental Western Europe reasonably consistently in second place. Much the same story is true in 1998, except that Scandinavia's lead position is much magnified and the Southern European grouping appears as a distinct tail to the distribution. This analysis confirms—or, more properly, replicates—the argument of Chapter 3 that state services provision is the distinguishing mark of the Scandinavian family of nations. In later chapters, we shall argue that aspects of the state services state may have an important role in counteracting the serious fertility decline currently being experienced in many European countries. In that context, the increasingly distinctive stances and very different expenditure priorities of the countries of Scandinavia and Southern Europe are clearly of the utmost policy relevance.

Conclusion

The findings of this chapter are detailed and complex, but can be readily summed up as answers to the questions with which we started. If Europe is taken as being Europe as a whole or EU membership as it stood after the 1996 enlargement, there is never, anywhere in our data, an instance where we encounter a distinct 'European social model' by our criterion of distinctiveness. Arguably, the nearest we come to such a model is in 1980, where the exclusion of Ireland from both aggregations does suggest that Europe is distinguished by its lower prioritization of poverty alleviation and health objectives. However, before this is reinvented as a story of a non-residual Europe of the 'golden age' from which we are now hastily retreating, it is worth noting that the virtuousness of low spending on poverty alleviation and health is a function of the extent of need in these areas. In 1980, and still perhaps today, Southern Europe's low priority on these programmes is not because there is no need, but because what need there is, is often ignored (see Ferrera 1996). According to the analysis of this chapter, the biggest aggregation with a clear identity is Northern Europe. At both the beginning of the period and the end, these countries were spending between 30 and 40 per cent of their welfare budgets on poverty alleviation and health. At the end of the period, they were consistently the countries with the highest levels of social expenditure and total outlays. These are countries in which social spending and the reach of government are sufficient to cater to basic need, without thereby necessarily sacrificing the wider objectives of the welfare state falling within the ambit of social security and state services provision.

Are European welfare states converging? The answer is that they are in some respects and not in others. Both wider European aggregations are converging in respect of expenditure levels and the Europe of fourteen is converging somewhat in respect of welfare standards. Pension provision is, if anything, diverging, while wider European trends are towards greater similarity in patterns of health spending. Finally, the wider European aggregations are becoming marginally more dissimilar in the size of their social security and poverty alleviation and health shares and somewhat more similar in the size of their state services shares. Are European welfare states harmonizing downward? The analysis in this and previous chapters suggests otherwise. In respect of aggregate spending, the trend of social expenditure is upward and of total outlays stationary. Admittedly, there has been a modest decline in welfare generosity within the Europe of fourteen—of approximately 4 per cent over eighteen years—but no sign that this trend owes anything to factors unique to EU membership. In this period, countries with exceptionally generous welfare states—whether inside the EU or Outside Europe—came back to the pack, while a number of the less generous countries caught up to varying degrees. It is possible to see the bigger cuts taking place in this period as a reflection of emergent forces inimical to excessive public spending, and this is an argument considered in the next chapter, but the evidence provided here does not suggest that these were forces in any way restricted to a European theatre of operations.

The comparative social policy literature's main counterpoint to the notion of an emergent or once existent 'European social model' is to emphasize the diversity of European welfare state types or regimes. Our analysis of family of nations sub-groupings offers considerable, but not wholly consistent, support for this idea. Families of nations cluster most strongly in respect of spending shares and aggregate spending, with the clearest patterning of all that of poverty alleviation and health in 1980. Clusters occur more sporadically in respect of particular programmes and spending adjusted for need. It is, perhaps, hardly surprising to note that wherever families cluster on aggregate and needs-adjusted spending measures, the distinctiveness of

Southern Europe and the English-speaking nations is to be towards the bottom of the expenditure distribution and of the countries of continental Western Europe and Scandinavia to be close to or above the expenditure mean. That, by 1998, Northern Europe as a whole can be characterized as a distinctive cluster in addition to Scandinavia and continental Western Europe is a consequence of the fact that Switzerland had by now joined these families of nations in the OECD social expenditure vanguard. Throughout the period under examination here, expenditure priorities in Switzerland were remarkably similar to those of countries in the continental Western Europe grouping and, by 1998, Switzerland had arguably become a typical member of this family of nations (cf. Bonoli and Mach 2000).

There are two final points, one relating to measurement strategy and the other to the future of the welfare state within the European Community. Our measurement strategy throughout this book has been to use multiple measures with the aim of coming to grips with the diverse complexity of welfare state trajectories. The value of such an approach is exemplified in this chapter. Convergence trends in aggregate expenditure may be accompanied by divergence trends in respect to generosity ratios and per capita spending per dependent. Northern Europe, for instance, is becoming more similar on the first dimension and less on the second. Tight clusters in respect of one measure dissolve in respect of another. The countries of Northern Europe are relatively similar in their poverty alleviation stances, but widely dissimilar in their social security and state services priorities. Comparative research on the welfare state needs to be more self-consciously aware of the multi-dimensionality of its subject matter and of the need to use a wide range of measures to identify the multi-faceted character of contemporary welfare state change.

Finally, it is worth noting the evanescence of some of the preoccupations of this chapter. In 2004, Europe is set to redraw its political and welfare state boundaries. The EU will over a period of transition become a Europe of twenty-five. For a time, at least, any notion of an encompassing 'European social model' will have to be set aside. Average aggregate expenditures and welfare standards are set to fall not because of any downward harmonization, but because poorer, economically peripheral nations will become half of the membership. If, over coming years, we eventually witness a broader European welfare state convergence, we should hope it is because structural adjustment initiatives and institutional rules stipulating minimum standards are bringing these countries closer to the realities now prevailing in much of Northern Europe. This, however imperfectly, is what took place in Ireland and the countries of the new Southern Europe when they joined the European Community. For many in the new Eastern Europe, it is the promise that makes EU membership appear so attractive.

5

Explaining Expenditure Outcomes

From Effects to Causes

The strategy of hypothesis testing employed in the first half of this book has been to examine a variety of measures of OECD aggregate expenditure development over a period of nearly two decades for evidence of adverse globalization effects. The results of our enquiry have been, almost entirely, negative in character. Contrary to prevailing crisis myths concerning the impact of globalization on the welfare state, we have found no evidence of a 'race to the bottom', only a modest degree of change in spending priorities and few signs of trends peculiar to the countries of Europe or the European Union.

In this chapter, we adopt an alternative strategy of enquiry. Rather than looking for effects, we look for causes. What we seek to do is to develop models capable of accounting for or 'explaining' the cross-national variation in expenditure outcomes we observe during this period. Clearly, identifying the causes of recent social expenditure change in the OECD is relevant to our broader goal of locating the factors likely to shape the future of the welfare state in advanced Western nations. It is no less relevant to our final assessment of the threat to the welfare state posed by developments in the international economy. There are two possible reasons why the globalization effects predicted by the crisis literature might have not shown up in our previous analysis. The first is that globalization may have had no such effects. The second is that whatever effects globalization may have had are obscured by a range of additional factors also influencing trajectories of welfare state change. The only way to adjudicate between these alternatives is to identify the factors accounting for welfare state change in this period and to locate what role, if any, the international economy has played in this process.

There is nothing new about modelling aggregate expenditure outcomes. Despite legitimate debate on how well social spending captures the 'theoretical substance' of welfare states, aggregate social expenditure clearly does tap into an important dimension of national 'welfare effort', a dimension readily mapped with data routinely provided by national governments and published in comparable form by international economic agencies. Cross-national data on aggregate social expenditure have been available from the International Labour Office (ILO) since the 1950s. Both the OECD and Eurostat (the statistical agency of the EU) now provide such data for member countries in a standardized form with extensive disaggregation of separate spending programmes.

Cross-national expenditure data have been the subject of statistical analysis since the 1960s and 1970s, when sociological researchers sought to demonstrate that countries were becoming more alike in their spending patterns as a consequence of the emergence of common welfare needs inherent to the processes of industrialization and economic modernization (see Cutright 1965; Wilensky 1975; Flora and Heidenheimer 1981; Pampel and Williamson 1989). Since that time, there have been many waves of comparative social policy scholarship, each pointing to a new range of factors potentially relevant to the extent of social spending. In the late 1970s and early 1980s, political scientists suggested that, in addition to socio-economic factors, ideology and partisanship mattered, with the Left outspending the Right on a wide range of social programmes and in aggregate terms (see Castles 1978, 1982, 1998; Stephens 1979; Hicks and Swank 1984, 1992; Schmidt 1996). In the 1990s, institutional differences were added to the mix, with scholars, again largely from political science, examining whether the institutional structuring of political systems influenced the propensity of governments to spend for welfare purposes (see Huber, Ragin, and Stephens 1993; Tsebelis 1995, 1999; Lijphart 1999). Recent work by Swank (2001, 2002) offers evidence that globalization and institutional variables interact, with economies structured on neo-liberal premises responding to pressures in the international economy with expenditure cuts and those organized along more corporatist lines responding to similar pressures by extending or at least maintaining the existing fabric of social protection.

Major topics of debate in the comparative literature during the past decade have included the impact of global economic forces (see references in Chapters 1 and 2) and the possibility that the 'old politics' of ideological partisanship has been superseded by a 'new politics of the welfare state' (see Pierson 1994, 1996, 2001; cf. Clayton and Pontusson 1998; Korpi 2003; Korpi and Palme 2003). For its protagonists, the notion of a 'new politics of the welfare state' explains why social spending has not declined in the manner predicted by globalization theory. The welfare state has strong constituencies of support amongst welfare recipients and welfare providers, which make it extremely difficult for governments to dismantle the welfare state, even where their economies are exposed to international pressures or where their ideological preferences are to cut spending. Moreover, and in a sense reminiscent of earlier industrialization theories, theorists of the 'new politics of the welfare state' suggest that post-industrial change in contemporary societies has produced new categories of need to which governments of all political complexions must necessarily respond. Unemployment, deindustrialization, and changes in the structure of the modern family all lead to new social expenditure programmes, each with its own constituency of support. As a consequence of these developments, 'there are good reasons to believe that the centrality of left party and union confederation strength to welfare state outcomes has declined' (Pierson 1996: 151). The purpose of the modelling undertaken in this chapter is to provide evidence against which we can assess the claims of both globalization theory and the 'new politics' hypothesis.

The strategy of model building adopted in this chapter is quite straightforward. The dependent variables that we model are measures of expenditure change drawn from our previous analysis. Because of its greater cross-national consistency, our preferred measure of change in aggregate social spending is the 12-component measure as in Table 3.1, rather than the standard total social expenditure measure as reported in the OECD Social Expenditure Database (SOCX) and Table 2.1. The other dependent variables are change in the total outlays of general government measured as a percentage of GDP as in Table 2.2, and the extent of welfare downsizing, here also measured as a percentage of GDP, rather than as a percentage of initial spending as in Table 3.2.

The initial step in the analysis is simple bivariate analysis, seen as a means of establishing a prima facie case for a significant linkage between variables. First, we look for bivariate links between international economy variables and expenditure change. Then having established that such linkages do, indeed, exist, we examine a range of domestic factors that have also been variously hypothesized as determinants of spending and establish whether they too are significantly associated with outcomes. Finally, we bring these variables together in best-fit multivariate models, which seek to maximize the degree of explained variation that can be obtained from variables each demonstrated as significantly related to expenditure outcomes (for a fuller discussion of this methodological criterion of variable inclusion, see Castles 1998: 18–19). These models identify the factors most probably associated with expenditure change in recent years. Where variables that are crucial to a given hypothesis do not feature in a model, or do not feature in the manner predicted, that is a reason for rejecting the hypothesis. As we shall see, this is a test that both globalization theory and the 'new politics' hypothesis ultimately fail.

International Economy Factors

We begin our analysis by presenting data measuring cross-national variation in respect of a variety of aspects of vulnerability to the international economy. That we have not had cause to examine such data previously in this analysis is a function of the fact that the globalization literature, in common with the vast bulk of crisis theorizing about the future of the welfare state, tends to make predictions that minimize the importance of cross-national differences. The assumption is that all countries will behave in a roughly similar fashion as a result of a common stimulus from the changing nature of the international economy. Once we move away from this common threat/ common response assumption to the more reasonable presumption that the extent of expenditure change is likely to be a function of the extent of the stimulus that gives rise to it, the question then becomes one of whether there is any correspondence between cross-national patterns of exposure to the international economy and the extent of change in aggregate spending. The causal logic of the crisis literature can readily be adapted to argue that cuts in aggregate spending will be proportional to the degree of globalization of the international economy. The counter argument noted in the introductory section of Chapter 2 that exposure to the world economy may lead to strong pressures on national governments to protect their citizens from economic vulnerabilities, suggests that internationalization of the economy is likely to be a stimulus to expenditure growth.

Table 5.1 contains data on the two main dimensions of international economic vulnerability identified in the globalization literature: the extent of trade openness and the extent of international capital movements. Trade openness is measured by imports plus exports as a percentage of GDP. Capital movement is measured by foreign direct investment flows also expressed as a percentage of GDP. For each dimension, we provide two separate indicators: one of the level of vulnerability to outside forces and the other of change in the degree of exposure to such forces. The first is measured by the average level of exposure for the period as a whole; the second by change in average levels of exposure between the first and second half of the period. In the case of the capital movement variables, the use of average measures is essential, since national capital investment flows fluctuate widely from year to year.

Table 5.1 Variables measuring exposure to the international economy in 21 OECD countries over the period 1981–98

	Imports + exports as a percentage of GDP		Foreign direct investment as a percentage of GDP	
	Average level	Change	Average level	Change
Australia	35.4	5.1	3.0	0.0
Canada	68.4	32.2	2.2	2.2
Ireland	118.8	25.0	2.9	4.5
New Zealand	58.9	−0.9	3.7	2.7
United Kingdom	52.8	0.8	5.1	1.3
United States	20.4	3.6	1.5	0.7
Family mean	*59.1*	*11.0*	*3.1*	*1.9*
Denmark	67.4	−0.9	2.2	2.7
Finland	57.9	4.5	3.3	3.8
Norway	72.9	−1.6	2.5	1.4
Sweden	66.0	1.9	4.6	5.1
Family mean	*66.1*	*1.0*	*3.2*	*3.3*
Austria	76.2	4.9	1.2	1.2
Belgium	137.0	1.2	6.0	6.2
France	44.0	0.3	2.5	2.3
Germany	53.0	−4.4	1.5	0.4
Netherlands	114.1	−6.7	6.3	5.4
Family mean	*84.9*	*−0.9*	*3.5*	*3.1*
Greece	44.4	0.8	1.5	−0.2
Italy	43.2	1.7	0.9	0.3
Portugal	66.4	0.4	2.4	1.6
Spain	40.4	5.1	2.1	0.9
Family mean	*48.6*	*2.0*	*1.7*	*0.7*
Switzerland	70.3	−1.2	4.6	2.5
Japan	21.0	−4.6	0.7	0.0
Overall mean	*63.3*	*3.2*	*2.9*	*2.2*
Coefficient of variation	*47.2*		*56.1*	

Notes and sources: Data on imports + exports as percentages of GDP come from OECD (various years), *Historical Statistics*, Paris. Data on inflows and outflows of foreign direct investment (FDI) as percentages of GDP are from OECD (various years), *Foreign Direct Investment in OECD Countries*, Paris, and IMF (various years), *Balance of Payments Statistics*, Washington, DC. Level variables are measured as averages for the period 1981–98. Change in both trade and investment variables is measured as the average annual level for the period 1990–8 minus the average annual level for the period 1981–9. All calculated figures subject to rounding errors.

Looking initially at the overall means of the variables featuring in Table 5.2 immediately makes apparent one key difference between these different aspects of vulnerability to the international economy. Between 1980 and 1998, international trade measured as a percentage of GDP only increased quite marginally. In the same period, flows of foreign direct investment more than doubled. If the thrust of the globalization argument is that there has been a major shift in the international economic environment in which government spending decisions are made, it would seem that changes in the extent of capital movements are a much better candidate for a causal stimulus than changes in exposure to international trade. That impression is strongly confirmed by a more detailed examination of the figures in the second column of Table 5.1 reporting changes in the extent of trade openness. With the exception of just two countries, Canada and Ireland, whose trade exposure increased spectacularly during this period, the picture is one of virtually unchanged cross-national variation. Without these countries, the correlation between the openness of the economy in the first and second halves of the period under examination here is 0.99. Increased vulnerability to world trade seems unlikely to be a source of any substantial aggregate expenditure change, since, contrary to the impression frequently given in the globalization literature (for a dramatic example of such hyperbole, see Milner and Keohane 1996), the trade exposure of Western welfare states has scarcely altered in recent decades.

Change in trade exposure apart, there are close similarities between the distributions of the other international economy variables featuring in Table 5.1. Belgium and the Netherlands manifest high levels of vulnerability irrespective of the measure under examination. Japan and the United States are invariably at the other end of the distribution. The former are relatively small economies highly reliant on international trade; the latter are huge economies with vast domestic markets. As a rough rule of thumb, the bigger the economy, the less the degree of international vulnerability, with the United Kingdom's high average level of capital flows the only major exception (see Dahl and Tufte 1973, for a discussion of the rationale for this relationship in respect of trade). These apparent similarities between different measures of exposure to the international economy show up clearly in bivariate correlations between the variables. Whereas correlations between change in trade and the other variables featuring in Table 5.1 are negligible, correlations amongst the remaining variables are substantial: 0.64 between the two levels variables, 0.77 between the average level of foreign direct investment and change in investment flows, and no less than 0.82 between levels of trade and change in investment flows. Given the lack of change in

Table 5.2 Patterns of association between expenditure change outcomes and variables measuring exposure to the international economy in 21 OECD countries over the period 1980–98

	12-component measure	Total outlays government	12-component of downsizing
Average level of imports + exports as a percentage of GDP	−0.52*	−0.63**	−0.61**
Average level of foreign direct investment as a percentage of GDP	−0.33	−0.57*	−0.55**
Change in average level of imports + exports as a percentage of GDP	−0.18	−0.17	−0.02
Change in average level of foreign direct investment as a percentage of GDP	−0.56**	−0.61**	−0.69**

Notes and sources: Correlations are Pearson's R.
  * Significant at 0.05 level.
  ** Significant at 0.01 level.
  Data on change in the 12-component measure of social expenditure from Table 3.1; data on change in total outlays of general government from Table 2.2. 12-component downsizing as measured here is calculated as the sum of cutbacks in expenditure measured as a percentage of GDP rather than as a proportion of initial spending as in Table 3.2. Data measuring exposure to the international economy are from Table 5.1.

patterns of trade in this period, and a modest correlation of just 0.30 between the extent of trade and of foreign direct investment in the first half of the period, it would appear that what we are witnessing here is a process of catch-up, in which investment flows adjusted to conform with patterns of trade exposure already established decades earlier.

The big question then is whether countries heavily dependent on trade and increasingly open to capital flows were simultaneously the countries in which aggregate spending changed most. Table 5.2, which reports bivariate correlations between measures of international economic vulnerability and expenditure outcomes, provides an initial answer. It suggests that there is at least a prima facie case for a negative linkage between greater exposure to the international economy and expenditure change in recent decades. All the reported bivariate relationships are negative, and change in trade openness apart, the only other instance of a relationship that is statistically insignificant is that between the average level of foreign direct investment and change in the

12-component measure. All the other relationships shown in Table 5.2 are moderately to strongly significant, with the strongest single association that between change in the extent of capital flows and 12-component downsizing. These findings appear more in tune with the notion that globalization is associated with cuts in welfare state spending than with the contrary position that international economic vulnerability creates pressures for higher levels of social protection.

Domestic Factors

By themselves, however, the findings reported in Table 5.2 are not a sufficient test of the globalization hypothesis. A proper test requires us to establish whether the extent of exposure to international trade and capital movements continues to predict lower rates of expenditure growth, when simultaneously controlling for a variety of other factors also presumed to be associated with spending trends. In the first section of this chapter, we noted the very considerable range of factors identified in the comparative literature as potential causes of cross-national expenditure variation, and that listing is but a subset of a much wider inventory of hypotheses concerning the determinants of welfare state and total public spending (for an enumeration of these hypotheses, see Castles 1998: 106–8). Space considerations restrict the number of control variables that can be used in this analysis. In what follows, we highlight variables that have featured conspicuously in previous comparative research or which appear particularly relevant to current debates on the factors impacting on aggregate expenditure development in recent decades. In contradistinction to the international economy factors discussed previously, all the factors examined here are domestic in character, relating to the maturation of existing national spending programmes to aspects of the domestic political economy and to the institutional and ideological structuring of domestic politics. Precise variable definitions and data sources are to be found in the notes and sources to Table 5.3.

1. *Initial levels of spending.* We use this measure of the maturation of social and public expenditure programmes as a means of assessing whether the trajectory of change is convergent in character, with a significant negative relationship between initial spending levels and subsequent expenditure change indicating that this is the case. Convergence, in this sense, means more than just an increasing similarity of the distribution as measured by a declining coefficient of variation at successive time points. Rather, convergence here

denotes an actual narrowing of the extent of the distribution, with high values tending to decline and low values to increase. The standard interpretation in the literature suggests that a change trajectory of this kind is most likely to occur as a consequence of the differential timing of the adoption of a common set of expenditure programmes in different nations. The argument is that early adopters will be the initial high spenders. Later, however, the laggards will also adopt these programmes and their levels of spending will ultimately catch up with those of the early leaders. Early debates in the literature focused on the possibility of such trends being driven by industrialization and population ageing. Democratization is another obvious candidate, with late programme adoption in Southern Europe clearly a part of any catch-up story in the period under discussion here. Convergence, however, is not just a function of catch-up by former laggards, but may also result from attempts to retrieve earlier expenditure overshoots by former expenditure leaders. Given that the decision to go ahead with a new programme implicitly assumes a particular rate of economic growth for the life of the programme, and that economic growth slowed markedly from the early 1970s onwards there is every reason to suppose that overshoot could provide an important impetus to retrenchment activity in recent decades. Data on initial levels of 12-component social spending are to be found in Table 3.1 and on initial levels of total outlays of general government in Table 2.2.

2. *1980 GDP per capita.* This variable is used to assess whether more affluent nations exhibit different patterns of expenditure growth than countries that are less affluent. Although the possibility of such an effect has been widely debated in the literature for many years (see Gemmell 1993), no determinate linear relationship has ever been uncovered (but see Castles 1998, for an account of curvilinear relationships between GDP per capita and *levels* of aggregate spending). In 1980, the average level of GDP per capita in these twenty-one OECD countries was US$10,745, with the United States at the top of the distribution on US$15,295 and Portugal at the bottom with US$4,982.

3. *GDP growth.* An account that did not demonstrate the negative impact of economic growth on expenditure change would be quite surprising. That is because all the expenditure measures used in this analysis are denominated as percentages of GDP. As GDP increases, all other things being equal, measured expenditure must fall. The levels of some social welfare benefits are automatically linked to the growth of wages or per capita incomes, but most require some administrative or political action to calibrate them to economic growth. In the absence of such action, the more rapid the increase in national income, the less likely it will be that expenditure will keep up.

The average OECD growth rate in the period under examination here was 2.3 per cent per annum, with Ireland at the top of the distribution with an average growth rate of 4.3 per cent per annum and Switzerland at the bottom with an average growth rate of 1.3 per cent per annum.

4. *Change in unemployment.* Increasing unemployment has clearly been one of the more important new demand-side factors influencing public spending since the early 1970s. Assuming the existence of unemployment benefit schemes, the link between growth of unemployment and growth in expenditure at a national level is axiomatic. Whether, however, that relationship shows up in cross-national analysis is likely to depend crucially on the differential generosity of provision in different nations. In order to smooth the effects of different national economic cycles, we measure change as the difference between average unemployment rates in the 1980s and 1990s. In the 1990s, the average OECD level of unemployment was 0.7 percentage points higher than in the 1980s, but cross-national variation was very considerable, with the Netherlands and Ireland experiencing reductions in unemployment of more than 3 per cent and Finland and Sweden experiencing increases in excess of 4 per cent.

5. *Change in deindustrialization.* This is a variable that seeks to provide an measure of the extent of welfare need resulting from the shift from an industrial economy based on agriculture and manufacturing to a post-industrial economy based on services. It captures not only the unemployment resulting from that transition, but also the extent of labour force withdrawal resulting from the low transferability of skills across employment sectors and the reduced demand for semi-skilled labour in the service sector. Iversen and Cusack (2000) and Iversen (2001) argue that deindustrialization has been the key factor shaping the development of Western welfare states since the 1960s, with the impetus to change originating in a structural transition of domestic labour markets rather than in changes in the international economy as asserted by globalization theory. Because deindustrialization is the source of new welfare needs and, hence, of new demands for government intervention, it supplies an important dimension of the supposed shift to 'a new politics of the welfare state' (see Pierson 2001). Between 1980 and 1998, the average level of deindustrialization in these twenty-one OECD countries went up from 77.2 to 83.9 per cent of the active population. Cross-national differences are, in large part, a function of a convergence of advanced economy employment patterns, with countries like the Netherlands and the United States, already substantially deindustrialized, experiencing little further change, and countries like Switzerland and Finland, still heavily dependent on manufacturing in the 1980s, experiencing a major transition in the 1990s.

6. *Constitutional structure*. The argument that the structure of political decision-making processes can influence the leverage for expenditure change goes
back to early comparative research on a possible link between federalism and
low spending (see Wilensky 1975; Cameron 1978; Castles and McKinlay 1979).
As formalized in more recent analysis, the idea is that a proliferation of veto-
points within decision-making structures makes it easier for conservative
elites to frustrate proposals for change (see Tsebelis 1995, 1999). The variable
used here derives from the work of Huber, Ragin, and Stephens (1993) as modified by Schmidt (1996) and itemizes the number of veto-points in contemporary constitutional structures. Federal arrangements tend to institutionalize
multiple veto-points, and so the high scorers are all federal nations including
the United States, Switzerland, Germany, Canada, and Australia.

7. *Corporatism*. The notion that corporatist organization of the economy is
in some way linked to welfare state development also dates back to early cross-
national research, with both Cameron (1978) and Katzenstein (1985) seeing the
emergence of such institutions as a factor mediating between trade exposure
and a variety of policy outcomes protective against external economic fluctuations. The implication is, as in more recent work by both Garrett (1998) and
Swank (2002), that corporatist economies will be more resistant to retrenchment pressures emanating from the international economy and, indeed, may
initiate new expenditure programmes in response to such pressures. The corporatism variable used here is a composite of twenty-three separate measures
in the literature (see Siaroff 1999). It locates Austria, Norway, Sweden, and the
Netherlands at the corporatist end of the spectrum and countries like Greece,
the United States, Canada, and Spain at the non-corporatist end.

8. *Left impact*. Finally, we turn to variables designed to assess somewhat different aspects of the proposition that class and party politics matters. This
proposition, which became the orthodoxy of the comparative public policy
literature in the 1980s, has recently been challenged by findings suggesting
that expenditure change over the last few decades has not been markedly
influenced by partisan differences. These are findings central to the argument
that we are now witnessing the emergence of a 'new politics of the welfare
state', but are not restricted to studies arguing for that case (see, for instance,
Ross 2000; Castles 2001b; Huber and Stephens 2001). Other studies have
argued that the influence of partisan incumbency remains as great as ever,
with Korpi and Palme (2003) most recently pointing to a statistically significant tendency for Left governments to make fewer benefit cuts in sickness,
industrial accident and unemployment benefits in the period 1975–95 than
governments of other ideological leanings. The Left impact variable used
in this analysis seeks to capture short- to medium-term partisan effects and

simply measures the number of years in which a country has had a democratic socialist Prime Minister during the period 1980–98. Countries toward the top of the distribution include Austria, Sweden, Australia, Spain, and Greece. Countries with no socialist governmental leadership whatsoever during this period include Belgium, Canada, Ireland, and the United States.

9. *Left legacy*. A possible reason that scholars have failed to find evidence of partisan effects in studies focusing on recent expenditure change might be that such effects are cumulative over longer periods of time than just a few decades. To take account of this possibility, we utilize a Left legacy variable that measures the extent of Left governmental leadership over the entire post-war period from 1950 to 1998. The implication is that partisanship effects, in certain countries, may go beyond the immediate impact of a party holding the reins of government for a given period of years. In some countries, parties that are in office for long periods may come to dominate the public policy culture by establishing programmatic priorities for many generations to come. In previous research, I have argued for such an effect in Sweden, Norway, and, to a lesser extent, Denmark, where a long-term social democratic ideological hegemony from the 1930s onward had a major influence on the trajectory of welfare state development in the immediate post-war decades (Castles 1978). Here we test whether recent expenditure change is also, in part, an outcome of such long-term partisan effects, with Austria and the countries of Scandinavia those in which we would expect these effects to be greatest.

Table 5.3 once again uses bivariate measures to test for the presence of prima facie relationships with expenditure change. The picture that emerges from the findings reported in this table is quite consistent across expenditure measures. In each case, expenditure change is significantly and negatively associated with initial levels of spending and significantly and positively associated with changes in unemployment and deindustrialization. However, since these latter variables capture aspects of the same phenomenon—namely, the impact on employment of the shift from an industrial to a post-industrial economy—it seems probable that these findings are not telling us anything very different about what is going on. The story is simply that expenditure change is associated with change in the structure of employment. Otherwise, the only linkage of any significance is the positive association between constitutional structure and 12-component downsizing, possibly indicative of the difficulty of effecting expenditure cutbacks in political systems characterized by multiple veto-points.

Considering the findings reported in Table 5.3 in conjunction with those of Table 5.2, three points appear worthy of mention. First, there is evidence of not just one prima facie relationship, but of three, with spending significantly

Table 5.3 Patterns of association between expenditure change outcomes and programmatic, socio-economic, and political variables in 21 OECD countries over the period 1980–98

	12-component measure	Total outlays of government	12-component downsizing
Initial level of spending	−0.55**	−0.73**	−0.73**
1980 GDP per capita	0.05	−0.30	0.07
GDP growth	−0.38	−0.25	−0.11
Change in unemployment	0.54*	0.47*	0.45*
Change in deindustrialization	0.71**	0.53*	0.46*
Constitutional structure	0.38	0.04	0.46*
Corporatism	−0.09	−0.29	−0.24
Left impact	0.32	0.41	0.13
Left legacy	0.07	0.03	−0.19

Notes and sources: Correlations are Pearson's R.

    * Significant at 0.05 level.

    ** Significant at 0.01 level.

Data on change in the 12-component measure of social expenditure from Table 3.1; data on change in total outlays of general government from Table 2.2. 12-component downsizing, as measured here, is calculated as the sum of cutbacks in expenditure measured as a percentage of GDP rather than as a proportion of initial spending as in Table 3.2. Initial level of spending is the level of the relevant expenditure measure in 1980—for data see Table 3.1 and 2.2. Data on 1980 GDP per capita from Real GDP per capita in 1985 US dollars from Summers and Heston (1991), 'The Penn World Table (Mark 5)', *Quarterly Journal of Economics*, 106: 2, 327–68. GDP growth is the average annual rate of growth of GDP calculated from OECD (various years), *Economic Outlook*, Paris. Change in unemployment is the average rate of unemployment 1990–8 minus the average rate for the period 1981–9 calculated from OECD (various years), *Economic Outlook*, Paris. Deindustrialization is defined as '100 minus the sum of manufacturing and agricultural employment as a percentage of the working age population' (Iversen 2001). Data are calculated from OECD (2001*b*), *Labour Force Statistics, 1980–2000*, Paris. Change in deindustrialization is calculated as average annual level of deindustrialization 1990–8 minus the average level for the period 1981–9. The corporatism measure used here averages a variety of scales from the literature and is from Siaroff (1999). Constitutional structure is an additive index designed to capture constitutional impediments to policy change and comes from Huber, Ragin, and Stephens (1993) as modified by Schmidt (1996). Left impact is measured as the number of years a social democratic Prime Minister was in office in the period 1980–98. Left legacy is measured as the number of years a social democratic Prime Minister was in office in the period 1950–98.

related to aspects of vulnerability to the international economy, to initial levels of expenditure, and to changes in the employment structure. Second, and crucially in terms of the probability of globalization emerging as the decisive factor shaping spending, in no instances are international economy variables those with the strongest relationships with outcomes. In the case of

12-component spending, the strongest relationship is with change in dein-dustrialization. For both total outlays and downsizing, the key variable is the level of initial expenditure, with evidence of a strong convergent tendency in respect of all three dependent variables. Third, despite the absence of signif-icant bivariate relationships in respect of a number of the variables in Table 5.3, it would be premature to assume that these variables will prove insignif-icant in subsequent multivariate modelling. The strongest variables identi-fied in Table 5.3 are sufficient by themselves to account for around 50 per cent of cross-national variation in expenditure outcomes. Controlling for effects of this magnitude may well completely alter the picture, allowing us to identify other factors related to the remaining expenditure variation.

Three Models of Expenditure Change

We now seek to provide a more complete account of the main determinants of recent aggregate expenditure trends by presenting multivariate models for each of the measures featuring in our earlier bivariate analysis. These are best-fit models that seek to maximize levels of 'explained' variation in spend-ing, including only variables that are themselves statistically significant. In effect, this means examining the huge range of potential accounts that can be modelled using the international economy and domestic sphere variables identified in Tables 5.2 and 5.3 and presenting those for which the statistical evidence is strongest. We concede what always has to be conceded in model-ling with so small a number of cases, that the account we end up with is only a broad-brush outline of reality. With only twenty-one cases, one cannot capture nuances. However, we reiterate the point made in Chapter 1, that the sample of countries analysed here is more extensive than in the majority of studies in the literature, and note also that our models have considerable explanatory power, accounting for a minimum of 75 per cent of the cross-national variance in expenditure outcomes, with all but one of the variables satisfying the 0.01 criterion of statistical significance. Our confidence in the models is further enhanced by the fact that they are basically consistent with one another in identifying much the same range of variables as shaping dif-ferent expenditure measures. Since these measures overlap considerably—social expenditure change is a subset of change in total outlays and downsizing is an aspect of social expenditure change—widely diverse models would make for real doubts as to the accuracy of the analysis.

All three models are to be found in Table 5.4. Consistency is at its strongest in respect of the 12-component expenditure and total outlays measures, with the only substantial difference between the models being the fact that change in deindustrialization features as a moderately strong determinant of social expenditure change, but not of total outlays change. Since the deindustrialization hypothesis is premised on the impact of a changing employment structure on welfare need, it is hardly surprising if this variable impacts more directly on social expenditure change than on public expenditure change as a whole. Otherwise, the models are essentially the same, with convergence effects of a quite novel magnitude combined with strong to moderately strong GDP growth and Left legacy effects. Growth in aggregate spending is lower in countries where existing expenditure levels are higher and also lower in countries with higher rates of economic growth. These effects combine powerfully, by themselves accounting for more than 60 per cent of cross-national variation in the 12-component measure and more than three-quarters of cross-national variation in total outlays.

The claim that the convergence trend of recent decades is of a novel magnitude is a potentially controversial one. Sociologists in the 1970s and 1980s celebrated the convergence of the welfare state as an accomplished fact. What had been occurring in the post-war decade was a 'growth to limits' impelled by processes of social and economic modernization stemming from the industrialization of Western societies (see Flora 1986; cf. Therborn 1995). Admittedly, the coefficients of variation in Table 2.1 tell us that, in the 'golden age' of the welfare state, OECD social expenditure patterns were already becoming more similar. However, no catch-up effects of the kind apparent in Tables 5.3 and 5.4 were observable during this period, with a correlation of only -0.07 between change in social expenditure 1960–80 and initial levels of spending (calculated from the data in columns 1 and 4 of Table 2.1). In the case of total outlays, the earlier period was actually one of growing diversity, with an increasing coefficient of variation over time (see Table 2.2) and a positive, although insignificant, correlation between initial spending and subsequent expenditure change (calculated from Table 2.2). Looking at patterns of aggregate spending over the period as a whole, it would, therefore, appear that welfare state convergence, ostensibly born of the process of industrialization, only really became the dominant trend of expenditure development in an era in which deindustrialization tendencies had finally triumphed.

If convergence on this scale was new, the carry over of partisan effects from the 'golden age' provides a degree of continuity. In countries in which Left incumbency has been strong, aggregate expenditure growth has been

Table 5.4 Best-fit models of change in 12-component measure of social expenditure, total outlays of general government, and 12-component downsizing for 21 OECD countries, 1980–98

	12-component measure			Total outlays of government			12-component downsizing		
	Coefficient	Standard error	t-value	Coefficient	Standard error	t-value	Coefficient	Standard error	t-value
Constant	17.797	2.990	5.96**	46.914	4.798	9.78**	1.597	0.707	2.26*
Initial level of spending	−0.660	0.084	−7.82**	−0.814	0.077	−10.56**	−0.155	0.045	−3.41**
GDP growth	−2.697	0.608	−4.44**	−5.916	1.119	5.28**			
Change in deindustrialization	0.401	0.120	3.34**						
Left legacy	0.150	0.036	4.22**	0.230	0.066	3.48**			
Change in FDI							−0.339	0.134	−2.53*
Change in unemployment							0.315	0.080	3.95**
Adj. R^2	0.87			0.87			0.76		

Notes and sources:
* Significant at 0.05 level.
** Significant at 0.01 level.

Sources and definitions for all variables are as in Tables 5.1 and 5.3. For total outlays of government, n = 19.

substantially higher, but this effect only becomes apparent controlling for convergence and economic growth effects. The fact that Left legacy features in both models does not mean that there were no short- to medium-term partisan effects. Both models can be successfully replicated including a Left impact term rather a Left legacy term, but these models account for a somewhat lower degree of variance than those reported in Table 5.4. The clear implication is that long- and short-term effects are cumulative. Finally, while on the subject of Left incumbency effects, it is worth mentioning that, in modelling unreported here, we have also employed alternative operationalizations of these variables using the proportion of Left cabinet seats rather than the number of years of Left governmental leadership as our measure of Left incumbency. The results obtained were virtually identical to those featuring in Table 5.4.

The downsizing model is similar to both other models in demonstrating a convergence effect, and to the 12-component expenditure model in showing the positive welfare expenditure effects of increased labour market stress, although here it is change in levels of unemployment rather than change in deindustrialization that features in the successful model. This positive effect of increasing unemployment is worthy of note because it contradicts recent findings that 'governments experiencing higher levels of unemployment were more likely to cut (expenditures)' (Huber and Stephens 2001: 213). The big differences between the downsizing model and both the other models are that GDP growth and partisan effects are absent, and that there is an apparent negative linkage between expenditure outcomes and increasing foreign direct investment flows. The absence of an economic growth effect is hardly surprising, since the downsizing measure automatically reduces the amplitude of such effects by ruling out of consideration expenditure increases occurring as a consequence of slow economic growth.

However, the absence of a partisan effect on downsizing in conjunction with a strong partisan effect on aggregate spending is of very great interest. This is because it suggests that the difference between countries in which long-term left incumbency has been pronounced and those in which this has not been the case is not that the Left made smaller cuts to existing programmes, but rather that such parties were more expansive in embarking on new expenditure initiatives. This is strongly confirmed by a separate bivariate analysis of the relationship between the partisanship variables figuring in this analysis and growth in the expenditure share types discussed in Chapter 3. Neither growth in spending on social security programmes nor on poverty alleviation and health care, both measured as percentages of GDP, are significantly related to partisanship, however measured. However, both

Left impact and Left legacy are strongly positively associated with growth in expenditure on state services for the elderly and for families, again measured as a percentage of GDP, with correlations of 0.64 and 0.77, respectively. Thus, it would appear that countries in which the Left has been strong not only exhibit higher levels of aggregate spending, but are also those in which the boundaries of welfare provision have been most rapidly transformed to respond to new needs associated with population ageing and a changing family structure.

Given this book's concern to test hypotheses relating to the negative expenditure effects of exposure to the international economy, the link between downsizing and capital flows might be seen as the most significant finding of this analysis. The substantive effect suggested by the coefficient of -0.339 is quite substantial. For the average OECD country, with an average increase in foreign direct investment flows of 2.2 percentage points between 1980 and 1998 (see Table 5.1), it implies a cut in existing expenditure programmes of 0.75 of a per cent of GDP, which amounts to approximately 40 per cent of average OECD downsizing occurring in the period. For the country with the biggest increase in foreign direct investment flows—Belgium with a 6.2 percentage point increase—it implies an expenditure cutback of just over 2 per cent of GDP. Given that Belgium's 12-component expenditure stood at 24.2 per cent of GDP in 1980, this suggests that increased exposure to capital flows cost the country in the order of 9 per cent of existing social expenditure over the course of the next eighteen years. If this were the true magnitude of the international economy effect, it is clear that for a small number of highly exposed OECD economies, the implications would be very serious indeed.

There must, however, be serious doubts about the statistical validity of this finding. Although the relationship between downsizing and change in foreign direct investment is statistically significant by the conventional 0.05 criterion, it fails a standard test of statistical robustness that all the other variables in this and the other models pass with flying colours: namely, that statistical significance is not a function of the inclusion of particular cases in the model. If either Austria and/or Ireland are excluded from the analysis, change in foreign direct investment ceases to be a statistically significant predictor of the extent of social expenditure downsizing. In earlier chapters, we have shown that predictions of major expenditure cutbacks and downward convergence resulting from economic globalization could not be sustained. Examining the three models of expenditure change elaborated in Table 5.4, we now find that, prima facie evidence to the contrary, two of the models contain no international economy term and, in respect of the third, the apparent evidence for a globalization effect does not pass statistical muster. This means that we must reject even the most modest of the variants of the globalization hypothesis. It would appear that expenditure change in recent decades is not proportionately and negatively related to changes in the international economy, but rather is very substantially a function of developments in the domestic sphere.

Pathways to Paradox

This is such an important conclusion that it is worth exploring in rather more detail. In a sense, what we wish to do is to expand the models of expenditure change we have been using to look not only at the relationships between the dependent and the independent variables, but also at the interconnections amongst the independent variables. Table 5.2 shows that a variety of aspects of international economic vulnerability are strongly negatively associated with each of our measures of expenditure change, yet, taking account of a range of factors in the domestic sphere, these relationships cease to be significant. Finding out why involves untangling the linkages between the international and domestic spheres. In Figure 5.1, we attempt to do this for the total outlays of government measure by means of a technique known as critical path analysis. This permits us to distinguish between the direct and the indirect effects of variables, using standardized regression coefficients as measures of the strength of association between variables and sequences of variables. Four independent variables are included in the model: initial levels of spending and GDP growth, the two domestic factors accounting for most of the variation in the relevant model in Table 5.4, plus the level of imports plus exports as a percentage of GDP and change in foreign direct investment as a percentage of GDP, the two international economy variables most strongly associated with change in outlays as shown in Table 5.2. Direct effects are represented by paths (arrows) directly linking independent and dependent variables. Indirect effects are represented by sequences of interconnected paths (sets of arrows) indirectly linking one variable to another. Asterisks indicate paths that are statistically significant. For an indirect effect to be statistically significant, all the steps in the pathway linking that sequence of variables must also be statistically significant.

Figure 5.1 replicates the findings of the relevant model in Table 5.4 in showing strong direct pathways between change in outlays and both initial outlays and GDP growth, and the complete absence of such pathways in the case of the international economy variables. There are, however, a variety of interesting indirect pathways linking aspects of the international economy

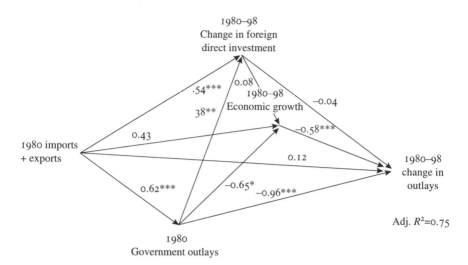

Fig 5.1 Critical path analysis of change in total outlays of general government in 19 OECD countries, 1980–98.

Notes and sources: Figures in path diagram are standardized regression coefficients. The value of the imports plus exports variable is for 1980 rather than the average for the period as a whole, so as to conform with the causal logic of path analysis. Otherwise, all variables are as referenced and described in previous tables.

   * Significant at 0.10 level.
  ** Significant at 0.05 level.
 *** Significant at 0.01 level.

and developments in the domestic sphere. One involves the revelation that, quite apart from a direct positive link between initial levels of trade openness and the subsequent growth in capital movements, there is a further linkage between these aspects of the international economy via the extent of government outlays in 1980. The school of thought suggesting that increased trade exposure leads countries to expand programmes of social protection might see both elements of this linkage as a vindication of their arguments. The strong positive association between the level of trade exposure in 1980 and outlays in the same year is precisely the relationship implied by such an analysis, and the fact that countries with higher levels of spending could lower the barriers protecting them from exposure to increased capital flows is, arguably, indicative of a resilience borne of the security afforded by such expenditure programmes.

There is no significant indirect pathway from change in foreign direct investment to expenditure outcomes, but two such pathways from trade openness to outcomes. One is a positive path via initial outlays and economic growth, but this is a pathway that is relatively weak and actually outweighed in substantive impact by the insignificant negative path via economic growth alone. This means that the key to the significant bivariate negative association between trade openness and expenditure change identified in Table 5.2 lies in the remaining path, in which the potential impact of trade exposure is mediated exclusively through prior expenditure level or convergence. Path analyses for change in the other measures unreported here demonstrate the existence of similar negative and significant indirect paths from trade openness to outcomes via prior spending levels. Such findings are seemingly paradoxical, since they appear simultaneously to confirm what are usually seen as rival hypotheses concerning the effects of exposure to the international economy. The story told by these path diagrams is one of trade openness leading to high levels of total public sector and welfare expenditure in the early 1980s, but of that very development leading to lower public sector growth and weaker welfare state expansion in the years thereafter.

This is a paradox which can only be resolved by recognizing that both hypotheses are at fault. That is because neither successfully captures a cross-national variation, which is simultaneously one of place and time. What we are observing here is not the working out of invariant economic laws linking exposure to international trade with expenditure growth, but rather stages in a process of programme maturation and convergence. Trade openness leads not so much to permanently higher levels of public and social expenditure as to the early adoption of public sector programmes designed to minimize the impact of exposure to the world market. A cross-sectional focus on a period in which only these early adopters have expanded their programmes necessarily gives the impression that trade openness is strongly associated with higher levels of expenditure, and that, of course, is why Cameron (1978) and Katzenstein (1985) identify such linkages in studies focusing on expenditure development up to the late 1970s and early 1980s. However, what such studies necessarily miss is what happens next. As programmes in the countries of early adoption mature, or where, under circumstances of reduced economic growth, they overshoot, subsequent rates of expenditure growth are likely to decline, while rates in later adopting countries accelerate. Convergence processes of this kind are captured by the negative association between prior expenditure levels and subsequent expenditure change. Where many of the early adopting countries are those most exposed to international trade, and where many of the later adopting countries are relatively insulated from such trade, the apparent link between trade openness and expenditure change will be strongly negative in character. Only when we control for initial expenditure levels, as in the models presented in Table 5.4, does this effect disappear.

Remaining Issues

Most of the implications of this analysis require no further extensive rehearsal at this juncture. The case for strong—and for that matter, weak—globalization effects has been the subject of virtually all our analysis to date, and no compelling evidence has been found that supports it. In our remaining chapters, we turn to other issues with potentially greater implications for the future of the welfare state. The identification in this analysis of a range of domestic factors strongly influencing recent social and public expenditure change clearly does have major implications for future expenditure development, but these we reserve for discussion in our concluding chapter. Here we restrict our concluding remarks to answering two important questions: first, are our findings secure against the possible charge that they are predetermined by our choice of cases and, second, what implications do our findings have for the notion of a 'new politics of the welfare state'?

In comparative research, it is always important to be certain that an idiosyncratic choice of cases does not lead to an idiosyncratic set of findings. The vast majority of quantitative studies of public expenditure development have excluded the countries of the new Southern Europe, generally because, for longer time-series, data on some topics and for some data-points are missing, most generally data for the 1960s and early 1970s. However, because our statistical analysis uses data only for a period commencing in 1980, it has been possible to include these nations in our data set. Our strongest finding concerns the extent of expenditure convergence in this period, a finding pivotal to uncovering economic growth and partisan effects not otherwise apparent in bivariate analysis. Arguably, however, the convergence effect might simply be a consequence of Southern European catch-up after a long period in which social spending was held back by late industrialization and late democratization. If that were so, real questions might be asked about the appropriateness of a sample base including countries at such markedly different stages of development.

This is, fortunately, an issue that can be settled quite simply. To test the effects of including the countries of the new Southern Europe in the analysis, we have reanalysed all three expenditure models in Table 5.4 excluding Greece, Portugal, and Spain as cases. In these models, levels of explained variance remain almost as they were in Table 5.4 and exactly the same variables feature as significantly related to outcomes, with change in foreign direct investment once again the only variable that fails to meet the 0.01 significance criterion. Unstandardized coefficients for initial levels remain very similar to those appearing in Table 5.4 and significance levels for this term are only diminished marginally. This reanalysis is decisive. These findings are not an artefact of an inappropriate sample base. As I have argued for some years now (see Castles 1995, 1998), it is time that the countries of the new Southern Europe were systematically included in quantitative analysis of public and social policy outcomes wherever possible.

Turning finally to the issue of the emergence of a 'new politics of the welfare state,' the implications of our findings are essentially negative. Admittedly, deindustrialization is amongst the variables that have been identified as creating new pressures and new constituencies for greater welfare state spending, and our analysis confirms a moderately strong positive impact of this factor on 12-component social expenditure. The downsizing model also suggests that new constituencies of need, produced by changes in the employment structure, are also relevant in this respect. However, the strong evidence for partisan effects in our analysis crucially undermines what has to be regarded as the fundamental premise of the 'new politics' argument: namely, that the old politics of the welfare state has been superseded. The king must surely be dead before we anoint his successor!

Almost as serious in its implications for the 'new politics' case is the very strong evidence for convergence, catch-up, and correction for overshoot throughout this analysis. The potential of big social expenditure programmes to produce constituencies of support for the welfare state is seen by protagonists of the 'new politics' hypothesis as central to the capacity of welfare states to resist pressures for retrenchment. What our analysis shows is that the countries with the initially biggest expenditure programmes were those that experienced the biggest cutbacks in aggregate spending and the most social expenditure downsizing. Since what is distinctive about the 'new politics' hypothesis is not the emergence of new needs as such—that a changing social structure produces new needs is a basic assumption of the sociological analysis of the welfare state—but rather the disappearance of traditional partisan effects and the role of welfare constituencies in resisting cutbacks, the case for the hypothesis appears fatally weakened.

6

Population Ageing and the Public Purse

The Demographic Threat

The focus of previous chapters has been on the supposed threat to the future of the welfare state posed by changes in the international economy. In this chapter and the next, we change gear and examine threats to the future of the welfare state and to the economic, social, and political fabric of Western societies more generally, which supposedly emanate from probable changes in the demographic structure of these societies. In this chapter, we look at evidence concerning recent expenditure trends in programmes catering to the needs of the aged as a basis for assessing the frequently made assertion that population ageing will pose intolerable burdens on public budgets in years to come. In the next, we look at changing patterns of fertility in economically advanced nations over recent decades and ask whether a change in social policy spending priorities is one way of countering a trend which some see as having the potential to bring about a radical decline in population in many countries of the OECD over the next century.

Population ageing is often presented as a threat to the welfare state no less potent than that posed by globalization. The World Bank, in the classic formulation of the case (1994), talks of 'the old-age crisis' and the OECD Secretariat (1996) of 'a critical policy challenge'. The Center for Strategic and International Studies (CSIS), in a recent report entitled *The Global Retirement Crisis*, sees the issues as a 'threat to world stability', and argues that 'the most certain impact of global ageing is the staggering fiscal cost' (CSIS 2002: 4). At the time of writing in October 2003, the OECD's home page headlines a story on 'Ageing Societies and the Looming Pension Crisis'. Other commentators note that whatever problems there may be in the short- to medium-term can only get worse as the fertility rates of many Western nations go into freefall. Op-ed pieces dwelling on the implications of 'the demographic timebomb' are commonplace, with one over-the-top piece suggesting that 'of all the threats to human society, including war, disease and natural disaster, one outranks all others. It is the ageing of the human population' (see Laurance 2002). Governments, too, are frequently prone to crisis rhetoric. National treasuries, irrespective of country-specific demographics, frequently use the supposedly ineluctable consequences of a 'greying' population as a mantra to be invoked against all proposals for enhanced public spending. New commitments are out of the question, when existing commitments to the old (and those who will become old) promise national ruin in a matter of decades. While some scholars, a few agencies of government, and the OECD in its less rhetorical moments provide a more measured analysis of national trends, their voices are often drowned out by the clamour of those who argue that the increased burden of aged spending means that the modern welfare state will no longer be able to pay its way.

Many of these views have some surface plausibility. The world's population is ageing and that of the advanced countries in particular. In the mid-1990s, it was estimated that between 2000 and 2030 AD, the elderly population (aged sixty-five and over) of the average OECD country would increase by 61.8 per cent, from 13.9 per cent of the population to 22.5 per cent (Bos et al. 1994). More recent estimates vector in the trend to declining fertility that has become more evident in recent years. Were period fertility rates to stabilize at a level of 1.6 children per woman, which was the OECD average rate in 1998 (see Table 7.1 Chapter 7), the proportion of the elderly could be expected to increase to around 28 per cent of the population (see Coleman 2001). At the same time, it is clear that the percentage of the old has direct budget implications. Many of the countries in the world, and all those featuring in the analysis here, have age pension systems with extensive coverage. All other things being equal, therefore, a more elderly population means proportionately greater income maintenance expenditure as a percentage of GDP.

Nor are these the only implications. Many commentators, including the World Bank, argue that ageing has a direct influence on health spending 'since health problems and costly medical technologies are concentrated among the old' (World Bank 1994: 3). The CSIS—at the present time, arguably, the most 'hawkish' of the think-tanks predicting demographic disaster— suggests that 'public health-care spending on the elderly in the typical developed country rises by 5.5 percent of GDP between now and 2050' (CSIS 2002: 22). Such predictions rest on often unexamined prior assumptions. The OECD has long conceded the possibility that 'the major increase in health costs in later life is actually determined by the lifetime remaining before death occurs' (Roseveare et al. 1996: 8), but the crisis literature continues to insist that the rise in costs will be proportional to the increase in the aged population. However, even if the crisis literature always assumes the worst, there obviously are real costs. As populations age, and a larger proportion survive into their late seventies, there clearly will be a need for greater provision of services to the frail elderly, such as nursing homes and home help, and these too must be factored into the financial equation resulting from an ageing population.

Finally, there is the question of how the costs of population ageing will be paid for. Some economists have argued that this is 'the single most important long run fiscal issue facing the developed world' (Gruber and Wise 2001: 1). International economic agencies and national economic policy-makers are deeply aware of the temptations facing democratic politicians confronted by demands for additional spending from relatively cohesive interest constituencies. For modern economists, as for their more orthodox forebears, spending without taxing is the primrose path of dalliance, leading on to eternal damnation. If politicians give way to their natural inclination to defer the inevitable fiscal consequences of increased public spending on the elderly by increased borrowing, the cost to the public treasury will ultimately be far greater. If, on the other hand, they adhere to the paths of financial righteousness, they will have to raise taxes and face the electoral odium likely to ensue. Confronted by the costs of population ageing, policy-makers find themselves caught in a cleft stick, with benefit cuts seemingly the only alternative to financial profligacy and widespread electoral unpopularity. As in the case of 'race to the bottom' arguments, the policy proponents of radical pension reform often like to suggest that 'there is no alternative' to what they are proposing.

Argued in general terms, these arguments seem persuasive. They appear to gain additional substance from comparative public policy research, which has demonstrated strong linkages between the age structure of the population and the bigger aggregates of welfare spending and public expenditure over the long run of the post-war period (see Pampel and Williamson 1989; Huber, Ragin, and Stephens 1993; Castles 1998). Harold Wilensky, a pioneer in this field of research, argued the case most strongly: 'If there is one source of welfare spending that is most powerful—a single proximate cause—it is the proportion of old people in the population' (Wilensky 1975: 47). There remain influential scholars who think much the same way. Having devoted a monograph to showing that globalization is not a threat to the achievements of social democratic corporatism, Geoffrey Garrett argues that 'demographic change will increasingly strain the public purse in all countries, including the ranks of social democratic corporatism' (Garrett 1998: 152). For commentators already convinced that the welfare burden is already far too great, the disastrous expenditure consequences of further substantial population ageing seem to follow inexorably.

There are, however, grounds for considerable scepticism. A number of economically literate commentators suggest that economic rather than demographic considerations are the key to the likely impact of population ageing. James Schulz, a leading figure in the economics of ageing, suggests that 'one of the biggest hoaxes perpetrated in the industrialized world today is the promulgation of the notion that the ageing of the population around the world has created a "crisis" ', going on to point out 'that relatively small changes in economic growth rates have the potential to substantially moderate the ill effects of other factors' (Schulz 2002: 86–7). Others note that the supposed 'burden' of supporting an aged population is substantially a function of the extent of labour market participation (see Shirer 1996). Coleman, for instance, points out that, if average European Union (EU) participation rates could be raised to the present Danish level, it 'would go a long way to meet future ageing changes' (Coleman 2001: 4). What both these arguments show is that the *ceteris paribus* clause in our earlier statement, that 'all other things being equal, a more elderly population means proportionately greater income maintenance expenditure as a percentage of GDP', simply cannot be assumed. Fixing the expenditure consequences of population ageing may be as much about fixing economic growth and labour markets as it is about pension reform and expenditure cutbacks (for a full listing of possible policy responses to population ageing, see Hinrichs 2001*b*: 177).

Still others suggest that crisis accounts are exaggerated. It is easy to forget that, in the course of the twentieth century, the population share of the elderly has increased hugely right across the Western world—in some cases, more than tripling—with few obvious adverse economic effects. Sometimes, too, the way in which issues are presented rigs the case in favour of a crisis interpretation. An interesting instance is the preference in much of the literature for using the 'old-age dependency ratio' (the ratio of the old to the active population) rather than the 'demographic dependency ratio' (the ratio of the old plus young to the active population) as the measure of the likely impact of demographic change on public spending. Estimates suggest that over the next twenty-five years Western European old-age dependency ratios will increase by 40 per cent, but that demographic dependency ratios will only go up by 10 per cent, because the percentage of children in the population has been diminishing as the percentage of the aged has risen (see Concialdi 2000: 18–21). The former calculation gives an impression of runaway change; the latter of a relatively gradual process that can be accommodated with only minor adjustments in public spending.

A further reason for scepticism is that, in common with crisis accounts in other areas, those relating to population ageing tend to focus on average figures, supposedly indicative of universal trends. In such accounts, and the policy recommendations stemming from them, there is little room for cross-national diversity. In its 1996 discussion of the 'critical policy challenge' arising from population ageing, the OECD argues forcefully and without qualification 'that if pension programmes are not changed, the tax or contribution rate required to finance transfers to the elderly will rise considerably' (OECD 1996a: 88). Yet the OECD Secretariat's own estimates show that some nations will be far more affected by this problem than others. For the English-speaking family of nations other than New Zealand, the average change in the tax/GDP ratio required to keep net debt constant in the years up to 2030, given the predicted effects of population ageing over that period, is around 3.3 per cent of GDP (calculated from OECD 1996a: table 5.3, 89–90). For the Scandinavian countries, the figure is 5.1 per cent; for the countries of continental Western Europe, it is 9.4 per cent; and for Southern Europe other than Greece, it is 9.0 per cent. The only difference between what the OECD is doing here in providing a one-size-fits-all solution to clearly quite diverse national circumstances, is that, unlike most other prophets of doom, it does at least locate the extent of national difference before proceeding to ignore it.

The exercise that follows is quite unlike those offered in the crisis literature. Rather than making forecasts of likely future developments on the basis of simplified models assuming standardized demographics and little or no change in economic policy parameters, we seek to establish how far and in what ways population ageing has impacted on public expenditure development in recent years. Once again, we adopt a comparative hypothesis-testing approach, seeking to test the validity of crisis accounts by examining whether cross-national differences in patterns of population ageing have translated into differences in aggregate expenditure in the years for which relevant data are provided by the OECD Social Expenditure Database (SOCX). Our analysis proceeds through four stages. First, we examine the post-war experience of population ageing in the twenty-one countries featuring in this study to locate similarities and differences in the trajectories of demographic change in different nations and groupings of nations. Second, we identify cross-national patterns of change in the extent and generosity of pension spending in these nations and groupings of nations in the period 1980–98, noting compelling evidence that programme generosity is a stronger driver of expenditure outcomes than population ageing. Third, we seek to establish whether, during this period, there is evidence of a significant association between variables measuring population ageing and pension generosity on the one hand and variables measuring the extent of individual programme and aggregate spending on the other. Finally, we reassess the models elaborated in the previous chapter to see if population ageing and pension generosity have influenced cross-national patterns of expenditure change in recent decades. Our finding that population ageing has had no discernable effect on either the growth of social expenditure or of total outlays in these years, but that generosity of provision does impact on both, implies conclusions quite different from those commonly arrived at in the crisis literature.

Population Ageing: 1960–2050

A likely a priori objection to using the experience of the past as a guide to likely future trajectories of development is that the scale of the problems to be encountered in the future is wholly without precedent in the past. Certainly, that would be the view of those who paint the direst picture of the consequences of population ageing. Much of the force of their argument rests on the fact that mankind faces a new and quite unprecedented problem, rather than an extension of an existing problem with which nations have been grappling with varying success over many years. The data presented in Table 6.1 on levels and growth in the aged population in twenty-one OECD countries over the period 1960–98 provide us with a benchmark for assessing the strength of this objection.

Calculations using the most recent UN population estimates (see UN 1998), which take some account of recent fertility trends, suggest that the average proportion of the elderly in OECD countries in the year 2030 will be of the order of 23.9 per cent, or 9.0 percentage points higher than the 1998 average shown in the third column of Table 6.1. Figures for average rates of change in the sub-periods 1960–80 and 1980–98 demonstrate that population ageing in the recent past has been of a lesser magnitude than that expected in coming decades. The average change of 5.3 percentage points over the entire period 1960–98 is only about 60 per cent of that projected for the coming three decades. In relative terms, however, the difference in the degree of change is less pronounced. Between 1960 and 1998, the proportion of the population that was elderly increased by around 55 per cent. Between 1998 and 2030, it is estimated that it will increase by a further 60 per cent. Admittedly, the former period is somewhat longer than the latter, but these differences hardly seem of sufficient magnitude to establish the existence of a problem on an entirely novel scale.

Those arguing for crisis scenarios are likely to want to use a different measure of the extent of the problem likely to be faced in coming decades. Data from the same UN source show the average OECD old-age dependency rate will

Table 6.1 Percentage of the population aged sixty-five years and over in 21 OECD countries 1960, 1980, 1998, and change over time

	1960	1980	1998	1960–80	1980–98
Australia	8.2	9.6	12.2	1.4	2.6
Canada	7.6	9.4	12.3	1.8	2.9
Ireland	11.1	10.7	11.3	-0.4	0.6
New Zealand	8.7	9.7	11.6	1.0	1.9
United Kingdom	11.7	15.0	15.7	3.3	0.7
United States	9.2	11.3	12.7	2.1	1.4
Family mean	*9.4*	*10.9*	*12.6*	*1.5*	*1.7*
Denmark	10.6	14.4	14.9	3.8	0.5
Finland	7.5	12.0	14.7	4.5	2.7
Norway	11.1	14.8	15.6	3.7	0.8
Sweden	11.8	16.3	17.4	4.5	1.1
Family mean	*10.2*	*14.4*	*15.7*	*4.1*	*1.3*
Austria	12.2	15.4	15.4	3.2	0.0
Belgium	12.0	14.4	16.5	2.4	2.1
France	11.6	13.9	15.8	2.3	1.9
Germany	10.2	15.5	16.6	5.3	1.1
Netherlands	8.6	11.5	13.5	2.9	2.0
Family mean	*10.9*	*14.1*	*15.6*	*3.2*	*1.5*
Greece	8.1	13.1	16.7	5.0	3.6
Italy	9.2	12.9	17.2	3.7	4.3
Portugal	8.1	11.4	14.8	3.3	3.4
Spain	8.1	11.2	16.3	3.1	5.1
Family mean	*8.3*	*12.1*	*16.2*	*3.8*	*4.1*
Switzerland	10.7	13.7	15.1	3.0	1.4
Japan	5.7	9.1	16.2	3.4	7.1
Overall mean	*9.6*	*12.6*	*14.9*	*3.0*	*2.2*
Coefficient of variation	*19.1*	*17.7*	*12.6*		

Notes and sources: Data for 1960 from OECD (1993), *OECD Health Systems*, Vol. II, Paris. Data from 1980 onwards from OECD (2001b), *Labour Force Statistics 1980–2000*, Paris. All means subject to rounding errors.

go up from 22.6 per cent in the year 2000 to 39.6 per cent in 2030, an increase of almost exactly 75 per cent. Clearly a measure which captures the capacity of society to bear the economic costs of ageing is to be preferred to one that does not, but, as we have already noted, the old-age dependency ratio may not be the most appropriate indicator in this respect. The denominator of the old-age dependency ratio is the population between the ages of fifteen and sixty-four or, so-called 'active population'. It is, however, a measure of the potentiality rather than the actuality of an economy's capacity to support the aged. Many of the active population are not active producers, including those in education above the age of fifteen, women who have withdrawn from the labour force to have children, and those who have withdrawn from the labour force before the age of sixty-five. This means that actual dependency rates are substantially higher than potential ones. Moreover, because countries differ very appreciably in their rates of post-15 educational enrolment, female employment, and early retirement, it is far from obvious that potential and actual dependency ratios will manifest anything like the same patterns of cross-national variation. Thus, the use of old-age dependency ratios as measures of the potential expenditure impact of population ageing is suspect not only because it ignores the dependency of children, but also because it takes no account of important labour market factors that influence the capacity of nations to bear the economic costs of ageing. Labour market reforms—cutting levels of early retirement, increasing levels of female employment, and raising the retirement age—are, arguably, easier and more effective ways of minimizing the fiscal consequences of population ageing than pension reforms aimed at cutting levels of entitlement.

Returning to the data in Table 6.1, it is very important to note how varied the experience of these OECD countries has been. Countries like Ireland, New Zealand, Austria, and the United States have aged relatively slowly over the period 1960–98. On the other hand, there are a number of countries in which the process of population ageing in the recent past has been of much the same order of magnitude that we may expect to be the norm in coming years. These countries include Japan, Greece, Spain, and Italy, all of which experienced a growth in the aged population of more than 8 percentage points. It should also be noted that, for the post-war period as a whole, the correspondence between rates of population ageing and social expenditure growth is hardly impressive. Table 2.1 in Chapter 2 shows that the four countries with the highest social expenditure growth in the period 1960 to 1998 were Switzerland, Sweden, Norway, and Denmark, yet, of these countries, only Sweden was above average in ageing terms, and then by only a small margin. There is more correspondence at the bottom of the spending distribution, with the United States, Ireland, and Canada all countries in which a relatively low increase in social expenditure went along with low or moderately low population ageing. A major exception, though, is Japan. The Japanese population has aged faster than anywhere else in the OECD, yet that country's rate of expenditure growth has been well below the OECD average. The Japanese experience of social expenditure growth over the past five decades should be a reality check for those inclined to accept the prognostications of the population ageing Nostradamuses too uncritically.

Two factors account for Japan's weak growth in social expenditure during the post-war period. The most important was Japan's exceptional economic growth rate in the four decades after the Second World War, which meant that it was simultaneously possible to restrain spending measured as a percentage of GDP while experiencing a growth rate in real spending higher than anywhere else in the OECD. The other was the persistence of an extended family support system, resting on Confucian values (Goodman and Peng 1996), which partially insulated the state from the impact of an ageing population. Other countries cannot possibly hope to emulate such an experience and, almost certainly, nor can Japan in future years. Our identification of Japan as a key case for the argument here is not because Japan is an exemplar of how to go about avoiding a future old-age crisis, but because it stands as an example of how economic, cultural, and other factors can get in the way of an automatic correspondence between the size of the aged population and public expenditure development over longish periods of time.

Finally, we should note differences in patterns of population ageing in different families of nations. In 1960, according to the data in Table 6.1, the countries of continental Western Europe had the oldest population structures, with an average of 10.9 per cent of the population aged sixty-five and over, with Scandinavia not far behind, on an average of 10.2 per cent. The countries at the bottom of the distribution covered a spectrum from the most economically advanced to the poorest nations, with the English-speaking family of nations averaging 9.4 per cent and the countries of Southern Europe 8.3 per cent. Nearly four decades later, the population ageing distribution had been radically transformed. The proportion of the aged population in the countries of Southern Europe had virtually doubled. With an average of 16.2 per cent of the population of sixty-five years and over, this was now the most elderly of these families of nations. Averages for the Scandinavian and continental Western European groupings were virtually identical at 15.7 and 15.6 per cent, respectively. The English-speaking countries were now much the most youthful grouping in the OECD, with the elderly averaging only 12.6 per cent of the population.

Long-term forecasts, again based on calculations from the latest UN data, suggest that the English-speaking nations' demographic advantage will continue. It is estimated that, in 2050, the proportion of the population of sixty-five years and over will be 22.8 per cent in the English-speaking world, 25.3 per cent in Scandinavia, 28.0 per cent in continental Western Europe, and an astounding 35.2 per cent in Southern Europe. Corresponding estimates for the aged as a percentage of the active population are 38.2 per cent (English-speaking), 43.2 per cent (Scandinavia), 48.8 per cent (continental Western Europe), and 64.6 per cent (Southern Europe). These differences essentially derive from the fertility differentials of earlier generations. The fact that the majority of English-speaking nations have been, throughout the post-war era, countries of overseas migration has been conducive to relatively high levels of fertility and a youthful population. More recently, Scandinavian social policies designed to permit women to combine labour force participation and family formation have promoted fertility rates rather higher than those typical of continental Western Europe and Southern Europe (for a fuller discussion, see Chapter 7), and this explains why Scandinavian old-age dependency rates are predicted to be lower than elsewhere on the European continent. These comparisons point to one very simple conclusion: that population ageing impacts, and will continue to impact, on different countries and groupings of countries to very differing extents. In itself, that casts serious doubts on the universalistic claims of the crisis literature.

Pension Spending and Pension Generosity

Of all the potential ways in which population ageing might impact on the public purse, the most obvious is through the enhanced costs of pension programmes as they expand to cope with an increasingly elderly population. Old-age cash benefit spending was, in most countries, the earliest major spending programme of the welfare state and, in most, remains the most expensive. In the absence of changes in the coverage and generosity of public pensions, it is axiomatic that as the proportion of the population of pensionable age increases, so too will cost to the exchequer (OECD 1985), although not necessarily the cost measured as a percentage of GDP, which also depends crucially on the rate of economic growth.

Table 6.2 provides data both on the cost of old-age cash benefits as a percentage of GDP and on the generosity of spending, measured by what we call the AGE ratio, which is simply cash spending as a percentage of GDP divided by the percentage of the population of sixty-five years and over. This ratio is

Table 6.2 Old-age cash benefit spending as a percentage of GDP and the AGE ratio (old-age cash benefit spending to aged population) in 21 OECD countries, 1980, 1998, and change over time

	Cash benefits			AGE ratio		
	1980	1998	Change	1980	1998	Change
Australia	3.2	4.3	1.1	0.33	0.35	0.02
Canada	2.8	5.1	2.3	0.30	0.41	0.11
Ireland	4.0	2.5	−1.5	0.38	0.22	−0.15
New Zealand	7.0	5.5	−1.5	0.72	0.47	−0.25
United Kingdom	5.1	6.4	1.3	0.34	0.41	0.07
United States	5.0	5.2	0.2	0.44	0.41	−0.04
Family mean	*4.5*	*4.8*	*0.3*	*0.42*	*0.38*	*−0.04*
Denmark	5.8	6.8	1.0	0.40	0.46	0.06
Finland	4.7	7.0	2.3	0.39	0.48	0.08
Norway	4.5	6.0	1.4	0.31	0.38	0.08
Sweden	6.7	7.5	0.8	0.41	0.43	0.02
Family mean	*5.4*	*6.8*	*1.4*	*0.38*	*0.44*	*0.06*
Austria	8.5	9.9	1.5	0.55	0.65	0.09
Belgium	6.1	7.4	1.3	0.42	0.45	0.02
France	7.6	10.6	3.0	0.55	0.67	0.12
Germany	8.7	10.5	1.8	0.56	0.63	0.07
Netherlands	6.5	6.2	−0.3	0.57	0.46	−0.11
Family mean	*7.5*	*8.9*	*1.5*	*0.53*	*0.57*	*0.04*
Greece	5.1	10.2	5.1	0.39	0.61	0.22
Italy	7.4	12.8	5.5	0.57	0.75	0.17
Portugal	3.4	6.3	2.9	0.30	0.43	0.13
Spain	4.6	8.1	3.5	0.41	0.50	0.09
Family mean	*5.1*	*9.4*	*4.3*	*0.42*	*0.57*	*0.15*
Switzerland	5.6	11.2	5.5	0.41	0.74	0.33
Japan	2.9	5.7	2.8	0.32	0.35	0.03
Overall mean	*5.5*	*7.4*	*1.9*	*0.43*	*0.49*	*0.06*
Coefficient of variation	*31.7*	*35.1*		*26.1*	*27.9*	

Notes and sources: Expenditure on old-age cash benefits spending as a percentage of GDP from OECD (2001a), *Social Expenditure Database, 1980–1998*, Paris. 1998 UK old-age cash benefits reduced by 3.3 per cent of GDP to take account of a definitional change in UK aged spending. The AGE ratio is calculated by dividing old-age cash benefit spending as a percentage of GDP by the percentage of the population aged sixty-five and over. Data on the aged population is from Table 6.1. All calculated figures subject to rounding errors.

equivalent in principle to the welfare state generosity measure appearing in Table 2.4. In reality, neither are pure measures of generosity, but capture the contribution to spending outcomes resulting from differential national levels of both programme coverage (the proportion of the relevant population receiving benefit) and programme generosity (the average amount of benefit received). In other words, they capture the degree of cross-national variation in benefit spending that cannot be attributed to population demographics (the size of the population category, in principle, entitled to benefit). In what follows, we frequently use the term generosity to cover both aspects of the non-demographic residual.

Table 6.2 shows that, between 1980 and 1998, pension spending in the OECD went up from an average of 5.5–7.4 per cent of GDP. In 1980, pensions represented around 30 per cent of aggregate 12-component social expenditure and, in 1998, around 33 per cent, hardly indicative of a marked tendency for pension growth to crowd out other kinds of expenditure programme. In 1980, Scandinavia was the region in which population ageing had proceeded furthest, but the first column of Table 6.2 shows that, at this date, continental Western Europe was the region with by far the highest levels of spending, with Germany, Austria, and France all with pension expenditure in excess of 7.5 per cent of GDP. At the other end of the distribution, the correspondence between population ageing and expenditure was greater, with the relatively youthful English-speaking countries spending even less than the poorer countries of Southern Europe, and very markedly less if the atypically high spending of New Zealand is left out of account.

As in the case of population ageing, by 1998, there had been a substantial change in pattern. Spending in continental Western Europe had continued to rise, but had been quite outstripped by expenditure growth in Southern Europe and Switzerland. In 1998, five countries were spending more than 10 per cent of their Gross National Product on age pensions: two in Southern Europe, two in continental Western Europe, and Switzerland, whose spending pattern was now analogous to that of the latter grouping (see also the discussion in Chapters 3 and 4). The populations of the Scandinavian countries were now only marginally less aged than those of Southern and continental Western Europe, but Scandinavian spending levels were much lower. Between 1980 and 1998, New Zealand cut back its pension spending quite dramatically and, on average, expenditures in the English-speaking countries remained almost stationary during these years. By the end of the period, spending in the English-speaking world was approximately half that of the big spending families of nations. As in the case of population ageing, the picture is not one of countries moving in step along a common developmental path, but of marked and persistent variation among countries and groupings of countries with common historical, linguistic, and cultural attributes.

The AGE ratio measure to be found in the last three columns of Table 6.2 provides an indicator of the extent to which cross-national variation in spending patterns corresponds to cross-national variation in population ageing. If all differences in spending were attributable to differences in population ageing, the coefficient of variation of the AGE ratio would be zero. As it is, the coefficient for the AGE ratio is somewhat less than that for spending both in 1980 and in 1998, but the reduction is only of the order of around 20 per cent. The clear implication is that generosity of spending, and in particular increasing benefit levels, is a far more significant determinant of levels of pension spending than the age structure of the population (Shirer 1996: 64; De Santis 2001: 13). Obviously, because ageing makes such a relatively small contribution to spending patterns, there are significant similarities between the distributions reported in the first three and last three columns of Table 6.2. Indeed, the only real difference is that patterns of variation are simplified. In 1980, the really generous countries were largely to be found in continental Europe and AGE ratios elsewhere were broadly similar. In 1998, Southern Europe had joined its continental Western European neighbours as the area of maximum generosity, with a very big gap to the countries of Scandinavia and the English-speaking world.

Looking at population ageing and the AGE ratio as separate factors together accounting for 1998 levels of spending, one observes what might, perhaps, best be described as a 'double whammy' effect. Ageing is greatest in Southern Europe, and so too is generosity. In the English-speaking world, the opposite is the case. As we have argued throughout, the extent of the fiscal problems or 'crisis' facing these countries is utterly different. In Southern Europe, the problem of a rapidly ageing population is compounded by an extremely generous pension system, and the dilemmas of the countries of continental Western Europe are essentially similar. The welfare states of the English-speaking world confront neither of these challenges in the short term, and their rates of population ageing will be lower than those of other groupings over the longer term. Scandinavia comes somewhere in between, but nearer the English-speaking end of the spectrum, with a relatively elderly population in the recent past, a level of expenditure generosity somewhat below the OECD mean, and a profile of future ageing less pronounced than that of either continental Western or Southern Europe.

Historically, the major sources of the differences in coverage and generosity, which contribute to patterns of cross-national variation in the AGE ratio, result from differences in the architecture or repertoires of social policy in these countries (see Palier 2001). In particular, they are a function of choices between universal or means-tested, flat-rate benefits and income-related, contributory benefits (see Overbye 1994; Myles and Quadagno 1997). Essentially, income-related benefits are more expensive than flat-rate or means-tested ones and the contributory principle creates a strong sense of entitlement to benefit. These are the characteristics of what, in Chapter 3, we described as the social security state. This potent combination, stemming from the original Bismarckian, institutional design of the welfare state, underlies the high pension expenditure levels of the core continental Western European states throughout the post-war period. It also helps to account for the substantial growth of the age pension systems of Southern Europe over the past two decades. Moreover, during this same period, the fiscal problems of continental Western European social systems have been exacerbated by using them as a source of funding for extensive early retirement schemes (see von Rhein-Kress 1993; Esping-Andersen 1999; Scharpf 2000). In these latter countries, a genuine case might be made for a 'triple whammy' effect.

The welfare states of the English-speaking family of nations are at the opposite extreme from such countries. The differences stem from the essentially Beveridgean design features of most of the English-speaking welfare states, with the majority of benefits provided on a flat-rate basis, either to all citizens or to groupings selected on the basis of need. The institutional objective of the system is not to replace earnings, but to prevent poverty, which is why, in Chapter 3, we designated systems emphasizing such goals as poverty alleviation states. In consequence, pensions tend to be ungenerous, typically replacing between 40 and 55 per cent of previous earnings rather than the 60–80 per cent more common in other systems (see Blöndal and Scarpetta 1998, whose estimates are for 1995). Given the English-speaking countries' relatively youthful age structures, this lack of generosity has translated into expenditure levels only around half of those prevailing in continental Western and Southern Europe.

The institutional designs of pension systems in Scandinavia can be seen as hybrids, with both Beveridgean and Bismarckian elements. Historically, these countries started out with flat-rate and/or means-tested provision and in the early post-war decades their pension systems were characterized by flat-rate universalism. However, from the 1960s onwards all, bar Denmark, added contributory and income-related second-tiers to their pension structures. This in-between status in terms of institutional design combines with an already noted in-between position in respect of demographic pressures. Consequently, it is not surprising that estimates of the likely cost burden of pensions in coming decades suggest that Scandinavia falls somewhere between the English-speaking and the continental Western European nations in severity of impact. It should be noted, however, that this underestimates the true costs of provision for the elderly in the Scandinavian countries. The Scandinavian emphasis on state services, which, in Chapter 3, we noted as the defining characteristic of the institutional design of the countries' overall systems of welfare provision, leads to substantial state spending on services to the elderly in a way that is not replicated in any other of the families of nations.

The lack of generosity and restricted coverage of age pension provision in the English-speaking family of nations follows directly from the institutional design of these nations' social policy systems. Although this makes for enduring contrasts with systems based on Bismarckian and social democratic principles, it is worth noting the recent trend of many European countries to adopt reforms aimed at limiting either the generosity or the coverage of existing age pension provision (for descriptions of reforms across Europe, see Feldstein and Siebert 2001). Strategies for reducing benefit levels have involved indexing pension benefits to the rate of inflation rather than to the rate of increase of real incomes and seeking to move away from income maintenance principles ('defined benefit' schemes) to the earlier notion of benefits in proportion to contributions ('defined contribution' schemes). Strategies for reducing coverage have included the introduction of partial means-testing and increasing the age at which individuals become eligible to receive benefit. Most of these reforms are of mid- to late-1990s provenance and do not yet show up as reduced AGE ratios in Table 6.2. However, calculations of changes in the AGE ratio between 1990 and 1998 not shown here indicate a distinct slowdown in the growth of average generosity across the OECD, with the countries of continental Western Europe averaging zero AGE ratio growth during this period.

The reforms that have been taking place are, of course, substantially motivated by an awareness of the dangers posed by high degrees of benefit generosity in the context of an ageing population. Nevertheless, the very fact that they have been enacted suggests that it may be possible to contain the public expenditure impact of age pensions in precisely those countries where the existing problems are greatest. It is also possible that governments may be able to provide for the income needs of the old in a manner that does not make use of the formal structures of public provision. At the same time as a number of countries have been trimming back on the generosity of their schemes, other countries have been redesigning their pension systems to provide greater cover and generosity through government mandated occupational provision. In the long run, anxieties about population ageing may actually lead to some partial convergence in overall spending totals, as historically generous public systems trim their provision and historically parsimonious ones use mandated schemes to cope with increasing need and growing expectations. Crisis theories frequently underestimate the capacity of governments to respond positively to the problems they confront, although it may be a legitimate riposte to argue that governments are the more likely to do so when faced with the prospect of a supposedly imminent crisis.

On the Correlates of Age-related Expenditures

It is beyond the scope of this study to offer a discussion of other age-related expenditures on the scale of that already provided for pension spending. Instead, we use bivariate analysis to provide a synoptic view of prima facie relationships between changes in the spending levels of a variety of age-related programmes and variables measuring the potential impact of population ageing and increased generosity of provision to the aged. Three variables feature in this analysis:

1. *Initial age structure* measured by the percentage of the population aged sixty-five years and over in 1980 (for data see the second column of Table 6.1). The use of this variable permits us to answer the question of whether age-related expenditures increase most rapidly in countries in which the population is already most elderly. The likely mechanism underpinning such a relationship is a political one whereby the elderly serve as a constituency of support for expenditure measures serving the interests of those in older age groups (see Pampel and Williamson 1989; Pierson 1996).

2. *Change in the age structure* measured here by increases or decreases in the percentage of the population aged sixty-five years and over in the period 1980–98 (see final column of Table 6.1). The standard interpretation of this variable would be that, as ageing increases, the population in need of age-related spending also increases. Such an effect might also occur as a consequence of enhanced political pressures for extended generosity and coverage, but is more likely to stem from automatic or quasi-automatic expenditure increases as the proportion of the population eligible for benefit under existing programmes increases in size.

3. *Change in the AGE ratio*, which, as explained in the previous section, should properly be regarded as a measure of change in the coverage and/or generosity of pension spending. As calculated here, the AGE ratio is the residual that results when pension expenditure is controlled for the extent of population ageing. However, although a residual, the sources of cross-national variation in programme generosity are well understood, emanating as they do

from fundamental differences in the architecture of social protection in diverse types of welfare system. In the case of pension spending, we are interested in whether the degree of association between generosity and spending is greater or smaller than the degree of association between ageing and expenditure. In the case of other spending programmes, an association between expenditure and the AGE ratio would suggest that the factors underlying the generosity of pension programmes flow through to other programmes catering to the needs of the elderly. Finally, in the case of the bigger aggregates of spending, the AGE ratio should be seen as an indicator of how far total social and public expenditure are shaped by the generosity of what is, in most countries, their largest single component programme.

The story told by Table 6.3 is not particularly complex. The figures appearing in the first column suggest no linkage between the initial size of the aged population and any of the age-related programmes of the welfare state or any of the wider aggregates of spending. Arguably providing additional evidence against the 'new politics' hypothesis, there is absolutely no sign that where the constituency of the elderly is greatest, there is any enhanced pressure for

Table 6.3 Patterns of association between expenditure change outcomes and age-related variables in 21 OECD countries, 1980–98

	Initial age structure	Change in aged 65+	Change in AGE ratio
Old-age cash benefits	0.15	0.48*	0.92**
Survivors' benefits	−0.09	0.28	0.54*
Health expenditure	−0.11	0.23	0.52*
Services to the elderly	0.42	−0.23	0.08
12-component measure	0.12	0.24	0.78**
Total outlays	−0.13	0.49*	0.78**
12-component downsizing	−0.12	0.56**	0.58**

Notes and sources: Correlations are Pearson's *R*.
   * Significant at 0.05 level.
   ** Significant at 0.01 level.
   Expenditures on old-age cash benefits and the AGE ratio from Table 6.2. Expenditures on survivors' benefits, public health, and services to the elderly and disabled from OECD (2001*a*), *Social Expenditure Database, 1980–1998*, Paris. Data on change in the 12-component measure of social expenditure from Table 3.1; data on change in total outlays of general government from Table 2.2. 12-component downsizing, as measured here, is calculated as the sum of cutbacks in expenditure measured as a percentage of GDP rather than as a proportion of initial spending as in Table 3.2. Data on initial age structure and the percentage of the population aged sixty-five and over from Table 6.1.

pensions to grow more rapidly. By contrast, the figures in the second column do suggest a positive linkage between an increasing aged population and increased pension spending, but the degree of association is quite modest. This relationship is replicated both for total outlays and for 12-component downsizing, the latter relationship indicating that expenditure cutbacks were least in countries where the population was ageing most rapidly. However, the population ageing effect is not apparent in respect of other programmes like survivors' benefits, health expenditure, and elderly services. Oddly, given the significant positive relationship with outlays, there is no positive association with the 12-component measure of total social spending.

The strongest relationships by far are those reported in the final column of Table 6.3 measuring the degree of association between change in the AGE ratio and change in expenditure outcomes. A 0.92 correlation with age spending itself confirms our earlier interpretation that change in pension spending is far more related to coverage and generosity change than to population ageing. In fact, a multiple regression of change in aged cash spending including both variables suggests that the substantive impact of AGE ratio change is more than twice that of population ageing. The AGE ratio effect is also apparent in respect of both survivors' benefits and health spending, suggesting that increasing expenditure in all these areas was, to some extent, responsive to the same range of factors. Increased expenditures on services to the elderly seem unrelated either to ageing or to whatever factors shape increased generosity to the aged. That fits with our earlier analysis, which sees state services spending as uniquely responsive to variables measuring partisan impacts. Finally, we note that the effects of change in the AGE ratio translate through strongly to 12-component social expenditure and to outlays and somewhat less strongly to downsizing. In no instances are population ageing effects greater than increased generosity effects, and the overall pattern of relationships revealed in Table 6.3 confirms the impression of our earlier analysis of pension spending, that cross-national differences are far more a function of differences in coverage and generosity than of ageing.

The Models Revisited

Contrasting the findings in Table 6.3 with earlier bivariate findings in Tables 5.2 and 5.3, we also note the remarkable fact that change in 12-component social expenditure and outlays is more closely associated with change in the AGE ratio than with any of the international or domestic variables featuring in these latter tables. This could simply mean that the factors explaining change in the expenditure aggregates also explain change in pension expenditures, which are, of course, a substantial component of change in those aggregates. However, it could also mean that pension generosity is independently a factor conditioning aggregate expenditure outcomes, implying, if our interpretation in the previous section is correct, that differences in the architecture of social protection influence the extent of provision as well as its structure. In order to find out if this is the case, and in order to establish whether population ageing variables fare any better in a multivariate than a bivariate context, we conclude our analysis by revisiting our Chapter 5 models and adding in the variables featuring in Table 6.3. Once again, our criterion of inclusion is the maximization of explained variance in models consisting only of statistically significant variables.

Table 6.4 replicates Table 5.4, and it is worth looking back to the previous chapter to identify the changes that result from the inclusion of new variables in the models. In regard to 12-component spending, the terms of the existing model are not altered. All four variables—catch-up, economic growth, deindustrialization, and Left legacy—remain significant predictors of outcomes, although the significance of the economic growth and deindustrialization terms are somewhat diminished. Nevertheless, it appears that the generosity of pension spending does make its own separate and significant contribution to outcomes. The coefficient for the AGE ratio seems large at 8.951, but given that the average increase in the AGE ratio over these eighteen years was only 0.06, this means that the average increase to 12-component spending contributed by this factor was only of the order of half a percentage point of GDP. The effect of remodelling on the outlays model is much greater, with the strong GDP growth effect from Table 5.4 disappearing and being replaced by an even stronger AGE ratio effect, with a substantive impact amounting to almost 3.1 per cent of GDP in the average OECD country over this period. Catch-up and Left legacy effects are effectively unchanged.

The disappearance of the economic growth term in the outlays model and its weakening in the 12-component expenditure model tell the same story. While there is an independent pension generosity effect on aggregate expenditure, much of the strong bivariate association between the AGE ratio and aggregate spending is a consequence of the strong impact of economic growth on change in pension expenditure. Pension spending increases fastest where GDP is growing most slowly and vice versa, with Ireland and Switzerland demonstrating the extremes of this process. There is nothing even faintly surprising about this. Because pension spending, just like aggregate spending, is denominated as a percentage of GDP, the effect of economic growth will, all other things being equal, be translated through into a decline in measured spending. In the outlays model in Table 6.4, this is captured exclusively by the effect of greater pension generosity on spending outcomes.

Table 6.4 Best-fit models of change in 12-component measure of social expenditure, total outlays of general government, and 12-component downsizing including age-related variables for 21 OECD countries, 1980–98

	12-component measure			Total outlays of government			12-component downsizing		
	Coefficient	Standard error	t-value	Coefficient	Standard error	t-value	Coefficient	Standard error	t-value
Constant	14.307	3.065	4.67**	16.408	3.126	5.25**	−0.335	1.060	−0.32
Initial level of spending	−0.569	0.085	−6.69**	−0.500	0.074	−6.73**	−0.306	0.042	−7.31**
GDP growth	−1.830	0.660	−2.77*						
Change in deindustrialization	0.306	0.115	2.67*						
Left legacy	0.138	0.032	4.31**	0.182	0.060	3.04**			
Change in FDI									
Change in unemployment							0.267	0.078	3.43**
Initial age structure							0.316	0.106	2.99**
Change in age 65+									
Change in AGE ratio	8.951	3.910	2.29*	51.587	8.111	6.36**			
Adj. R^2	0.90			0.90			0.79		

Notes and sources:
* Significant at 0.05 level.
** Significant at 0.01 level.
Sources and definitions for all variables are as in Tables 5.1 and 5.3. For total outlays of government, $n = 19$.

In the 12-component model, the effect is shared between the negative impact of GDP growth and positive effect of increased pension spending.

In many ways, the most interesting model changes are to be observed in respect of downsizing. What happens here is that the statistically suspect change in foreign direct investment effect from Table 5.4 disappears to be replaced by a positive initial age structure effect. With the disappearance of a negative international economy term goes the last smidgeon of evidence supportive of a globalization interpretation of recent expenditure change. A further effect of the model respecification is that the catch-up term becomes more pronounced, and now comparable in strength to those featuring in the other aggregate expenditure models. All three models are now entirely consistent in showing programme convergence as much the strongest factor driving outcomes.

The question that then remains is whether the emergence of an ageing term in the downsizing model should make us re-evaluate our negative appraisal of the ageing hypothesis, and the answer is, almost certainly, not. The downsizing measure captures not what is happening to expenditure as a whole, but the extent to which existing expenditure programmes escape cuts. What the revised model in Table 6.4 tells us is that, in broad terms, the countries most vulnerable to downsizing were those with the biggest aggregate expenditure programmes, but that, within those parameters, cuts were minimized where the needs of pensioners and the unemployed were greatest. Put like that, the story sounds suspiciously like the oft-told tale of the 'frozen landscape' (Esping-Andersen 1996), 'immovability' (Pierson 1998), or 'maladjustment' (Manow and Seils 2000) of the countries of continental Western Europe finding it difficult to cope with the compound challenges of an ageing population and labour market rigidities. An analysis of the residuals in this model suggests, however, that these findings are very largely driven by what happened at the other end of the downsizing distribution, with the deepest cuts in existing programmes occurring in Ireland and the Netherlands, countries with relatively youthful populations and very markedly declining unemployment levels. The appropriate lesson is the hardly astonishing one that reform initiatives are easier where demographic and labour market conditions are most propitious.

A Crisis for Some

This chapter has utilized a comparative analysis of age-related expenditure change in recent decades to test propositions concerning the likely consequences of population ageing for public expenditure development in coming years. Its conclusion is quite clear. There is an effect on the cross-national distribution of pension spending, but one of relatively minor significance compared to that of coverage and generosity changes combined. There is also an initial age structure effect, which inhibits expenditure downsizing. However, neither of these effects flows through to influence change in total social and public expenditure totals, presumably because countries with higher spending on pensions compensate by spending less on other kinds of programme (for a discussion of the ageing bias in the welfare states of Southern Europe, see Castles and Ferrera 1996; Ferrera 1996; Esping-Andersen and Sarasa 2002). Our conclusion, therefore, is that the countries confronting major fiscal difficulties as a consequence of high levels of pension expenditure are not so much those with aged and ageing populations, but rather those with extremely generous levels of pension provision. Contrary to the universalistic claims of the crisis literature, these are problems restricted to a quite small minority of countries.

Now that age pension provision in New Zealand has been so radically pruned, these countries are to be found exclusively in Southern and continental Western Europe, including, for these purposes at least, Switzerland in this latter grouping. Not only are these the families of nations in which generosity of provision and population ageing are greatest, they are also those in which labour market activity rates are generally lowest, thereby making the future support base of public provision for the elderly that much more problematic. This is why a number of commentators with a more nuanced understanding of national differences than the World Bank have identified the real welfare expenditure malaise of these countries as one of Eurosclerosis rather than of population ageing. However, even this diagnosis may be too sweeping. A point that is often neglected is that it is the countries with the most expensive pension systems that have the most scope and motivation for pension reform. Of the continental Western European countries, the Netherlands has markedly reduced the generosity of its provision in recent years, and France has adopted structural reforms involving the abandonment of key aspects of the existing Bismarckian institutional design of the pension system (see Palier 2000).

In Southern Europe, the Italian experience of the 1990s provides a further instance of purposive policy reform under the most adverse of circumstances. Of all the countries in the OECD facing serious difficulties arising from the combined effects of population ageing and, arguably, excessive generosity to beneficiaries, Italy constitutes the most extreme example. Table 6.2 shows that, in 1998, both pension spending and pension generosity were higher in Italy than anywhere else in the OECD. Table 6.1 shows that, in the same year, Italy's population was the most aged in the region, with UN projections implying that this will continue to be the case for many decades to come. Prior to the Italian reforms of 1995 and 1997, expenditure projections suggested a pensions' bill peaking in 2040 at more than 23 per cent of GDP. As a consequence of the reforms, the projected spending peak has been revised downward to 15.8 per cent of GDP in 2032, with spending levels gradually declining in the years thereafter (Ferrera 2000; 176–7). Reforms of the kind occurring in the Netherlands, France, and Italy should not be over-interpreted to suggest that anything like a structural convergence of Western pension systems is occurring. On the contrary, changes in New Zealand and Switzerland have, if anything, made family of nations profiles more distinctive. They do, however, challenge the notion that democratic politicians are powerless in the face of demographic change. The evidence of expenditure development in the area of pensions over the past two decades simply does not sustain such an interpretation (see also Hemerijck 2002; 201–5).

Finally, from the point of view of those countries which are actually low spenders on pensions—and all members of the English-speaking family of nations fall into this category—to talk of crisis and to read lessons on the potential effects of population ageing from the experience of those countries with the most extensive and generous pension programmes involves a serious distortion. By almost any criteria, including those of the OECD Secretariat and the World Bank—the existing age structure of the population, generosity levels, recent expenditure trends, and existing levels of public indebtedness—most of these countries are well placed to cope with the public expenditure impact of population ageing in the coming decades. To use the spectre of population ageing in these countries as a means of combating the growth of public expenditure is to transform social science analysis into ideological rhetoric. Arguably, what the extremely low AGE ratios of some these countries demonstrates is not the necessity for cuts in spending, but rather the basis of the case for pension reform to increase the generosity of provision to the aged. What the relatively youthful age structures of these same countries suggest is that such increases are unlikely to bankrupt public budgets any time in the foreseeable future. As in the case of the crisis literature on the implications of globalization, one is forced to conclude that much of the rhetoric about the budgetary consequences of population ageing is motivated more by short-term considerations of containing or cutting back public budgets than by justified anxieties concerning the consequences of demographic change.

7

Birth-rate Blues: A Real Crisis in the Making?

The Possibility of Population Decline

This chapter takes a radically different approach from those that have preceded it. Earlier we have been concerned with the validity of hypothesized threats to the future of the welfare state. Here, we examine a supposed threat to the very fabric of the societies in which we live and ask whether social policy initiatives could be a part of the solution. The supposed threat to the viability of existing societies is that we are entering an era in which insufficient children will be born to replace populations at anything like current levels. Those with a concern for an environmentally sustainable future may see a gradual decline in population as a blessing rather than a threat, but the prospect of population decline implied by current fertility rates is anything but gradual, threatening to halve or even quarter the populations of some Western nations over the course of the next century.

It is, therefore, a question of some considerable significance whether the process of fertility decline can be slowed down or reversed by the deliberate policy actions of the state. This is a question of great interest to demographers, but it is also one in which comparative policy research has a legitimate interest. Fertility rates differ markedly from country to country and that suggests that the kind of comparative hypothesis testing approach utilized throughout this book may be of value in locating reasons for cross-national differentials in fertility decline. Moreover, we have every reason to believe that national social policy differences may be amongst the factors most likely to affect fertility outcomes. In many countries, there are policies in place designed to make it easier for women to combine work and family. An obvious hypothesis—and one that is the central focus of this chapter—is that it is the countries in which such policies are best developed that have been most successful in countering the factors making for fertility decline.

Table 7.1 Period total fertility rates in 21 OECD countries, 1960, 1980, 1998, and change over time

	1960	1980	1998	1960–80	1980–98
Australia	3.48	1.89	1.76	−1.59	−0.13
Canada	3.90	1.73	1.62	−2.17	−0.11
Ireland	3.73	3.24	1.93	−0.49	−1.31
New Zealand	4.24	2.01	1.92	−2.23	−0.09
United Kingdom	2.69	1.90	1.71	−0.79	−0.19
United States	3.65	1.85	2.07	−1.80	0.22
Family mean	*3.61*	*2.10*	*1.83*	*−1.51*	*−0.28*
Denmark	2.54	1.55	1.72	−0.99	0.17
Finland	2.71	1.63	1.70	−1.08	0.07
Norway	2.90	1.72	1.81	−1.18	0.09
Sweden	2.13	1.68	1.50	−0.45	−0.18
Family mean	*2.57*	*1.65*	*1.69*	*−0.92*	*0.04*
Austria	2.69	1.65	1.34	−1.04	−0.31
Belgium	2.58	1.68	1.59	−0.90	−0.09
France	2.73	1.95	1.76	−0.78	−0.19
Germany	2.36	1.56	1.36	−0.80	−0.20
Netherlands	3.12	1.60	1.63	−1.52	0.03
Family mean	*2.69*	*1.69*	*1.54*	*−1.00*	*−0.15*
Greece	2.28	2.22	1.29	−0.06	−0.93
Italy	2.41	1.64	1.20	−0.77	−0.44
Portugal	3.01	2.25	1.46	−0.76	−0.79
Spain	2.86	2.20	1.16	−0.66	−1.04
Family mean	*2.64*	*2.08*	*1.28*	*−0.56*	*−0.80*
Switzerland	2.44	1.55	1.47	−0.89	−0.08
Japan	2.00	1.75	1.38	−0.25	−0.37
Overall mean	*2.88*	*1.87*	*1.59*	*−1.01*	*−0.28*
Coefficient of variation	*21.1*	*20.5*	*15.6*		

Notes and sources: 1960 period total fertility rates are from World Health Organization, *World Health Statistics Annual*, WHO, Geneva, 1993. 1980 and 1998 figures are from J.-P. Sardon (2002), 'Recent Demographic Trends in the Developed Countries', *Population* (English edition), 57: 1, 111–56. All calculated figures subject to rounding errors.

Since 1960, period total fertility rates (PTFRs) in advanced industrialized societies have declined precipitously. As shown in Table 7.1, in all but a few of these societies, the bulk of that decline occurred between 1960 and 1980, with a drop in average PTFRs for the twenty-one OECD countries featuring in this study from 2.88 to 1.87 children per woman in the age group 15–44. All of these countries experienced some fertility decline in this period, but its extent varied widely from as little as 3 per cent in Greece to as much as 40 or 50 per cent in all the English-speaking nations of Oceania and North America. After 1980, the process of decline continued, but at a much slower rate and with greater variability of trend. By 1998, average PTFRs for these countries had fallen to 1.59. However, a number of countries in both Scandinavia (Denmark, Finland, and Norway) and the English-speaking world (New Zealand and the United States) bucked the downward trend and experienced some (generally modest) recovery from their 1980 levels.

Although fertility decline between 1960 and 1980 was far more rapid than in the period 1980–98, it is change in the latter period that is widely seen as the more problematical by contemporary demographers. The prevailing 'demographic transition' model of population change sees fertility decline as a function of reductions in disease and mortality that make it possible for couples to have fewer children without a reduction in the number surviving to maturity (see Chesnais 1992; van de Kaa 1996). In terms of this model, the fact that major post-war decreases in infant mortality in the industrialized countries were accompanied by substantial reductions in fertility is no surprise. What is more puzzling is that fertility rates, having reached the level— approximately 2.08 children per woman—required for population replacement have, in many countries, continued to fall, and this despite consistent opinion poll evidence that the majority of women in these countries continue to see a family with two children as optimum (see Coleman 2001: 5).

To understand why below replacement fertility could be a real cause for concern about the future viability of Western societies, it is necessary to extrapolate over time. McDonald notes (2002: 2) that, other things being equal, a PTFR of 1.3 sustained over a period of a century implies a decline in population of 1.5 per cent per annum and an eventual population only a quarter the original size at century's end. Four of the countries featuring in Table 7.1—Austria, Greece, Italy, and Spain—are presently on track for such outcomes, and two others—Germany and Japan—face population decline almost as great. The implications of population decline on this scale are potentially extremely serious. Initially, it would lead to reduced rates of growth of the labour force and national product. Thereafter, it would mean labour market contraction and negative rates of economic growth. Employers and governments, concerned about the social expenditure demands of an ageing population, are likely to see such trends as reasons to encourage migration, and, where fertility decline is only modest, this could be a solution. However, as McDonald (2002: 2), echoing a recent United Nations Report (2001), points out, 'where fertility is below about 1.6, the levels of migration required for replacement of the population become impossibly large'. As Table 7.1 shows, this is a level to which average OECD fertility rates have already fallen.

These immediate economic implications are, however, but the tip of the iceberg. Substantial increases in migration could well lead to political tensions and provide a platform for anti-immigrant populist movements with a real potential to destabilize the political systems of Western democracies. The overnight emergence of the List Pim Fortuyn as the Netherlands' second largest political party in the aftermath of its founder's assassination in May 2002 may only be a foretaste of what is to come. Population decline is also likely to affect the balance of geopolitical power over the course of the next hundred years. The United States, with a PTFR almost spot-on replacement rate, is currently the only one of the major OECD countries that seems relatively immune from population decline. As earlier noted, in terms of population size alone, many of the other big players in the contemporary international arena are going to find themselves downgraded to what amount to bit-parts well before the end of the coming century.

Economic stagnation resulting from rapid population decline will also make it harder and harder for other countries to compete on even terms with what is likely to remain a continuingly dynamic US economy. Amongst likely consequences may well be a 'brain drain' westwards and the depletion of much of Europe's and north Asia's human capital base. At the same time, Europe, on its eastern and southern borders, will be facing nations with rapidly growing populations and declining living standards, both resulting from high (or at least much higher than European) levels of fertility. Under these circumstances, the prospect for increasing jealousies, mounting tensions, and ultimately, perhaps, armed confrontation between have and have-not nations would be very real indeed. Extrapolating mechanically from present trends and looking forward over the coming century, the potential threat can readily be presented as being of, almost literally, apocalyptic proportions.

These are visions of a distant future seen 'through a glass darkly' and not yet the subject of active policy debate. Increasing awareness of the phenomenon of below replacement fertility has produced two kinds of scholarly response. The first has been to question whether existing low levels of total fertility are likely to continue in the long term. This avenue of inquiry follows naturally from the fact that period total fertility is a synthetic measure designed to capture in a single number the current fertility behaviour of all women at a given point in time. Compared with measures of cohort fertility, which are counts of the average number of children born to women in a given age group, the analytical advantage of period rates is in providing the best estimate of the number of children currently being born to those younger women who will shape tomorrow's patterns of fertility. The disadvantage of period rates is that they fluctuate not only with changes in couples' underlying preferences for children but also in response to changes in the timing of those children's births. Given that an important manifestation of fertility decline in recent decades has been a marked increase in the average age at which mothers have their first child, it seems probable that some part of the trend to below replacement fertility is a temporary phenomenon due to later family formation and the deferral of first births.

This has been extensively discussed in the recent demographic literature, along with the additional possibility of differential national rates of fertility 'recuperation' after the birth of the first child (see Lesthaeghe and Moors 2000). It is now widely agreed that, in periods when the age of first births is increasing, PTFRs are likely to exaggerate the extent of long-term fertility decline. However, although with some exceptions (see Bongaarts and Feeney 1998), there also appears to be a consensus emerging that deferral of first births is insufficient to account for anything like the full decline of PTFRs in those countries in which they are lowest (see Lesthaeghe and Willems 1999: 226; McDonald 2002: 4). Apparently, what we are witnessing in these countries is a long-term change in preferences concerning family size, partly manifested in the increased number of women who have no children at all, but, ultimately more significantly, in a secular decline in the proportion of second and especially third births.

Hence, the obvious alternative response to issues raised by the widespread shift to below replacement levels of fertility in advanced industrialized societies has been predicated on the proposition, explicitly argued or otherwise, that observed differences in period fertility rates are genuinely indicative of underlying fertility differences amongst countries. Given such a view, an obvious strategy of enquiry is to focus on the factors associated with cross-national variance in fertility levels, using comparative analysis to establish their relative importance. For governments under pressure to come up with 'solutions' to impending population decline, this strategy holds out at least some promise that it could lead to the identification of policy instruments with a potential for reversing current adverse trends.

Research along these lines has focused largely on the implications of women's changing labour market attachment and on policies supportive of combining female employment and maternity. However, while this literature has frequently adduced contrasts between nations in support of its arguments, its use of comparative evidence has generally been quite limited (partial exceptions are Ahn and Mira 1998; Castles 1998; Esping-Andersen 1999). Partly, that is because population researchers in the demographic tradition have been methodologically more inclined to focus on the factors shaping individual choice and behaviour than on those shaping aggregates of behaviour at a national level. Partly, it is because economists interested in accounting for fertility behaviour have often been more concerned with theoretical exposition than with the need for empirical testing of whether hypothesized relationships exist in the real world.

Arguably, however, the greatest obstacle to comparative research in this area has been the fact that cross-national data pertaining to certain of the policies imputed to influence female labour force participation and fertility have not, until recently, been available for a sufficient number of countries to permit even a rudimentary comparative analysis. Essentially, we have had data on public spending for family policy purposes and little else. Information on such matters as the availability of childcare places and family-friendly working practices has only been available for particular countries in particular years. This is now changing. What makes the analysis of this chapter possible is the recent publication by the OECD of a far more comprehensive data set on family-friendly policy measures than has hitherto been available. These data permit us to assess the extent to which family-friendly public policy influences current fertility outcomes and, hence, whether it offers a potential way of combating fertility decline in coming decades.

The World Turned Upside Down

A comparative account of the factors associated with below replacement fertility starts not from the brute fact of fertility decline, but from the observation that in a period of somewhat less than two decades there has been a dramatic change in the cross-national incidence of fertility in advanced societies. Chesnais (1996: 729), amongst the first to note the extent of this change, identifies it as a Western European phenomenon involving a reversal of 'the longstanding differential in fertility between the north and south of Europe'. Table 7.1 makes it possible to map the contours of this change as it has occurred in the most economically advanced countries of the Western world. In 1960, of the exclusively European families of nations, continental Western and Southern Europe had quite similar average fertility rates, in both instances well above replacement level. However, between 1960 and 1980, rates in continental Western Europe declined appreciably, leaving Southern Europe as the only European family of nations with replacement level fertility. In the most recent period, Southern European fertility rates have declined very steeply, and, by the late 1990s, were markedly lower than elsewhere in the OECD.

Table 7.1 also confirms a turnaround of comparable magnitude in the countries of Scandinavia. Until 1980, these countries had the lowest average fertility rates in the OECD. Thereafter, Scandinavian birth rates began to recover, so that by 1998 they were appreciably higher than those of continental Western and Southern Europe. Providing data only for time points almost two decades apart makes the Swedish case appear to diverge from the general Scandinavian pattern. In fact, given that the Swedish period fertility rates actually increased from 1.68 in 1980 to 2.13 in 1990, at that time the highest rate in the OECD bar Ireland, before declining to 1.50 in 1998, the real question seems to be why the Swedish fertility rate rose so rapidly during the course of the 1980s and why it then manifested a no less dramatic decline in the 1990s. These are questions we address in our later analysis.

The timing and trajectory of fertility decline in the English-speaking world was different again, with the bulk of change occurring earlier, but having less impact on family of nations relativities. Table 7.1 shows that, at the beginning of the period, average PTFRs were extremely high as a consequence of the early post-war 'baby boom' fertility of the countries of North America and Oceania, all with high levels of migration and consequently extremely youthful populations. However, between 1960 and 1980, these countries experienced an average drop in fertility more precipitous than any other grouping in the OECD, only remaining in replacement rate territory because Ireland was a significant outlier in terms of the late onset of fertility decline. After 1980, and again with the exception of Ireland, the trajectory of decline became much shallower, with the consequence that, by the end of the period, the average fertility of the English-speaking countries was once again markedly higher than that of any other grouping.

These comparisons of OECD countries illustrate the extent of change in cross-national patterns of fertility in the advanced nations during the post-war period. As the declining coefficients of variation in Table 7.1 indicate, the general trend of the post-war period has been one of convergence towards a low fertility profile. If anything, the data in Table 7.1 underestimate the scope of the change in international terms. The source from which the data is derived (Sardon 2002) also shows that, since 1980, many of the countries of Eastern Europe and the former Soviet Union have experienced a decline in period fertility rates from levels at and around replacement rate to ones comparable to those of contemporary Southern Europe. Fertility rates in a number of newly industrialized countries in north-east Asia have followed a similar trajectory, with, as Table 7.1 shows, Japan leading the way. The dramatic nature of the change that has occurred is, perhaps, most clearly revealed in the North/South reversal, but its scope is now worldwide, progressively affecting industrialized societies in every continent.

This transformation is more than just a matter of altered cross-national fertility patterns. Commentators have also noted seismic shifts in the historic relationships between fertility rates and other variables often seen as shaping cross-national variation in those rates to a greater or lesser degree. The variables most frequently highlighted in this context are cultural values emphasizing the primacy of the family and employment structures. For Chesnais (1996: 729), the truly revolutionary nature of what has taken place lies in the fact that the Southern countries of exceptionally low fertility are precisely those 'still commonly labelled as traditional, Catholic, and family oriented'. The changed implications of traditional cultural values are also noted by Monnier and de Guibert-Lantoine (1996). They point out that, under contemporary conditions, the relatively higher fertility rates of the English-speaking and Scandinavian countries go along with higher divorce rates, higher rates of cohabitation, and higher rates of extra-marital births, and that the ultra low fertility of the countries of Southern Europe occurs precisely in those countries in which an emphasis on the family remains strongest.

My own earlier work on the correlates of fertility in OECD countries (Castles 1998: 272–3) identifies a shift from statistically significant positive to statistically significant negative findings for Catholic adherence between 1974 and 1993 and shifts of comparable magnitude but opposite signs for both female labour force participation and service employment during the same period. Narrower studies focusing exclusively on the impact of economic variables identify similar labour market trends. Ahn and Mira (1998), examining a panel of OECD labour market and fertility data, locate the timing of the reversal as the mid-1980s and its likely determinants as changes in women's wages and the growth of unemployment in the countries of Southern Europe. An OECD study (1999: 17) shows that a similar pattern of reversal can be identified using cohort rather than period fertility rates. Finally, Esping-Andersen (1999: 67–70) links the cultural and economic aspects of the transformation by arguing that the 'familialistic' social policy typical of countries in which Catholicism remains culturally salient makes it extremely difficult for women to combine work and family, leading to lower rates of fertility than in countries where the obstacles are less daunting.

Cultural Values and Employment Structures

Our purpose here is not to challenge the main thrust of these findings, but to elaborate a model capable of accounting for cross-national variation in advanced nation fertility levels taking advantage of the recent availability of data on family-friendly policies in OECD countries. The first step we take in building such a model is to focus on relationships between fertility rates in 1980 and 1998 and a wide range of variables drawn from the relevant literature. The strength and direction of these relationships is assessed by the correlation coefficients appearing in the first two columns of Table 7.2. Variables

Table 7.2 Patterns of association between period total fertility rates and variables measuring cultural values and employment structure in 21 OECD countries, 1980 and 1998

	Correlation with PTFR		Correlation between values of independent variables in 1980 and 1998
	1980	1998	
Catholic adherence	0.47*	−0.43*	0.99**
Total divorce rate	−0.43*	0.49*	0.88**
Service employment	−0.44*	0.55*	0.94**
Female employment	−0.47*	0.53*	0.81**
Female labour force	−0.47*	0.50*	0.80**
Female tertiary education	−0.26	0.53*	0.80**
Female unemployment	0.17	−0.53*	0.49*
PTFR	—	—	0.21

Notes and sources: Correlations are Pearson's *R*.
 * Significant at 0.05 level.
 ** Significant at 0.01 level.
  Data on Catholic adherence as a percentage of the population in 1975 from *World Christian Encyclopedia*, 1st edn., Nairobi: Oxford University Press, 1983, and for 1995 from *World Christian Encyclopedia*, 2nd edn., New York: Oxford University Press, 2001 (for the purposes of this analysis, Greek Orthodoxy is counted as equivalent to Catholicism). Data on total divorce rates come from J.-P. Sardon (2002), 'Recent Demographic Trends in the Developed Countries', *Population* (English edition), 57: 1, 111–56. Data on female employment and female labour force participation as percentages of the female population aged 15–64 come from or are calculated from OECD, *Labour Force Statistics* 1980–2000, Paris, 2001. Data on female unemployment as a percentage of the female labour force and on service employment as a percentage of total civilian employment come from the same source. Data on the percentage of females educated to tertiary level come from the *UNESCO Statistical Yearbook*, various numbers. Data on 1980 and 1998 PTFRs from Table 7.1.

capturing the continued salience of traditional cultural values are adherence to the Catholic faith and rates of divorce, although only the former can be reasonably interpreted as potentially being causally related to fertility outcomes. Direct measures of the modernity of the employment structure are female employment, female labour force participation, and total service employment. Although discussed separately in the literature, employment and labour force participation as measured here are virtually identical, with correlations as high as 0.99 in 1980 and 0.98 in 1998. Service sector employment is included as a variable potentially relevant to fertility outcomes because it has been widely identified as an important determinant of the post-war growth of female employment (see OECD 1984; Bakker 1988; Castles 1998).

Two other variables are less easy to classify in terms of a traditional values/ employment structure dichotomy. The first is female tertiary educational enrolment, here taken as a proxy for a wider expansion of female educational opportunities during the post-war era and as an approximate measure of women's enhanced equality during this period. Increased access to education captures aspects of both changing cultural values and a changing employment structure, allowing women to escape from the thrall of outmoded beliefs (Sen 2001), while simultaneously providing them with the skills required to participate in a modern economy. The second is the level of female unemployment. This is not a measure of the modernity of the employment structure as such, but may be regarded as an indirect indicator of how well that structure caters to women's labour market preferences. Where women's rates of unemployment are high, prospects for labour market re-entry after maternity are diminished. A strong negative relationship between female unemployment and fertility could be interpreted as indicating a disinclination to further risk employment prospects through maternity under circumstances where labour market entry is already problematical.

The picture that emerges from the figures presented in the first two columns of Table 7.2 is about as unambiguous as one could hope to get. Every single variable is significantly associated with fertility in 1998 and every single variable changes signs between 1980 and 1998. Five variables—the two measures of traditional cultural values and the three direct measures of the modernity of the employment structure—are statistically significant in one direction in 1980 and in the other in 1998. The findings for 1980 are entirely congruent with received expectations that traditional values and traditional employment structures are likely to be associated with relatively high levels of fertility. The findings for 1998 suggest a world turned upside down, in which the highest levels of fertility are to be found where the institutional support for traditional family values is weakest, where women's educational opportunities and, arguably, gender equality are greatest, and where employment structures are most welcoming to female workers.

The figures in the final column of Table 7.2 report bivariate correlations between the 1980 and 1998 values of each of the independent variables featuring in the table. By providing a measure of the extent to which these variables have changed over these years, they allow a preliminary assessment of how far transformed patterns of relationships were a function of fertility reversal and how far of changes in employment structures and traditional values. The answer is once again unambiguous. With the single exception of levels of female unemployment, the cross-time correlations between the values of the variables measuring traditional values and employment are extremely high (0.80 and above), indicating that patterns of cross-national variation changed relatively little during the period. In contrast, the cross-time correlation between PTFRs in 1980 and 1998 (see final row of Table 7.2) is a mere 0.21, indicative of a very substantial change in the cross-national incidence of fertility over time.

The findings reported in Table 7.3 seek to shed more light on the factors associated with fertility change in these twenty-one OECD countries over the period 1980–98. The first column of the table reports correlations between initial 1980 values of the same variables featuring in Table 7.2 and fertility rate change in the ensuing period. The second column reports correlations between change in those variables and change in fertility rates. Clearly, the findings featuring in the first column have less direct causal implications than those featuring in the second. Where theory suggests a linkage between two variables, a significant correlation between change in one and change in the other may be, at least, tentatively interpreted as implying the possibility of a direct causal connection between them. By contrast, the existence of a statistically significant association between the initial value of one variable and subsequent change in another variable, however strong that relationship is, tells us only about the prior attributes of the cases which have changed most and those which have changed least. Such correlations do not provide us with explanations, only with more focused clues as to the phenomena that must be accounted for.

It is in this light that the findings in Table 7.3 should be interpreted. The extremely strong relationships reported in the first column tell us much about the characteristics of the countries in which fertility declined most sharply. They were the countries in which adherence to traditional values, as measured by the degree of Catholic adherence and the infrequency of divorce, was strongest. They were simultaneously the countries in which

Table 7.3 Patterns of association between 1980 and 1998 change in period total fertility rates and initial and 1980–98 change values of variables measuring cultural values and employment structure in 21 OECD countries

	Correlations with change in PTFRs	
	Initial value	Change value
Catholic adherence	−0.70**	0.27
Total divorce rate	0.75**	0.05
Service employment	0.76**	−0.58**
Female employment	0.64**	−0.01
Female labour force	0.64**	−0.15
Female tertiary education	0.48*	0.15
Female unemployment	−0.24	−0.35
PTFR	−0.80**	—

Notes and sources: Correlations are Pearson's *R*.
   * Significant at 0.05 level.
   ** Significant at 0.01 level.
   All initial and change values are from or calculated from data with source references as provided in Table 7.2.

female labour force participation and service employment were weakest. To a somewhat lesser degree, they were also the countries in which women had the least educational opportunity. Finally, the strongly negative relationship between fertility rates in 1980 and change in fertility thereafter is indicative of the last stages of a catch-up process in which Ireland and the countries of Southern Europe emulated the earlier fertility trends of the other OECD nations. In measurement terms, the strength of the reported associations with the variables capturing aspects of cultural values and economic structure comes as no surprise, following axiomatically from the sign reversal of statistically significant relationships reported in Table 7.2. In substantive terms, the strength and coherence of the patterns revealed by these variables suggest that links between fertility change, cultural values, and economic structure are likely to prove anything but fortuitous.

Arguably, the same may not be true of the one significant finding reported in the second column of Table 7.3: the apparently anomalous, because traditionally assumed, link between growth in service employment and decline in fertility. Almost certainly, this relationship is an artefact of the much stronger positive association between high initial levels of service employment and subsequent fertility growth. This was a period in which service sector growth was taking place largely in those countries where it had previously been weakest, with a catch-up correlation of −0.77. Hence, rather than seeing this single finding as an exception to the general rule that modern employment structures now tend to be associated with higher rather than lower levels of fertility, it seems more appropriate to view it as deriving from the fact that it was precisely those nations with the weakest service sector development at the beginning of the period which were most likely to experience substantial fertility decline in the years thereafter. The finding is again not a causal one, but part of the pattern we are trying to explain.

The strong correlations reported in the first column of Table 7.3 and the absence of transparent causal linkages that might explain them suggest two possibilities. Either the variables measuring aspects of traditional cultural values and employment structure have changed their meaning for social actors, leading to a shift in preferences regarding the trade-off between work and family, or, alternatively, the reported correlations appearing in Table 7.3 are spurious in the sense of serving as proxies for relationships between fertility change and other variables as yet unidentified in the analysis. The obvious candidate variables are those relating to the impact of family-friendly public policy. In the account that follows, we argue that an adequate account of recent fertility change almost certainly involves both kinds of mechanism.

Changing Preference Patterns

The mystery of the great reversal is the more perplexing since both of the main economic theories which seek to account for the trend to below replacement fertility in recent decades are agreed in attributing this change to increasing levels of female education and rising levels of female employment, variously seen as increasing the 'opportunity costs' of maternity (Becker 1991) or as increasing the financial rewards flowing from postponing parenthood (Easterlin 1976; Easterlin and Crimmins 1991). It is, moreover, an axiom of popular commentary on the trend to later marriage that this phenomenon is a function of young women's wishes to complete their education and establish themselves in careers prior to embarking on family formation. Yet, the relationships assumed by these hypotheses appear, on the surface at least, to contradict those demonstrated in our cross-national analysis. In that analysis, negative relationships between fertility and labour market modernity are a thing of the past, with the highest rates of fertility apparent in precisely those nations in which female educational attainment and female employment are highest.

The standard account of the traditional relationship between fertility rates and employment structure and of the declining trend of fertility in response to educational and employment change is generally articulated in terms of a trade-off between work and maternity at the level of individual behaviour (Sorrentino 1990; Blau and Ferber 1992), with the contradictory demands of working life and motherhood seen as restricting the capacity of female employees to have children and of mothers to work. Clearly, this is an argument that must be true at the margin. All other things being equal, more paid employment or more maternity will increase the demands on a woman's time and will be likely to influence her choices as to her preferred employment/ maternity mix. Clearly too, it is an argument which we know to be true at the extremes. Busy female executives find it extremely hard to balance the demands of work and family. Mothers with several small children find it difficult to hold down full-time jobs. However, while the trade-off implied by these stereotypical instances is real enough, the considerations shaping individual fertility choice have almost no bearing on patterns of cross-national fertility variation. What matters in this connection is the wider context within which the trade-off takes place.

The theories of economists, including those concerning fertility, proceed from the notion of actors seeking to maximize their preferences, but take the nature of those preferences as given. Women and couples choose their preferred mix of employment and fertility in light of their own aspirations and of the obstacles they anticipate encountering in fulfilling those aspirations, but they do so in a manner that is hugely constrained by the values that society defines as (and sometimes enforces as) appropriate to their situation. These values can and do change. What made the context of the immediate post-war decades quite different from that of the present era, and what produced a negative relationship between female employment and fertility on a cross-national scale throughout that period, was not any fundamental difference in the character of the trade-off between work and maternity in these two epochs, but rather a set of values and attendant preferences concerning work and maternity quite different from those common in contemporary post-industrial societies. In a world where female employment was widely regarded as inimical to child-bearing and to the proper nurture of the young, countries in which, for whatever reasons, female employment was greatest were inevitably going to be those with the lowest levels of fertility.

However, a preference for a complete separation of the spheres of employment and maternity does not follow axiomatically from the logic of trade-off, nor has such a preference characterized most hitherto existing societies. The widespread assumption of Western developed societies in the early post-war decades that women would withdraw from paid employment either on marriage or with the onset of maternity must, almost certainly, be regarded as a historical aberration (see Hudson and Lee 1990). It was made possible by the fact that these societies were the first in human history to produce an economic surplus sufficient to allow the majority of women to concentrate exclusively on tasks within the household economy. Before new educational opportunities and new ideas about careers for women again changed the terms of trade back towards female labour force participation, the fact that so many women stayed at home to look after their children from birth to maturity can, with only some minor hyperbole, be likened to a form of conspicuous consumption on the part of industrialized societies made suddenly prosperous by post-war productivity growth.

But if the cross-national outcomes of the trade-off between female employment and fertility are influenced by the context of values within which the trade-off takes place, the obvious place to look for a source of cross-national fertility reversal is in a widespread shift in preferences relating to the appropriate balance between women's work and maternity (for an extremely interesting, if idiosyncratic, account of this transformation, see Hakim 2000). Although studies differ somewhat in their accounts of the mechanisms involved, all are broadly agreed as to its nature. Progressively replacing preferences built around the assumption that women's primary role is motherhood, and that work and motherhood are largely incompatible, are a new set of preferences proceeding from the assumption that women have the same right and often the same financial need to work as men and that fertility must somehow be combined with the demands of working life. One can readily see why such a shift in preferences is likely to produce an overall decline in fertility of the kind observed in Western nations since 1960. Whether premised on women's increased education and employment (Esping-Andersen 1996, 1999; Lesthaeghe and Willems 1999), a decline in the salience of breadwinner models of family interdependence and increasing demands for gender, equity (McDonald 2000; and, in a somewhat different context, Sen 2001), or the victory of the feminist agenda of the 1970s and 1980s (Castles 1998), such a shift necessarily implies a much increased valuation of women's work and a consequently greater willingness on the part of women to make temporary or permanent adjustments to fertility aspirations in order to pursue valued career goals.

Paradoxically, this same preference shift also provides important reasons why countries characterized by modern employment structures and modern cultural values are likely to be characterized by higher fertility levels than countries that do not. Given such preferences, strong employment prospects for women become an important precondition for family formation. Strong educational qualifications and tight labour markets are the best possible guarantee that such prospects will be realized. Moreover, while the difficulties confronting modern working mothers are as great as at any time in history, a decline in traditional family values means that their lives are no longer governed to the same extent as in the past by social and legal norms premised on the complete separation of work and family. It is also precisely in those countries where traditional values have the weakest grip that we might expect to see the strongest push to implement policies designed to help women overcome these difficulties. By contrast, in countries where women find it more difficult to obtain employment, and where combining work and family is still regarded as culturally inappropriate, women are likely to be tempted to defer maternity until they have launched their careers and, perhaps, then to have fewer children than they might otherwise have contemplated with the aim of resuming those careers with the least possible disruption. Thus, the same set of changes in women's preferences around work and family helps to account for both the post-war trajectory towards below replacement fertility and for the great reversal in the cross-national incidence of fertility rates in the industrialized nations that has accompanied it.

Diverse Policy Contexts

The wider context of the trade-off between work and maternity is not just a matter of changing preferences. For individuals and couples, questions concerning work and family always involve either/or choices, but these choices are likely to be more or less difficult depending on the policy environment in which they are made. Under this heading fall a wide range of the nostrums of contemporary family policy, although the focus of the literature in this area has, until recently, been far more concerned with the identification of factors promoting high levels of female employment than with the location of policy determinants of cross-national fertility variation. The linkages here are commonsensical. If individuals have the means to purchase services that reduce the additional workload consequent on maternity, it will be easier to combine employment and fertility. The same applies where childcare services are cheaply available or are freely provided by the state. Where governments provide significant numbers of employment opportunities in the welfare sector, women are likely to view their re-employment prospects more favourably than where this is not the case. Women are also likely to feel more secure in temporarily absenting themselves from the labour force to have children if their right to re-entry is written into law and if their absence from work is compensated by generous parental leave arrangements. If state schemes of parental leave are unavailable, it will be easier to juggle work and family where work hours are flexible and where there are arrangements for part-time working.

This is the point where the concerns of demographers and social policy specialists become complementary. It is also the point where policy-makers with a concern to stem the tide of declining fertility have reason to take note of the academic debate. An underlying premise of all these propositions is that pre-existing differences in labour market arrangements—anything from the wage scales of service employees to the flexibility of work arrangements—and the policy choices of national governments—anything from visa restrictions on overseas domestic servants to the free provision of childcare services—can modify the terms of the trade-off between work and maternity and, hence, potentially influence the aggregate fertility behaviour of a given country.

Chesnais (1996), arguing in this mode, suggests that the ultimate paradox is how little countries professing to uphold traditional family values do to support actual families, pointing to the diminished share of child benefits in the Italian budget and the weakness of 'institutions complementing the childrearing function of the family' in Germany. Esping-Andersen (1996b) argues more generally that a neglect of family service provision in the countries of continental Western and Southern Europe is a major factor discouraging women from seeking to combine work and fertility. In an earlier work (Castles 1998), I have argued that Catholic adherence serves as a proxy for the absence of a range of family-friendly policies including the availability of childcare, the integration of work and school hours, the taxation of dual-earner families, and the encouragement of part-time work, all with important implications for cross-national variation both in female labour force participation and fertility.

Commentators on Scandinavia, and in particular on Sweden, seeking to account for the fertility recovery in these countries during the course of the 1980s, have similarly stressed the role of the policy environment. Key factors identified have included the availability of sheltered public sector employment in the area of the caring services (see Esping-Andersen 1999) and expanded provision for childcare, parental leave benefits, and flexible working time arrangements (see Hoem 1993; Gustavsson and Stafford 1994). The expansion of state services spending in Scandinavia noted in earlier chapters has played a major role in underwriting both the expansion of female employment and the availability of childcare in these countries. Confirming a similar policy logic, research on the dramatic fertility downturn in Sweden in the mid-1990s suggests that the most crucial factors were the downturn in female employment in these years and cuts in family benefit levels initiated by a government desperately in need of reducing public expenditure levels (see Hoem 2000).

The thrust of all these arguments is that public policy matters for both female employment and fertility. Moreover, the argument applies even where the factors involved are ostensibly shaped by the market rather than by the state, since the implication is that governments could, if they so wished, intervene to modify the operations of the market. That, of course, is an immediate lesson from comparative studies revealing the wide range of family policy variability characterizing even countries as otherwise similar as those belonging to the OECD. Viewed in comparative perspective, the policy environment is defined not by what governments do or do not do, but by what they could do if they were so minded. A prominent theme in much of the literature is that governments are far more likely to be so minded in cultures where traditional values are no longer dominant.

Contextualizing the trade-off relationship by allowing for changing preferences and diverse policy environments makes the cross-national fertility transformation of recent decades appear less anomalous in theoretical terms. If the account offered here has any substance, the world has been turned upside down because women in the industrialized countries have changed their views as to their proper role in society, and because governments, in at least some of these countries, have changed their policies to accommodate those views. However, the evidence so far provided is incomplete. The findings reported in the second column of Table 7.2 tell us that by the late 1990s there were modestly significant relationships of a kind consonant with the preference shift hypothesis. The much stronger relationships reported in the first column of Table 7.3 offer further indirect evidence with the same import. What we are so far lacking is direct evidence as to the impact on fertility of variation in the policy environment. That is required if we are to establish which of a wide variety of supposedly family-friendly policies has the greatest influence and how far preference shift and policy impact accounts can be separated in practice.

Measuring the Impact of Policy

Family-friendly policy comes in a wide variety of forms (see Kamerman and Kahn 1981; Gornick, Meyers, and Ross 1997), each with somewhat different implications for encouraging higher rates of fertility amongst working women. At one end of the spectrum are measures capturing aspects of traditional population policy making it possible for women to leave the labour force on a more or less permanent basis. Prominent amongst these are child benefits and tax allowances compensating for a woman's loss of income when she stays at home to look after children. At the other end of the spectrum are measures underwriting the capacity of women to find employment and stay in the labour force when they have children. Prominent here are the public provision of caring sector employment and the provision of childcare facilities, with viable arrangements for children between the ages of nought and three crucial to early labour force re-entry. At various points in between are measures actively or passively facilitating maternity amongst female employees. Active measures include maternity and childcare leave, with longer leave periods allowing women (and, more recently, parents) the time needed to cater for the special needs of younger infants and higher replacement rates compensating for temporary loss of income incurred in doing so. Passive measures include a variety of flexible workplace arrangements enabling couples to arrange their lives in a manner compatible with the conflicting demands of work and family.

Assessing the impact of family friendly policy on fertility rates is not altogether a straightforward matter. Causal ordering is, again, part of the difficulty. Insofar as governments see particular policies as having the potential to address problems of unduly low fertility, they are most likely to employ those measures when fertility is low, reversing the expected order of causality and the expected sign of the relationship. It is also natural to suppose that measures of aggregate spending on child benefits, maternity and parental leave, childcare, and other services to families will, all other things being equal, be higher where the population is most youthful, again making these measures, at least in part, outcomes rather than determinants of fertility. This is, however, a difficulty that can be overcome by calculating rates of expenditure per capita, with the imputed causal link to fertility through the generosity of spending.

It might seem that there are also causality problems in attributing higher fertility to higher childcare coverage and more flexible workplace arrangements. However, while there is an obvious sense in which these policy outcomes can be seen as products of maternity, that sense is not properly causal. Given the quite different cultural values prevailing across the industrialized world in the early post-war decades, much higher levels of fertility than at present were commonplace with next to nothing in the way of formal childcare facilities and flexible work arrangements, simply in virtue of a normatively enforced separation of the spheres of work and maternity. Of course, in a society like our own, in which the normatively assumed default position is that mothers will continue working after childbirth, it is a truism that fertility on any scale is largely a function of such policies being in place. But what that really means is that women will generally only choose to have children where childcare facilities are available and where flexible workplace arrangements are in place. This makes these policies prerequisites or preconditions of fertility, rather than its consequences.

In fact, the greatest problem for comparative research has not been the issue of causality, but rather a lack of appropriate data. While we now possess a comprehensive picture of the development of most of those aspects of family-friendly policy which arise out of public expenditure programmes, those where the information required must be collected from business enterprises, private organizations, and individuals are far less well documented. Important instances are the prevalence of flexi-time working, voluntary part-time working, and childcare provision outside the public sector. The choice of work hours is often crucial to the capacity of couples to organize working life in a way that accommodates the childrearing needs and workforce participation of both partners. Part-time working can reasonably be taken as a measure of workplace flexibility enabling women to combine work and family needs, but only where it is voluntary. Where part-time working is involuntary, a wish to gain a competitive edge in obtaining full-time employment may serve only as a further motive for deferring fertility. Childcare data as hitherto reported in the comparative literature have focused exclusively on variations in publicly funded provision, doubtlessly because those are the data governments tend to collect and, hence, to report. However, there is absolutely no reason to suppose that cross-national variation in private provision is irrelevant to fertility outcomes, with much the simplest hypothesis that fertility is a positive function of the extent of childcare provision however provided.

The OECD has recently published a survey of policies designed to help parents into paid employment (OECD 2001c), which includes questionnaire-based data on various aspects of workplace flexibility as well as information on formal childcare provision across all sectors for between eighteen and twenty nations for a time period in the late 1990s. The data provided in this survey, together with other routinely available information on publicly funded childcare and spending on cash benefits and services, allow us to explore which of a reasonably wide range of the instruments of family-friendly policy are most closely related to present-day fertility rates. The fact that the survey also contains a composite index of policies for the reconciliation of work and family life also makes it possible to test the hypothesis that integrated policy packages influence outcomes more decisively than the separate policy impacts of which they are constituted.

Table 7.4 reports correlations between measures of policy and 1998 PTFRs. The strongest relationships are the positive associations between fertility and formal childcare for the under-3s and between fertility and average levels of formal provision, the latter finding being, effectively, a derivative of the former. Not only are these relationships much stronger than those pertaining to publicly funded provision, but, in the case of provision for the over-3s, they have the opposite sign, with high levels of public provision significantly associated with lower levels of fertility. It has been argued by Gauthier (1996: 181) that, in countries like France, Belgium, and Italy, high levels of childcare for the over-3s have little to do with encouraging women's employment, but, instead, reflect a belief in the benefits of early education. This finding seems to capture that effect.

Only two other relationships are statistically significant. The first is between fertility and the percentage of employees reporting that they work flexi-time, suggesting that what happens in the workplace may be as relevant to outcomes as are deliberately crafted public policies. The second is the relationship between fertility and the composite index of work/family reconciliation policies. Given, however, that the composite index has among its components the extent of formal childcare for the under-3s and the extent of flexi-time working, and that the index's relationship with fertility is weaker than that between childcare and fertility and roughly comparable with that between flexi-time working and fertility, there seems no evidence for the hypothesis that integrated packages of family-friendly policy measures have an impact above and beyond their separate components. All other associations reported in Table 7.4 are either negligible or perverse, with the negative and almost significant link between fertility and maternity benefit replacement rates providing possible evidence that this is an area in which governments have recently been active in using family-friendly policy to turn the tide of low fertility.

The extremely strong positive relationship between fertility and formal childcare provision, and the somewhat lesser one with flexi-time, constitute strong evidence that cross-national differences in the policy environment have an important impact on the cross-national incidence of fertility. Moreover, although a lack of systematic comparative data on formal childcare provision prior to the late 1990s means that part of the necessary evidence is missing, it does seem highly probable that the growth of childcare facilities was prominent amongst the factors making for the great fertility reversal of the 1980s and 1990s. Clearly, the mechanism proposed makes sense of the very strong linkages with pre-existing levels of female employment and traditional family values reported in the first column of Table 7.3, with women workers an obvious source of political pressure for the expansion of childcare

Table 7.4 Patterns of association between 1998 period total fertility rates and various measures of family-friendly public policy in 21 OECD countries

	Correlation with PTFR
Proportion of children using formal childcare arrangements[a,b]	
• Aged 0–3	0.73**
• Aged 3 to mandatory school age	0.37
• Average	0.69**
Proportion of children using publicly funded childcare arrangements[c]	
• Aged 0–3	0.44
• Aged 3–6	−0.52*
• Average	−0.30
Maternity/childcare leave	
• Duration of maternity leave (weeks)	−0.07
• Replacement rate (per cent average wages)	−0.44
• Total maternity/childcare leave (weeks)	−0.32
Social expenditure on families[d]	
• Percentage of GDP on family cash benefits	0.14
• Family cash benefits per capita	0.18
• Percentage of GDP on family services expenditure	0.07
• Family services expenditure per capita	0.01
Flexible workplace arrangements[e]	
• Percentage of employees working flexi-time[c]	0.50*
• Percentage of women voluntarily working part-time	0.01
Composite index of work/family reconciliation policies[c,f]	0.51*

Notes

Correlations are Pearson's *R*.

* Significant at 0.05 level.

** Significant at 0.01 level.

[a] No data for Switzerland.

[b] Data on the proportion of children covered by formal childcare arrangements include both public and private provision in childcare centres and in residential care homes. They also include care by childminders based in their own homes and by carers who are not family members but live with the family in question.

[c] No data for Japan, New Zealand, and Switzerland.

[d] Social expenditure on families as defined by the OECD consists of family cash benefits programmes (family allowances for children, family support benefits, benefits for other dependents, lone parent cash benefits, family other cash benefits, and maternity and parental leave benefits) plus family services expenditure programmes (formal day care, personal services, family other services, and family other benefits in kind). Per capita expenditure is obtained by

places and traditional values a cultural obstacle to such demands being translated into policy. Moreover, what evidence we do have on the growth of childcare provision strongly supports this thesis. The four countries of Scandinavia, all of which were successful in reversing the downward trend of fertility in the 1980s, were simultaneously the four countries with the highest levels of female employment in the OECD at the beginning of the period, and the countries with the strongest push to expand publicly funded childcare places in the years thereafter (see Gauthier 1996: 182). This commitment to family-friendly policy costs money. The OECD Social Expenditure Database shows that, already by 1980, the four Scandinavian countries spent more on family services than any other countries in the OECD and that this remained the case in 1998.

Because we only have adequate data on cross-national variation in family-friendly public policy for the late 1990s, we are not in a position to model the relationship between policy change and changing fertility outcomes over the period 1980–98. However, we are in a position to provide a best-fit model of cross-national variation in PTFR in 1998. This model is to be found in Table 7.5. It brings together variables featuring in the second column of Table 7.2, reporting linkages between fertility and aspects of cultural tradition and employment structure, and those featuring in Table 7.4, reporting linkages with aspects of family-friendly public policy. The criteria for model inclusion are as stipulated in Chapters 5 and 6.

Table 7.5 identifies three factors accounting for PTFR variation in 1998. They are the average level of formal childcare provision, the extent of female

---

dividing expenditure as a percentage of GDP by the percentage of the population under the age of fifteen.

   [e] Information on flexible workplace arrangements are from questionnaire responses from national surveys conducted in OECD countries.

   [f] The composite index of work/family reconciliation is calculated by the OECD as the sum of a variety of indicators of family-friendly policies by government and employers. These indicators include formal childcare coverage under the age of three, maternity pay entitlements, the extent of flexi-time working, the extent of voluntary part-time working and the extent to which firms provide voluntary family leave (this latter indicator having half the weight of the others included in the index).

Sources: All data bar that for publicly funded childcare and social expenditure on families are from or calculated from OECD (2001a), 'Balancing Work and Family Life: Helping Parents into Paid Employment', *OECD Employment Outlook*, Paris, 129–66. Data on publicly funded childcare are from or calculated from Daly, M. (2000), 'A Fine Balance: Women's Labor Market Participation in International Comparison'. In F. W. Scharpf and V. A. Schmidt (eds.), *Welfare and Work in the Open Economy*, Oxford: Oxford University Press, 488. Data on social expenditure on families as percentages of GDP are from or calculated from OECD (2001a), *Social Expenditure Database, 1980–1998*, Paris.

Table 7.5 Best-fit model of the determinants of cross-national variation in 1998 period total fertility rates in 20 OECD countries[a]

	Coefficient	Standard error	t-value
Constant	0.993	0.154	6.36**
Female tertiary education	5.53E−03	0.002	3.03**
Female unemployment	−1.75E−02	0.005	−3.21**
Average level of formal childcare	8.77E−03	0.002	4.23**
Adj. R^2 = 0.73			

Notes and sources: [a] Missing data for Switzerland for childcare variables means that this case cannot be included in the model.

** Significant at 0.01 level.

Sources for all variables as referenced in the previous tables in this chapter.

tertiary enrolment, and the level of female unemployment. The model accounts for 72 per cent of cross-national variance and manifests no signs of multi-collinearity, with the strongest correlation between its component elements of less than 0.3. Excluding Ireland and Sweden, earlier variously located as outliers, the figure for explained variance goes up to 82 per cent. The variable with the greatest impact is childcare coverage, but all three variables are significant at the 0.01 level. However, jackknifing the equation, that is, serially removing each case in turn, shows that the unemployment finding is entirely dependent on the inclusion in the model of Spain, the OECD country in which unemployment rates have been highest in recent decades. Removing the four Southern European cases of exceptionally low fertility leaves a model accounting for 51 per cent of the variation in which childcare retains its former significance and educational enrolment remains significant at the 0.05 level. With the exception of the unemployment variable, it is, therefore, safe to argue that these rather impressive findings are not an artefact of individual cases and are not dependent on the distinctiveness of the exceptionally low fertility countries of Southern Europe. Further support for the basic thrust of the model is also provided by unreported multivariate findings, which show that fertility change in the period 1980–98 can be successfully modelled using a catch-up term plus a positive term for change in female tertiary enrolment and a negative term for change in female unemployment. Hence, despite our lack of information on changing family policy parameters in this period, we do know that some of the factors shaping fertility levels in 1998 appear also to have been among the factors driving change in the preceding two decades.

The model in Table 7.5 also appears to fit exceptionally well with the theoretical account we have derived from the literature. The robust evidence that high fertility is in part a function of women's access to educational opportunity fits well with the idea of a preference shift in which the possession of resources guaranteeing a niche in the employment structure makes it easier rather than more difficult for women to embark on maternity. The finding concerning the importance of educational access also provides strong support for the view that, under modern conditions, gender equality promotes rather than hinders higher levels of fertility. Clearly, to the extent that the unemployment finding is a real one, it also supports a resources-based interpretation, with unemployment serving as a direct measure of ease of female access to employment. The even more robust relationship between fertility and formal childcare provision clearly underlines the role of family-friendly public policy in shaping present day fertility behaviour, singling out the factor most directly relevant to women's early labour market re-entry after childbirth. That a variable measuring family-friendly policy turns out to be more important in shaping present outcomes than any single variable capturing preference shift is hardly surprising, but is not to be interpreted as meaning that policy change is, in some sense, more important than preference shift as an agency of cross-national transformation. Clearly, one would expect the two to be closely linked. It is, surely, a measure of the true significance of preference shifts in democratic societies that they ultimately lead to policy changes of comparable magnitude.

A Verdict Deferred

In the earlier chapters of this book we have been dismissive of general crisis claims. Such claims tend to extrapolate from averages and fail to take into account the possibility of policy action to redress emergent problems. The same is true in respect of declining fertility, although it is fair to note that if the benchmark for potential crisis is a fertility rate of 1.60 or less, this is the one instance in this book where the evidence supports the view that roughly half the countries of the OECD are in deep trouble. The risk of rapid population decline is not a crisis myth, but nor yet is it an established reality. There are two reasons for rejecting a general crisis interpretation at this time. The first is that, in many countries, declines in PTFRs are too recent to be certain that some partial recuperation is impossible. Unlike data for social expenditure, we have data on fertility for years after 1998 and we know that, by 2000, there had been some minor recovery in fertility rates in a number of countries, and in France a more substantial rebound in rates, with an increase in that country's PTFR from 1.76 to 1.89 in a matter of just two years. The evidence is not yet available to demonstrate the existence of a general crisis; only that some countries face huge problems if things stay the way they are.

A further reason for reserving judgement is that the analysis here provides strong evidence that, even where the continuation of existing low rates of fertility presents an apparent problem, there are potential policy remedies available to modern governments. What Table 7.5 tells us is that fertility outcomes are shaped not just by one policy relevant variable, but by three. Family-friendly policy is the most obvious parameter because governments can deliberately use it as a means of making work and maternity more compatible, as Leftist governments have done in Scandinavia. However, if the evidence of our model is to be believed, measures which enhance women's access to education and to employment have similar indirect effects. If this is true, it means that governments have more levers at their disposal in combating below replacement fertility than family-friendly policy alone, including policies to extend female education and training and to make labour markets function more efficiently.

An optimistic reading of the evidence might note that the latter are policies to which virtually all OECD governments are already signed up, so that the only task remaining is to get across the message that family-friendly policy is at least part of the answer to slowing down or reversing the extent of fertility decline. A more pessimistic reading of the evidence might suggest that many of the countries with the worst fertility prospects are precisely those demonstrated in Chapter 6 as having the strongest bias towards generosity to the aged, indicative perhaps that policy change favouring the young is likely to come into conflict with fundamental principles of these countries' systems of social provision. The story, then, would not be one of general crisis, but of deeply entrenched problems peculiar to certain of the countries of continental Western and Southern Europe. The diversity of the problems and challenges facing welfare states of different types is one that is taken up in the concluding section of our final chapter.

8

Towards a Steady-state Welfare State?

Introduction

In this final chapter, we seek to identify some of the main implications of the foregoing analysis. The chapter is relatively brief because the intention is not to introduce new material, but rather to draw out what our findings can tell us about the likely future of the welfare state and social policy in the twenty-one OECD countries that have been the focus of analysis throughout this book. Here, we quite explicitly attempt to argue from the experience of the recent past to the likely experience of coming decades. Such a procedure is, of course, fraught with very real danger. As we saw in the previous chapter on fertility decline, societies can experience sudden change and all our assumptions can be turned upside down almost overnight. An alternative to the inductive path of arguing from recent experience is to argue from theory, but, if there is one lesson this book should have taught us, it is that theory, unless rigorously tested against empirical reality, frequently leads to unwarranted conclusions.

It is precisely the use of theory untested against the experience of recent welfare state development that has given rise to the kinds of all-embracing crisis myths that have been the subject of this analysis, often in the process leading to policy diagnoses of contemporary and future trends that are wildly inaccurate and likely to make problems worse, not better. That being so, we prefer the inductive route of making inferences from trends demonstrated accurately to describe trajectories of development in the recent past, offering only the standard caveat that the predictions that we make on such a basis are likely to become progressively less faithful to reality with the passage of time. In what follows, we discuss how much patterns of welfare state expenditure are likely to change in coming decades and the kinds of problems and challenges that welfare states of different types are likely to confront during those years.

Steady-state Spending

The crisis literature we have discussed and tested in this book suggests that the welfare state has been and will be subject to substantial pressures from both international economy and demographic factors. The clear implication of this literature is that the welfare state, as a result, will change fundamentally in character. Expenditures in aggregate, or across a range of programmes, will be cut back either because that is the decree of international financial markets or because such curtailments in some programmes are necessary to release the resources required to meet the needs of an increasingly aged population. However, the evidence of the past two decades of expenditure development indicates that these pressures have not, so far, been translated into any general tendency for aggregate expenditures either to decline or to increase on a major scale. Crisis threats made with increasing stridency since the mid-1970s have remained uniformly unfulfilled.

On the contrary, the strongest tendency of the past two decades has been a convergence towards what may, perhaps, most appropriately be described as a 'steady-state' welfare state, with a number of expenditure laggards substantially increasing their spending and some previous expenditure leaders making significant, but somewhat smaller, spending cuts. In our analysis in Chapter 5, we argued that the extraordinarily strong convergence trajectory of both 12-component expenditure and total outlays detected in our modelling was a result of two trends. The first was a process of catch-up by countries that adopted expenditure programmes later than others. The second involved corrections for expenditure overshoot in countries where predicted expenditure outcomes had been premised on levels of economic growth greater than later turned out to be the case. Expenditure convergence on the scale of recent decades is entirely novel, displacing a far more dispersed pattern of cross-national expenditure growth in the 1960s and 1970s, in which the countries initiating their programmes earliest were often those most exposed to high levels of international trade. Much of the catch-up occurring in the period under review was by countries left behind in this initial process of post-war programme development. As we sought to demonstrate in our discussion of the path analysis featuring in Figure 5.1, this coincidence of high expenditure growth in countries with low exposure to international trade is one of the reasons that a 'race to the bottom' argument has had some surface plausibility in recent decades.

When we talk about the emergence of a steady-state welfare state, we do not mean that expenditure by the state for social purposes has ceased to grow or that it will not grow further in future. On the contrary, in Chapter 2, we noted that real spending per capita and per dependent had increased significantly in virtually all of the OECD nations between 1980 and 1998. If future trends conform to those of the recent past, we would expect rates of real expenditure growth to keep pace with rates of economic growth in coming years. Nor by a steady-state welfare state do we mean that welfare state spending measured as a percentage of GDP—'welfare effort'—has necessarily peaked. Rather the notion we are seeking to capture is that Western welfare states have now, for the most part, moved beyond their initial growth trajectories. The 'golden age' of the welfare state, when welfare programmes were growing from small beginnings, is no longer with us, and we now live in an era in which the vast majority of social programmes have attained their mature form. As a result, aggregate expenditure levels can, in future, be expected to move within narrower bounds and, where pressures for expenditure growth continue to be experienced, that growth is likely to be more gradual than in the past. Depending on circumstances—in particular, differing rates of economic growth, differing stages in the economic cycle, and differing profiles of partisan control of government—peaks and troughs of total social expenditure measured in GDP terms may still vary by as much 10–15 per cent over periods of perhaps as little as a decade, but such change is likely to be, in large part, cyclical in character, and of an extent that does not disturb existing cross-national relativities to any substantial degree. The correlation between 1980 and 1998 total social expenditure levels was higher than that between 1960 and 1980 expenditure levels. We would expect the correlation between 2000 and 2020 levels to be higher still.

The convergence trend of recent decades has been accompanied by an overall moderate growth in social spending that, to some extent, has displaced other categories of public expenditure, and has, almost everywhere, established the welfare state sector as the primary focus of modern public policy. In consequence, the Marxist night watchman state, resting on the primacy of spending for external defence and domestic law and order, has increasingly become a thing of the past, even in the lower spending countries of the English-speaking and Southern European families of nations. One of the few possibilities of a reversal in this trend would be a renewed emphasis on the external security functions of the state, possibly occasioned by a real or imagined threat to the internal and/or external security of nations posed by international terrorism. How mass publics would respond to an explicit trade-off between reductions in accustomed social benefits in order to pay for the costs of greater security is uncertain. Given the range of international responses to demands for the men and material to defeat what President Bush called the 'Axis of Evil', the probability must be that a threat of this kind would disturb the convergence pattern of recent decades, downgrading the salience of the welfare state in those few nations in which the preference was for more internal and/or external security and less social policy.

This, of course, is the kind of 'world turned upside down' scenario in face of which the inductive method is helpless. However, assuming that apocalypse is not now, and that the trends of the recent past are extrapolated over coming decades, including the trend for the rate of expenditure growth to diminish with increasing programme maturity, we can expect future aggregate spending patterns to cluster even more tightly than they do today and to be only a few percentage points higher than at present. Table 2.1 shows that the coefficient of variation for total social expenditure has been nearly halved in the four decades since 1960. The modelling of Chapters 5 and 6 demonstrated the strength of catch-up and correction for overshoot tendencies in respect of all major aggregates of spending in recent decades. Change of a comparable order in coming years would suggest that, perhaps in another three or four decades, most of these countries will be devoting resources to welfare on much the same scale as at present, with aggregate public expenditure on the categories of social spending covered by the OECD Social Expenditure Database, perhaps, somewhere in the region of 25–27 per cent of GDP.

The average increase in expenditure of between 2 and 4 percentage points of GDP, which this represents over 1998 figures, arguably allows sufficient room for the expenditure growth likely to be required by population ageing in the majority of OECD countries during this period. If we further extrapolate the virtually stationary trend of total outlays demonstrated in Table 2.2 across coming decades, some of this growth seems likely to come from a further attenuation of non-social items of expenditure. Those who view education, law and order, and public infrastructure investment as vital to a properly functioning society, must hope that the category of spending that will bear the brunt of further social expenditure development will be net debt interest payments. As the Scandinavian Social Democrats, who have run big welfare states with low levels of borrowing over many years, know very well, there are some aspects of financial orthodoxy that are matters of fiscal prudence rather than proper grounds for ideological disputation. Big deficits make countries hostages to financial markets while simultaneously reducing the resources available for needed public spending over the long term.

Convergence to Type

Almost certainly, however, future social expenditure convergence will be more limited than is suggested by the mechanical extrapolation of present trends. A possible interpretation of the analysis offered in Chapters 3 and 4 is that, rather than a common process of aggregate expenditure convergence across the OECD region, what has taken place in these decades has been a process best described as a convergence to type. This trend is apparent both in respect of the expenditure share types identified in Chapter 3 and the family of nations types that have guided our analysis throughout. What appears to have been occurring during this period was that aggregate spending levels within expenditure share types and families of nations were becoming internally more homogeneous, without the spending levels of the types themselves necessarily becoming markedly more similar to each other.

This trend of intra-type convergence can be readily established by looking at the expenditure trajectories of those countries that changed their spending patterns most dramatically during this period. In 1980, Ireland, although the poorest—or, perhaps, because it was the poorest—of the English-speaking nations, was amongst that grouping's biggest spenders. In 1980, New Zealand had one of the world's most generous welfare states, particularly in the area of pensions. However, between 1980 and 1998, both of these poverty alleviation states reverted to type, with Ireland radically pruning its spending and New Zealand its generosity. Intra-Scandinavian convergence tendencies were even more marked than those of the English-speaking world. Table 2.1 shows that between 1960 and 1980, Sweden and Denmark's welfare state expenditures grew more rapidly than anywhere else in the OECD. In the decades after 1980, Finnish and Norwegian social expenditure programmes grew at a comparable rate, with Table 4.1 demonstrating that, by 1998, the Scandinavian countries had attained a degree of similarity in spending levels unparalleled elsewhere in our analysis. Given also the strong state services bias of these countries' spending, this is the family of nations which now has much the most distinctive overall spending pattern in the OECD.

Table 4.1 shows that, already in 1980, the aggregate spending levels of the social security states of continental Western Europe were extremely similar to each other. These were, after all, the pioneer welfare states of the early post-war era, whose social programmes, because initiated earlier, were tending to mature before those of other nations. It is, therefore, reasonable to suppose that the changes taking place within this grouping would already conform to a steady-state pattern in the period we are discussing here. This, indeed, appears to have been the case, with the Netherlands providing a nice example of expenditure change within already established family of nations parameters. Between 1980 and 1998, 12-component expenditure in the Netherlands declined by about 15 per cent, and that country went from being the highest to the lowest aggregate spender in the grouping. Despite the magnitude of this change, Table 4.1 shows us that the coefficient of variation of the continental Western European family of nations was virtually unchanged. A major factor contributing to the Netherlands' expenditure decline in this period was that country's exceptional economic performance from the mid-1980s onward—the Dutch 'economic miracle' (see Visser and Hemerijck 1997)—which made it possible to cut 'welfare effort' without seriously affecting the country's status as being amongst the most generous of the OECD's welfare states. These are just the kinds of changes that we should expect to encounter in a steady-state universe of advanced welfare states in which the process of convergence to type is all but complete. Having said that, it should also be noted that a case can be made for arguing that, during this period the continental Western European family of nations actually acquired a new member through what might well be regarded as the most dramatic instance of convergence to type of all. Switzerland, which in 1980 already closely resembled the countries in this grouping in expenditure share terms, but which spent far less as a percentage of GDP, hugely expanded its spending over the following two decades, ending up with a clearly continental Western European spending profile on all counts.

Finally, Greece and Italy, also with a strong social security bias in their patterns of provision increased their aggregate social spending to levels comparable to those of the countries of continental Western Europe, a trajectory of development nicely conforming with earlier findings of a close association between levels of economic development and welfare effort in the Catholic countries of Western Europe (Castles 1998, 160–1). If, in coming years, the trajectory of change elsewhere in Southern Europe follows the same pattern, the emergent similarity of spending levels in northern Europe noted in Chapter 4 is likely, ultimately, to extend to Western Europe as a whole, excluding only Ireland and, perhaps, the United Kingdom. In these latter countries, as elsewhere in the English-speaking world, a structure of spending focusing primarily on poverty alleviation and health care seems likely to continue to serve as a constraint on expenditure growth.

It is this cleavage between low spending, poverty alleviation states and high spending, social security and state services states that makes it highly unlikely that, in the foreseeable future, convergence trends will ever be carried through to their logical conclusion of cross-national expenditure uniformity. What seems far more probable is the emergence of a more or less bipolar distribution of aggregate expenditure levels, with spending in the Scandinavian, continental Western European, and some of the Southern European nations clustering somewhere between 25 and 30 per cent of GDP, and spending in the English-speaking nations and Japan clustering at and around 20 per cent. Of course, in coming decades, the number of advanced welfare states is likely to be substantially greater than it is today, and it seems quite probable that, ultimately, the countries of the 2004 European Union enlargement will also be arrayed between these poles, with the extent of their spending depending on whether their primary orientation to social provision focuses on social security and state services or on poverty alleviation and health care.

If further dramatic convergence of expenditure levels is unlikely, such a development is still more improbable in respect of expenditure share types. The analysis of Chapter 3 shows that the patterning of expenditure shares has changed far less than the patterning of aggregate expenditure in the period under review here. The English-speaking nations tend to spend less because they seek to do less, but, although social security and state services states devote similar proportions of their national resources to welfare state purposes, those purposes are substantially different. A Bismarckian welfare architecture that preserves work-related status differentials leads to quite different outcomes from a more social democratic and egalitarian attempt to tackle the emergent welfare problems of a post-industrial society. Indeed, looking at the evidence in Tables 3.3 and 3.4, it seems perfectly sensible to conclude that, in terms of expenditure types, the OECD countries had already arrived at something akin to a steady state by 1980, and have changed very little since that time.

It may be objected on the basis of the analysis presented in Chapter 7 that the urgent need in certain countries to adjust policies in ways that make them more family-friendly will, in future, lead to a generalized shift towards the Scandinavian pattern, where the availability of jobs in the caring sector and of highly subsidized childcare, both underwritten by the state services state, play a prominent role in enabling women to combine employment and maternity. However, although Table 3.4 does show a gradual shift to state service provision, the pace of change has been extremely slow. That is because countries generally prefer to adopt policies which conform to their already established structural parameters. Certain English-speaking nations—conspicuously the United States—provide access to cheap childcare by tolerating, or even in effect licensing, private provision by low wage carers in their own homes. This is a route that minimizes direct state intervention and involves no direct social expenditure. In contrast, other countries with a more statist orientation, but with reservations about a one-size-fits all policy of public childcare provision, have opted to provide income-support to mothers of young children to be used either to enable them to stay at home with their children or as a subsidy for privately provided childcare. This is a route that uses quasi-income maintenance principles to allow couples to choose the family-friendly package that suits their particular needs. There is nothing new in such processes of welfare state adaptation. Over more than a hundred years, welfare states have expanded their reach to cater to an ever-increasing range of needs with only modest and usually quite gradual change in their structural forms. There is no reason to suppose that, in coming years, as welfare states of different types tackle new problems and challenges, the structure of their spending or the character of their welfare mixes (c.f. Powell and Barrientos 2004) will become more similar than is presently the case. The diversity of welfare state regimes and families of nations is with us for the long-term.

Factors Shaping Welfare Futures

However, before turning to the problems and challenges likely to preoccupy policy-makers in different families of nations in decades to come, we need to discuss whether there are other factors likely to disturb the future predicted here of steady-state spending and further muted expenditure convergence? The model in Chapters 5 suggests possible candidates, of which the strongest in terms of statistically demonstrated effects is economic growth. Clearly, high levels of economic growth contributed to the contraction of the Irish and Netherlands welfare states in the period under review here. No less clearly, slow growth in Switzerland magnified other forces making for expenditure growth in this period, and, in Sweden, countered other factors conducive to expenditure contraction. If, in coming decades, all OECD countries were to be able to emulate the 1990s Irish experience of 6 per cent plus economic growth, Western welfare states would, doubtlessly, become substantially smaller, with Finance Ministers gleefully availing themselves of what is much the most painless and, for all but the most doctrinaire defenders of welfare provision levels, infinitely the most welcome route to social expenditure contraction. On the other hand, if the Swiss experience of slow economic growth were to be the norm for future development over an extended period, total social and public expenditure denominated in GDP terms would grow very markedly indeed, and the notion of an imminent crisis of the welfare state might suddenly move from the status of crisis myth to that of crisis reality.

Neither scenario, however, is likely to describe the shape of things to come. The levels of growth experienced by Ireland in the 1990s were quite aberrant and, almost certainly, as in Japan earlier in the post-war period, were part of a wider process of income convergence that has brought GDP per capita levels in most OECD nations relatively close to each other over recent decades (see Dowrick and Nguyen 1989). If income convergence is the major factor determining future economic growth rates, the only countries featuring in this analysis with prospects of growth on this scale in future are Greece, Portugal, and Spain, all of which still remain relatively poor by Western European standards. The idea of a generalized trend to lower aggregate expenditure premised on a substantial increase in average OECD economic growth rates has no basis in anything we know about the trend of economic expansion in the West over the past half century.

In reality, during the period 1980–98, the OECD average annual rate of economic growth was 2.5 per cent, rather less than half that experienced by Ireland in the 1990s, with rates very marginally lower in the second half of the period than in the first. There is no obvious reason to expect average rates to be much lower than this in coming years and every reason to suspect that, over a period as long as several decades, national growth relativities will fluctuate quite considerably. Certainly, that has been the experience of the recent past. Japan, the economic growth paragon of the post-war era, became an economic cripple in the 1990s, with its growth rate declining from 4.1 per cent in the 1980s to 1.4 per cent in the 1990s. The United States, which, conforming to the per capita income convergence regularity, experienced generally quite muted expenditure growth in the immediate post-war decades, recovered in the 1980s and 1990s to become the powerhouse of OECD area economic expansion. Obviously, in future years as in past ones, there is a real potential for periods of low economic growth to produce adverse expenditure effects, with cyclical downturns in economic activity leading to cyclical upturns in social expenditure. However, we do not have any reason to assume that such effects will be anything other than cyclical, with expenditure once again declining as economic conditions improve. Economic growth trends will contribute to aggregate social expenditure fluctuations in the future as in the past, but there is no reason to believe that the effects will decisively transform the trajectory of expenditure development of recent years.

A similar conclusion seems appropriate in respect of the likely effects of deindustrialization. Further deindustrialization is unlikely to lead to a dramatic expansion in OECD social expenditure levels in coming years, simply because there is very little scope for further deindustrialization in these OECD countries. By 1998, the average percentage of the population employed in agriculture and manufacturing in the OECD countries was marginally over 16 per cent of the working age population, and only in two countries—Japan and Portugal—was that figure in excess of 20 per cent. The average change in levels of deindustrialization between 1980 and 1998 of countries with less than

20 per cent of their working age populations in these employment sectors in 1980 was a further decline of 3.6 percentage points, implying, on the basis of the relevant coefficient in Table 5.4, an average expansion of aggregate social expenditure of one and a half per cent of GDP. If that were to be the contribution of deindustrialization to future social expenditure growth, the outcome would remain well within the ambit of steady-state continuity. Moreover, since both Japan and Portugal are well below the OECD average in aggregate social and total public expenditure terms, deindustrialization on a much greater scale in these countries would simply speed up the rate of future OECD expenditure convergence. Arguably, however, deindustrialization effects will be far more pronounced in many of the countries of Central and Eastern Europe, with significant implications for the convergence of expenditure levels in the wider European Community created by the enlargement of 2004. Virtually all of Germany's above average 12-component expenditure growth shown in Table 3.1 took place after 1990, with dramatic deindustrialization in the area of the former East Germany clearly an important contributory factor.

We have argued above that the biggest single obstacle to the completion of the convergence trend of the aggregate social expenditure levels of the OECD nations is the continuing gap between the welfare aspirations of the poverty alleviation states on the one hand and the social security and state services states on the other. Our modelling in Chapter 5 strongly suggests that the factor primarily accounting for the difference in the spending levels of the English-speaking poverty alleviation states and the Scandinavian state services states is partisan incumbency and, in particular, the long-term, cumulative effects of Left legacy. These are effects that we would not expect to diminish in the short term. The hegemony of social democracy in the Scandinavian countries is no longer as pronounced as formerly, but social democratic parties remain, in each of these countries, the natural parties of government. In contrast, in the United States, democratic socialism still does not have a political voice and, in Canada, what voice it has is heard only at provincial level. In Ireland, the party system condemns Labour to a permanently ineffectual role. Elsewhere in the English-speaking world, adversarial alternation of governments seems to guarantee that the social policy gains of any lengthy period of Left incumbency are cancelled out by an equal and opposite incumbency of the Right in succeeding years. There is absolutely no sign that these political differences between the English-speaking and Scandinavian countries are beginning to unravel, but, even if there were, their welfare state effects are likely to live long after them—certainly for the duration of the period we are considering here.

If partisanship accounts for differences between the English-speaking and Scandinavian expenditure levels, differences between the English-speaking and continental Western European countries would appear to be primarily a matter of differential levels of generosity. In Chapter 6, we modelled this effect in terms of differences in the AGE ratio of pension generosity, but it is clearly a difference that applies more broadly across all categories of income maintenance expenditure. Given that benefit generosity is intrinsically linked to the contributory structure of provision that characterizes the social security state, these, too, are effects that under normal circumstances we would expect to be extremely long-lasting. It is because Bismarckian welfare states implicitly make promises to contributors—and, hence, to voters—concerning future levels of benefits, that generosity inflation is built into the system. It is not just pension systems built on such principles that are like 'elephants on the move'. The same applies to all categories of income-maintenance benefits in which entitlements are a function of prior contributions.

However, in Chapter 6, we have already noted that circumstances in coming decades may be far from normal, insofar as a number of the countries with the most generous pension systems are precisely those that face the prospect of the most rapid population ageing during the next fifty years. We have also noted that in a number of these countries—with Italy, perhaps, the most conspicuous example—there have been concerted attempts throughout the 1990s to bring about pension reform. If these reform efforts ultimately prove to be successful, convergence tendencies within the OECD are likely to be reinforced. If they are unsuccessful, there is a real possibility that this combination of pension generosity and extreme population ageing could lead to the emergence of a new ultra-high spending grouping of countries consisting of some, but only some, of the countries constituting the existing continental Western and Southern European families of nations.

Future Challenges

This discussion of the potential for pension reform brings us naturally to our final topic: the challenges confronting the welfare state in coming years. Here—by now, we hope utterly predictably—our main point is that, just as generalizations concerning the crises likely to beset the welfare state in coming decades are wholly inappropriate, so too are generalizations concerning challenges for the welfare state. The reason is, of course, the same: that welfare states in different nations experience different problems and therefore confront different challenges. This does not mean, however, that each country's problems and challenges are wholly unique. Different families of nations have developed their welfare institutions in different ways, and this means that they often confront problems which differ only in degree from those of other family members, although radically from the problems prominent in other families. The issues confronting advanced welfare states in the coming years are neither universal nor wholly unique, but patterned by their historical and cultural inheritance, including, most prominently, sets of institutional preferences peculiar to the welfare state types to which they belong. It is not our claim that the linkages here identified between welfare state types and particular problems and challenges are in any way novel to this analysis. Rather, it would be our contention that, insofar as these linkages follow immediately from the evidence presented in earlier chapters, our findings serve as systematic backing for the conclusions of recent scholarship in this area (see, in particular, Esping-Andersen 1996a; Scharpf and Schmidt 2000a,b; Esping-Andersen et al. 2002).

The primary problem confronting the English-speaking welfare states is the well-known tendency for these countries to manifest higher levels of poverty and inequality than most other countries in the OECD (for the latest evidence confirming this regularity, see Smeeding 2002). Whether we describe the premises of welfare provision in these countries as 'liberal', 'residual', or poverty alleviating, the implication is the same: that the institutional settings of the welfare state in these countries lead to systematically lower expenditure and generosity levels than in other families of nations (see Tables 2.1, 2.2, 2.4, and 6.2). Admittedly, the comparative welfare state literature often tends to overdraw the contrast between English-speaking nations and other advanced welfare states. A major reason for a poverty alleviating stance in social policy is a distaste for state intervention, and this, in turn, means that these are the countries in which we are most likely to encounter forms of mandated provision and regulatory intervention that avoid direct state provision (see Castles 1994). For analogous reasons, they are also the countries least likely to tax welfare recipients, with some real implications for the validity of cross-national poverty and expenditure relativities (see Whiteford 1995; Castles 1997; Adema 1999). Differences in aggregate expenditure, therefore, sometimes exaggerate differences in welfare outcomes. Nevertheless, it remains a fact that there is a very major gap between these countries' spending and generosity levels and those of most other OECD nations, despite high levels of affluence and demographic pressures that are markedly less than in other families of nations.

The main social policy challenge for these countries is almost the reverse of that implied by the crisis literature. It is to take advantage of their favourable demographic position to move beyond minimum levels of benefit and service provision or, in other words, to cease to be poor welfare states, catering only, and then inadequately, to the needs of the poor. A minor challenge—but an important one—is for these countries also to cease serving as the primary intellectual hothouses for the propagation of crisis theories of the welfare state. It is not accidental that the most strenuous claims that 'there is no alternative' but to cut back welfare state spending because of international economic and demographic pressures originate in the countries that are least generous to the poor. A major function of crisis myths of the welfare state—applying certainly to much popular commentary on the impacts of globalization and population ageing—is in providing a rationale for minimal state intervention and the lowest possible rates of taxation. Here, if anywhere, is a justification for what I have, on occasions, described as the 'awfulness of the English' (see Castles and Merrill 1989).

The challenges for the countries of Southern Europe, which are nearest to the English-speaking world in average levels of spending and generosity, are quite different. Partly that is because the Bismarckian institutional architecture of transfers provision in these countries suggests that, as programmes mature and as per capita incomes increase, these countries will end up spending far more than the countries of the English-speaking world. The lack of generosity of the Southern European countries documented in Table 2.4 is not, as in the English-speaking world, intrinsic to their preferred mode of social provision. Moreover, because the countries of Southern Europe embarked on the process of welfare state building decades later than the other OECD countries, their programmatic development, in many instances, is still incomplete. It is these countries that are most likely to supply any further OECD convergence and catch-up potential in coming decades.

The biggest problems for the Southern European welfare states are problems of imbalance (see Ferrera 1996). Two issues stand out. First, more than anywhere else in the OECD, the Southern European welfare states are pensioners' welfare states. They are, in general, the countries in which the disproportion between spending on aged and middle aged (early retirees) workers and on women and children is greatest (for a more nuanced discussion, see Lynch 2002). These imbalances can be seen both in their disproportionate spending on age cash benefits (see the first three columns of Table 6.2) and in the difference in overall generosity of their welfare provision and their AGE ratio generosity to the elderly (contrast Table 2.4 and the last three columns of 6.2). Second, the Southern European countries are also those with both the most rapidly ageing populations and the greatest prospects of imminent population implosion as a consequence of rapidly declining fertility. The challenge for these countries is to rebalance their welfare states with a view to rebalancing their societies. Pension reform is urgently required, with a shift in resources from the elderly to family-friendly policies designed both to enhance levels of female employment and to promote greater fertility. The premises of Southern European familialistic social policy still see these objectives as contradictory (see Esping-Andersen 1999). Our analysis here suggests that they are not, and that both, in different ways, are required to reduce the social policy impact of population ageing in the long term.

The welfare states of continental Western Europe, although at the opposite end of the spectrum in terms of programme maturity from those of Southern Europe, share some of the same problems and challenges. Ageing populations, high levels of pension generosity, and plummeting fertility rates are characteristics as frequently encountered north of the Alps as on the Mediterranean seaboard (see Tables 6.1, 6.2, and 7.1). In countries like Austria and Germany, the same shift of resources from pensions to family-friendly policy is required if these countries are to avoid the more serious implications of population decline. The countries of Southern and continental Western Europe also share a common institutional architecture based on the contributory principle, which is intrinsically more difficult to modify than systems funded from general taxation. Pension reform is extremely high on the policy agenda in both of these families of nations and, in both, it is an issue with the potential to undermine the stability of reforming governments.

A major difference, however, is that, in the countries of continental Western Europe, there is a lesser degree of imbalance between different programmes, with generosity to those within or with recent attachments to the labour force of a similar order to the generosity afforded the aged. This is again a contrast made abundantly plain by comparing the figures in Tables 2.4 and 6.2. It is in the continental Western European welfare states that the goal of income maintenance through social security has been most nearly achieved. Arguably, however, at some cost. This undifferentiated generosity between categories of claimants, and its potential impact in reducing labour force participation, can be seen as the defining problematic for these countries' welfare states, creating labour market inflexibilities on a substantial scale and contributing to persistent long-term unemployment and underemployment (see Esping-Andersen 1996*b*; Scharpf 2000; c.f. Kenworthy 2003). The fundamental challenge for the social security state in coming years is to find a way of combining high income replacement levels with high levels of labour market participation for both men and women.

Finally, we turn to the problems and challenges confronting the Scandinavian welfare states. Here, at first sight, we encounter an imbalance which is the mirror image of that in Southern Europe, with pension generosity levels not nearly as high in comparative terms as the generosity of welfare programmes as a whole. However, the implication of a lesser emphasis on the needs of the aged is illusory, since the Scandinavian countries are the OECD's biggest providers of services to the elderly as part of a package of state service provision unparalleled in other types of welfare system. As Esping-Andersen has argued over many years, free or highly subsidized service provision on this scale makes the Scandinavian countries very different, potentially solving many welfare state problems simultaneously (see Esping-Andersen 1990, 1999). Free service provision—not just to the elderly, but also in the form of national health services and, as we have seen, extensive systems of publicly funded childcare—provides a uniquely equalizing component to the welfare state, while simultaneously bolstering employment and, because much of that employment is female, simultaneously underwriting high levels of gender equality. Moreover, by providing family services that further encourage female employment, the Scandinavian welfare states have a unique bias that serves as a potential counter to the factors in modern societies conducive to low fertility.

In principle, the Scandinavian welfare states end up generous, egalitarian, employment conducive, and family-friendly, a combination of labour market and social policy pluses unrivalled in other systems. There are, however, challenges here too. Most frequently articulated is the extent of the fiscal burden of financing such high levels of expenditure substantially from general taxation rather than from contributions. More serious, probably, is a vulnerability to high levels of unemployment that potentially challenges most aspects of the Scandinavian welfare architecture. In Sweden, in the mid-1990s, the country's first serious encounter with mass unemployment since the 1930s led to rapidly increasing poverty (see Palme 2000) and rapidly declining fertility (Hoem 2000). More recently, unemployment in both Finland and Sweden has abated, and poverty and fertility trends reversed, suggesting, despite the anxieties of some about difficulties of managing labour markets in the context of a single European market (see Korpi 2003), that Scandinavian goals of egalitarian social policy and full employment remain compatible, at least in the short term.

We have argued that spending levels in the advanced welfare states are unlikely to change appreciably in the coming years and that the spending priorities of different welfare state types and families of nations are still more firmly entrenched. Obviously, this suggests that problems endemic to welfare provision in different families of nations will be difficult to overcome. However, it does not mean that such problems are wholly intractable. The history of the Western welfare state is littered with problems that policy-makers found intractable at the time. Yet, over the past hundred and twenty odd years since Bismarck instituted the first contributory social security schemes, welfare states with diverse architectures have evolved successively to cope with a range of new problems. They did this by proliferating programmes and very markedly increasing their aggregate spending as a percentage of GDP. The great challenge for Western welfare states in the coming decades will be to find ways of solving their problems—particularly their demographic problems—within the context of what looks likely to be, essentially, steady-state spending.

References

Abrahamson, P. (1999), 'The Welfare Modelling Business', *Social Policy and Administration*, 33(4): 394–415.

Adema, W. (1999), 'Net Social Expenditure', *Labour Market and Social Policy Occasional Papers*, 52, 2nd edn. (Paris: OECD).

Ahn, N. and Mira, P. (1998), 'A Note on the Changing Relationship Between Fertility and Female Employment Rates in Developed Countries', *Fundación de Estudios de Economía Aplicada (FEDEA)*. Working Paper No. 13.

Aldenderfer, M. S. and Blashfield, R. K. (1984), *Cluster Analysis*. Sage University Papers, No. 44 (Newbury, Park, CA: Sage Publications).

Anttonen, A. and Sipila, J. (1996), 'European Social Care Services: Is it Possible to Identify Models', *Journal of European Social Policy*, 6(2): 87–100.

Armingeon, K. (2001), 'Institutionalising the Swiss Welfare State'. In J-E. Lane (ed.), *The Swiss Labyrinth. Institutions, Outcomes and Design* (Special issue of *West European Politics*) (London: Frank Cass), pp. 145–68.

Aspinwall, M. (1996), 'The Unholy Trinity: Modelling Social Dumping Under Conditions of Capital Mobility and Free Trade', *West European Politics* 19(1): 125–50.

Bakker, I. (1988), 'Women's Employment in Comparative Perspective'. In J. Jenson, E. Hagen, and C. Reddy (eds.), *Feminization of the Labour Force* (Cambridge: Polity Press), pp. 65–84.

Beaujot, R. and Liu, J. (2002), 'Children, Social Assistance and Outcomes: Cross-National Comparisons'. *Discussion Paper No. 01-20*, Population Studies Centre, University of Western Ontario.

Beck, N. and Katz, J. N. (1995), 'What To Do (and Not to Do) with Time-Series-Cross-Section Data in Comparative Politics', *American Political Science Review*, 89(3): 634–47.

Beck, W., van der Maesen, L., and Walker, A. (eds.) (1997), *The Social Quality of Europe* (The Hague: Kluwer Law International).

Becker, G. S. (1991), *A Treatise on the Family*, 2nd edn. (Boston: Harvard University Press).

Blau, F. D. and Ferber, M. A. (1992), *The Economics of Women, Men, and Work*, 2nd edn. (Englewood Cliffs, NJ: Prentice Hall).

Blöndal, S. and Scarpetta, S. (1998), 'The Retirement Decision in OECD Countries'. OECD Economics Department Working Paper No. 202.

Bongaarts, T. and Feeney, G. (1998), 'On the Quantum and Tempo of Fertility', *Population and Development Review*, 2(24): 271–91.

—— and Mach, A. (2000), 'Switzerland: Adjustment Policies Within Institutional Constraints'. In F. W. Scharpf and V. A. Schmidt (eds.), *Welfare and Work in the Open Economy, Vol. II: Diverse Responses to Common Challenges* (Oxford: Oxford University Press), pp. 131–74.

Bonoli, G. and Taylor-Gooby, P. (2000) *European Welfare Futures: Towards a Theory of Retrenchment* (Oxford: Polity).

Bos, E., Vu, M. T., Massiah, E., and Bulateo, R. (1994), *World Population Projections, 1994–95* (New York: World Bank).

Boston, J. and Uhr, J. (1996), 'Reshaping the Mechanics of Government'. In F. Castles, R. Gerritsen and J. Vowles (eds.), *The Great Experiment: Labour Parties and Public Policy Transformation in Australia and New Zealand* (Sydney: Allen and Unwin), pp. 48–67.

Brittan, S. (1977), *The Economic Consequences of Democracy* (London: Temple Smith).

Cameron, D. (1978), 'The Expansion of the Public Economy: A Comparative Analysis', *American Political Science Review*, 72(4): 1243–61.

Castles, F. G. (1978), *The Social Democratic Image of Society* (London: Routledge and Kegan Paul).

—— (ed.) (1982), *The Impact of Parties* (London: Sage Publications).

—— (1994), 'Is Expenditure Enough? On the Nature of the Dependent Variable in Comparative Public Policy Analysis', *Journal of Commonwealth and Comparative Politics*, XXXII(3): 349–63.

—— (1995), 'Welfare State Development in Southern Europe', *West European Politics*, 18(2): 291–313.

—— (1997), 'The Institutional Design of the Australian Welfare State', *International Social Security Review*, 50(2): 25–42.

—— (1998), *Comparative Public Policy: Patterns of Post-War Transformation* (Cheltenham: Edward Elgar).

—— (2001a), 'Reflections on the Methodology of Comparative Type Construction: Three Worlds or Real Worlds?' *Acta Politica*, 36: 140–54.

—— (2001b), 'On the Political Economy of Recent Public Sector Development', *Journal of European Social Policy*, 11(3): 195–211.

—— and Ferrera, M. (1996), 'Home Ownership and the Welfare State: Is Southern Europe Different?', *South European Society and Politics*, 1(2): 163–85.

—— and McKinlay, R. (1979), 'Does Politics Matter? An Analysis of the Public Welfare Commitment in Advanced Democratic States', *European Journal of Political Research*, 7(2): 169–86.

—— and Merrill, V. (1989), 'Towards a General Model of Public Policy Outcomes', *Journal of Theoretical Politics*, 1(2): 177–212.

—— Gerritsen, R., and Vowles, J. (eds.) (1996), *The Great Experiment: Labour Parties and Public Policy Transformation in Australia and New Zealand* (Sydney: Allen and Unwin).

Center for Strategic and International Studies (CSIS) (2002), *The Global Retirement Crisis* (Washington, DC: Center for Strategic and International Studies).

Chassard, Y. and Quentin, O. (1993), 'Social Protection in the European Community: Towards a Convergence of Policies', *International Social Security Review*, 45(1/2): 91–108.

Chesnais, J-C. (1992), *The Demographic Transition: Stages, Patterns, and Economic Implications* (Oxford: Clarendon Press).

—— (1996), Fertility, Family, and Social Policy in Contemporary Western Europe', *Population and Development Review*, 22(4): 729–39.

Clayton, R. and Pontusson, J. (1998), 'Welfare State Retrenchment Revisited', *World Politics*, 51(1): 67–98.

Coleman, D. (2001), 'Population Ageing: An Unavoidable Future', *Social Biology and Human Affairs*, 66: 1–11.

Comité des Sages (1996), *For a Europe of Civic and Social Rights* (Brussels: European Commission, Directorate-V).

Concialdi, P. (2000), 'Demography, the Labour Market and Competitiveness'. In G. Hughes and J. Stewart (eds.), *Pensions in the European Union: Adapting to Economic and Social Change* (Boston: Kluwer Academic).

Corrado, L., Londoño, B., Mennini, F., and Trovato, G. (2003), 'The Welfare States in a United Europe', *European Political Economy Review*, 1(1): 40–55.

Council of the European Union (2000), *Document 14011/00*, SOC 462 (Annex).

Crozier, M., Huntington, S. P., and Watanuki, S. (1975), *The Crisis of Democracy: Report to the Trilateral Commission on the Governability of Liberal Democracies* (New York: New York University Press).

Cutright, P. (1965), 'Political Structures, Economic Development and National Security Programs', *American Journal of Sociology*, 70(5): 537–50.

Dahl, R. and Tufte, E. (1973), *Size and Democracy* (Stanford, CA: Stanford University Press).

Daly, M. (1997), Welfare States Under Pressure: Cash Benefits in European Welfare States Over the Last Ten Years', *Journal of European Social Policy*, 7(2): 24–59.

—— (2000), 'A Fine Balance: Women's Labor Market Participation in International Comparison'. In F. W. Scharpf and V. A. Schmidt (eds.), *Welfare and Work in the Open Economy, Vol. II: Diverse Responses to Common Challenges* (Oxford: Oxford University Press), pp. 467–510.

Delors, J. (1992), *Our Europe* (London: Verso).

De Santis, G. (2001), 'Population Ageing in Industrialized Countries: Challenges and Issues'. Policy and Research Paper, No. 19. Paris: International for the Scientific Study of Population (IUSSP).

Dowrick, S. and Nguyen, D (1989), 'OECD Comparative Economic Growth 1950–85: Catch-up and Convergence', *American Economic Review*, 79(5): 1010–30.

Drache, D. (1996), 'From Keynes to K-Mart: Competitiveness in a Corporate Age'. In R. Boyer and D. Drache (eds.), *States Against Markets: The Limits of Globalization* (New York: Routledge), pp. 31–61.

Drezner, D. (2000), 'Bottom Feeders', *Foreign Policy*, 171(Nov/Dec): 64–70.

Easterlin, R. A. (1976), 'The Conflict Between Aspirations and Resources', *Population and Development Review*, 2(3/4): 417–25.

—— and Crimmins, E. M. (1991), 'Private Materialism, Personal Self-fulfillment, Family Life and Public Interest: The Nature, Effects, and Causes of Recent Changes in the Values of American Youth', *Public Opinion Quarterly*, 55(4): 499–533.

Ebbinghaus, B. (1999), 'Does a European Social Model Exist and Can it Survive?' In G. Huemer, M. Mesch, and F. Traxler (eds.), *The Role of Employer Associations and Labour Unions in the EMU. Institutional Requirements for European Economic Policies* (Aldershot: Ashgate), pp. 1–26.

Emerson, M. (1988), *What Model for Europe?* (Boston: MIT Press).

Esping-Andersen, G. (1990), *The Three Worlds of Welfare Capitalism* (Cambridge: Polity Press).

—— (1993), 'Budgets and Democracy: Towards a Welfare State in Spain and Portugal, 1960–1986'. In I. Budge and D. McKay (eds.) *Expanding Democracy: Research in Honour of Jean Blondel* (London: Sage Publications).

Esping-Andersen, G. (ed.) (1996a), *The Welfare State in Transition* (London: Sage Publications).

—— (1996b), 'Welfare States Without Work: The Impasse of Labour Shedding and Familialism in Continental European Social Policy'. In G. Esping-Andersen (ed.), *The Welfare State in Transition* (London: Sage Publications), pp. 66–87.

—— (1997), 'Hybrid or Unique? The Distinctiveness of the Japanese Welfare State', *Journal of European Social Policy*, 7(3): 179–89.

—— (1999), *Social Foundations of Post-Industrial Economies* (Oxford: Oxford University Press).

—— and Sarasa, S. (2002), 'The Generational Confict Reconsidered', *Journal of European Social Policy*, 12(1): 5–21.

—— Gallie, D. Hemerijck, A., and Myles, J. (2002), *Why We Need a New Welfare State* (Oxford: Oxford University Press).

Falkner, G. (1998), *EU-Social Policy in the 1990s: Towards a Corporatist Policy Community* (London: Routledge).

Feldstein, M. and Siebert, H. (eds.) (2001), *Social Security Pension Reform in Europe* (Chicago: Chicago University Press).

Ferrera, M. (1996), 'The "Southern Model" of Welfare in Social Europe', *Journal of European Social Policy*, 6(1): 17–37.

—— (2000), 'Reconstructing the State in Southern Europe'. In S. Kuhnle (ed.), *The Survival of the European Welfare State* (London: Routledge), pp. 166–81.

—— and Rhodes, M. (eds.) (2000), 'Recasting European Welfare States', *West European Politics* (Special Issue), 23(2).

—— Hemerijck, A., and Rhodes, M. (2001), 'The Future of the "European Social Model" in the Global Economy', *Journal of Comparative Policy Analysis*, 3(2): 163–90.

Flora, P. (1986), 'Introduction'. In P. Flora (ed.), *Growth to Limits: The Western European Welfare States Since World War II*, Vol. 1 (Berlin: De Gruyter), pp. XI–XXXVI.

—— and Heidenheimer, A. (eds.) (1981), *The Development of Welfare States in Europe and America* (New Brunswick, NJ: Transaction Books), pp. 37–80.

Furniss, N and Tilton, T. (1977), *The Case for the Welfare State* (Bloomington: Indiana University Press).

Ganghof, S. (2000), 'Adjusting National Tax Policy to Economic Internationalization: Strategies and Outcomes'. In F. W. Scharpf and V. A. Schmidt (eds.), *Welfare and Work in the Open Economy, Vol. II: Diverse Responses to Common Challenges* (Oxford: Oxford University Press), pp. 597–645.

Garrett, G. (1998), *Partisan Politics in the Global Economy* (Cambridge: Cambridge University Press).

Gauthier, A. H. (1996), *The State and the Family* (Oxford: Clarendon Press).

Gemmell, N. (1993), 'Wagner's Law and Musgrave's Hypotheses'. In N. Gemmell (ed.), *The Growth of the Public Sector: Theories and International Evidence* (Aldershot: Edward Elgar), pp. 103–20.

Goldthorpe, J. (ed.) (1984), *Order and Conflict in Contemporary Capitalism* (Oxford: Clarendon Press).

Goodman, R. and Peng, I. (1996), 'The East Asian Welfare States: Peripatetic Learning, Adaptive Change, and Nation-Building'. In G. Esping-Andersen (ed.), *The Welfare State in Transition* (London: Sage Publications), pp. 192–224.

Gornick, J., Meyers, M., and Ross, K. (1997), 'Supporting the Employment of Mothers: Policy Variation Across Fourteen Welfare States', *Journal of European Social Policy*, 7(1): 45–70.

Gough, I. (1979), *The Political Economy of the Welfare State* (London: Macmillan).

Grahl, J. and Teague, P. (1997), 'Is the European Social Model Fragmenting?', *New Political Economy*, 2(3): 405–26.

Green-Pedersen, C. (2004), 'The Dependent Variable Problem Within the Study of Welfare-State Retrenchment: Defining the Problem and Looking for Solutions', *Journal of Comparative Policy Analysis*, 6(1).

Green-Pedersen, J. (2002), *The Politics of Justification: Party Competition and Welfare-State Retrenchment in Denmark and the Netherlands from 1982 to 1998* (Amsterdam: Amsterdam University Press).

Gruber, J. and Wise, D. (2001), *An International Perspective on Policies for an Aging Society*. NBER Working Paper No. W8103 (Cambridge, MA: National Bureau of Economic Research).

Guillén, A. and Álvarez, S. (2001), 'Globalization and the Southern Welfare States'. In R. Sykes, B. Palier, and P. Prior (eds.), *Globalization and European Welfare States* (Basingstoke: Palgrave), pp. 103–26.

Gustavsson, S. and Stafford, F. (1994), 'Three Regimes of Childcare: The United States, the Netherlands, and Sweden'. In R. Blank (ed.) *Social Protection versus Economic Flexibility* (Chicago: University of Chicago Press), pp. 333–62.

Hakim, C. (2000), *Work-Lifestyles Choices in the 21st Century* (Oxford: Oxford University Press).

Hemerijck, A. (2002), 'The Self-Transformation of the European Social Model(s)'. In G. Esping-Andersen, D. Gallie, D. Hemerijck, and J. Myles (eds.), *Why We Need a New Welfare State* (Oxford: Oxford University Press), pp. 173–213.

Hicks, A. and Swank, D. (1984), 'On the Political Economy of Welfare Expansion', *Comparative Political Studies*, 17(1): 81–119.

—— and —— (1992), 'Politics, Institutions, and Welfare Spending in Industrialized Democracies, 1960–1982', *American Political Science Review*, 86(3): 658–74.

Hinrichs, K. (2001a), 'Elephants on the Move: Patterns of Public Pension Reform in OECD Countries'. In S. Liebfried (ed.), *Welfare State Futures* (Cambridge: Cambridge University Press), pp. 77–102.

—— (2001b), 'Ageing and Public Pension Reforms in Western Europe and North America: Patterns and Politics'. In J. Clasen (ed.), *What Future for Social Security? Debates and Reforms in National and Cross-national Perspective* (The Hague: Kluwer Law International), pp. 157–78.

Hirst, P. and Thompson, G. (1996), *Globalization in Question* (Cambridge: Polity Press).

Hodges, M. and Woolcock, S. (1993), 'Atlantic Capitalism versus Rhine Capitalism in the European Community', *West European Politics*, 16(3): 329–44.

Hoem, B. (2000), 'Entry into Motherhood in Sweden: The Influence of Economic Factors on the Rise and Fall in Fertility, 1986–1997', *Demographic Research*, 2(4) (www.demographic-research.org/Volumes/Vol2/4).

Hoem, J. (1993), 'Public Policy as the Fuel of Fertility: Effects of a Policy Reform on the Pace of Childbearing in Sweden in the 1980s', *Acta Sociologica*, 36(1): 19–31.

Hood, C. and Wright, V. (eds.) (1981), *Big Government in Hard Times* (Oxford: Martin Robertson).

Huber, E. and Stephens, J. (2001), *Development and the Crisis of the Welfare State* (Chicago: University of Chicago Press).

—— Ragin, C., and Stephens, J. (1993), 'Social Democracy, Christian Democracy, Constitutional Structure and the Welfare State', *American Journal of Sociology*, 99(3): 711–49.

Hudson, P. and Lee, W. R. (1990), 'Introduction'. In P. Hudson and W. R. Lee (eds.), *Women's Work and the Family Economy in Historical Perspective* (Manchester: Manchester University Press), pp. 2–47.

IMF (various years), *Balance of Payments Statistics* (Washington, DC).

—— *Financial Statistics* (Washington, DC).

Iversen, T. (2001), 'The Dynamics of Welfare State Expansion: Trade Openness, De-industrialization, and Partisan Politics'. In P. Pierson (ed.), *The New Politics of the Welfare State* (Oxford: Oxford University Press), pp. 45–79.

—— and Cusack, T. (2000), 'The Causes of Welfare State Expansion: Deindustrialization or Globalization?', *World Politics*, 52(2): 313–49.

Jessop, R. (1996), 'Post-Fordism and the State'. In B. Greve (ed.), *Comparative Welfare Systems: The Scandinavian Model in a Period of Change* (New York: St Martin's Press), pp. 165–83.

Kamerman, S. and Kahn, A. (1981), *Child Care, Family Benefits and Working Parents* (New York: Columbia University Press).

Kangas, O. (1991), *The Politics of Social Rights* (Stockholm: Swedish Institute for Social Research).

Katzenstein, P. (1985), *Small States in World Markets* (Ithaca, NY: Cornell University Press).

Kautto, M., Fritzell, J., Hvinden, B., Kvist, J., and Uusitalo, H. (eds.) (2001), *Nordic Welfare States in the European Context* (London: Routledge).

Kelsey, J. (1993), *Rolling Back the State* (Wellington: Bridget Williams Books).

Kenworthy, L. (2003), 'Do Affluent Countries Face an Incomes—Jobs Tradeoff?', *Comparative Political Studies*, 36(10): 1180–209.

Keohane, R. O. and Milner, H. V. (eds.) (1996), *Internationalization and Domestic Politics* (Cambridge: Cambridge University Press).

Kittel, B. (1999), 'Sense and Sensitivity in the Pooled Analysis of Political Data', *European Journal of Political Research*, 35(2): 225–53.

Korpi, W. (1989), 'Power, Politics, and State Autonomy in the Development of Social Citizenship: Social Rights During Sickness in Eighteen OECD Countries Since 1930', *American Sociological Review*, 54(2): 309–28.

—— (2001), 'Contentious Institutions: An Augmented Rational-Action Analysis of the Origins and Path Dependency of Welfare State Institutions in Western Countries', *Rationality and Society*, 13(2): 235–83.

—— (2003), 'Welfare-State Regress in Western Europe: Politics, Institutions, Globalization, and Europeanization', *Annual Review of Sociology*, 29: 589–609.

—— and Palme, J. (2003), 'New Politics and Class Politics in the Context of Austerity and Globalization: Welfare State Regress in 18 Countries, 1975–95', *American Political Science Review*, 97(3): 425–46.

Kriesi, H. (1999), 'Note on the Size of the Public Sector in Switzerland', *Revue Suisse de Science Politique*, 5(2): 106–9.

Kuhnle, S. (ed.) (2000), *Survival of the European Welfare State* (London: Routledge).

Lane, J-E. (1999), 'The Public/Private Distinction in Switzerland', *Revue Suisse de Science Politique*, 5(2): 94–105.

Laurance, J. (2002), 'Why an Ageing Population is the Greatest Threat to Society', *Today*, International Youth Care Network (www.cyc-net.org/today/today020410.html).

Lesthaeghe, R. and Moors, G. (2000), 'Recent Trends in Fertility and Household Formation in the Industrialized World', *Review of Population and Social Policy*, 9: 1–49.

—— and Willems, P. (1999), 'Is Low Fertility a Temporary Phenomenon in the European Union?', *Population and Development Review*, 25(2): 211–28.

Liebfried, S. (1993), 'Towards a European Welfare State?' In C. Jones (ed.), *New Perspectives on the Welfare State in Europe* (London: Routledge).

—— (ed.) (2001), *Welfare State Futures* (Cambridge: Cambridge University Press).

—— and Pierson, P. (eds.) (1995), *European Social Policy: Between Fragmentation and Integration* (Washington, DC: Brookings Institution).

Lijphart, A. (1999), *Patterns of Democracy: Government Form and Performance in Thirty-Six Countries* (New Haven, CT: Yale University Press).

Lindberg, L. and Maier, C. (eds.) (1985), *The Politics of Inflation and Economic Stagnation: Theoretical Approaches and International Case Studies* (Washington, DC: Brookings Institution).

Lynch, J. (2002), *The Age of Welfare: Citizens, Clients, and Generations in the Development of the Welfare State*. Ph.D. Dissertation (Berkeley: University of California).

Manow, P. and Seils, E. (2000), 'Adjusting Badly: The German Welfare State, Structural Change, and the Open Economy'. In F. W. Scharpf and V. A. Schmidt (eds.), *Welfare and Work in the Open Economy, Vol. II: Diverse Responses to Common Challenges* (Oxford: Oxford University Press), pp. 264–306.

McDonald, P. (2000), 'Gender Equity, Social Institutions and the Future of Fertility', *Journal of Population Research*, 17(1): 1–16.

—— (2002), Low Fertility: Unifying the Theory and the Demography. Paper Presented to a Meeting of the Population Association of America, Atlanta, 9–11 May.

Miller, P. and Wilson, M. (1983), *A Dictionary of Social Science Methods* (New York: John Wiley and Sons).

Milner, H. and Keohane, R. (1996), 'Internationalization and Domestic Politics: An Introduction'. In R. Keohane and H. Milner (eds.), *Internationalization and Domestic Politics* (Cambridge: Cambridge University Press), pp. 3–24.

Mishra, R. (1990), *The Welfare State in Capitalist Society* (Toronto: University of Toronto Press).

—— (1999), *Globalization and the Welfare State* (Cheltenham: Edward Elgar).

Monnier, A. and de Guilbert-Lantoine, C. (1996), 'La conjoncture démographique: l'Europe et les pays développés d'outre-mer', *Population*, 16(4): 1005–30.

Moran, M. (1988), 'Crises of the Welfare State', *British Journal of Political Science*, 18(3): 397–414.

Myles, J. (2002), 'A New Social Contract for the Elderly?' In G. Esping-Andersen with D. Gallie, A. Hemerijck, and J. Myles (eds.), *Why We Need a New Welfare State* (Oxford: Oxford University Press).

Myles, J. and Quadagno, J. (1997), 'Recent Trends in Public Pension Reform: A Comparative View'. In K. Banting and R. Boardway (eds.), *Reform of Retirement Income Policy: International and Canadian Perspectives*. Queen's University, Kingston, ON: School of Policy Studies.

Obinger, H. and Wagschal, U. (2001), 'Families of Nations and Public Policy', *West European Politics*, 24(1): 99–111.

O'Connor, J. (1973), *The Fiscal Crisis of the State* (New York: St Martin's Press).

OECD (1981), *The Welfare State in Crisis*. Paris.

—— (1984), 'The Contribution of Services to Employment', *OECD Employment Outlook*. Paris, pp. 39–54.

—— (1985), *Social Expenditure 1960–1990. Problems of Growth and Control*. Paris.

—— (1993), *OECD Health Systems*, Vol. II. Paris.

—— (1994), 'New Orientations for Social Policy', *Social Policy Studies*, No. 12. Paris.

—— (1996a), *Ageing in OECD Countries: A Critical Policy Challenge*. Social Policy Studies, No. 20. Paris.

—— (1996b), *Social Expenditure Statistics of OECD Member Countries* (Provisional Version). Paris.

—— (1999), *A Caring World: The New Social Policy Agenda*. Paris.

—— (2001a), *Social Expenditure Database, 1980–1998*, CD-Rom. Paris.

—— (2001b), *Labour Force Statistics, 1980–2000*. Paris.

—— (2001c), 'Balancing Work and Family Life: Helping Parents into Paid Employment', *OECD Employment Outlook*. Paris, pp. 129–66.

—— (various years), *Economic Outlook*. Paris.

—— (various years), *Foreign Direct Investment in OECD Countries*. Paris.

—— (various years), *Historical Statistics*. Paris.

Offe, C. (1984), *Contradictions of the Welfare State* (London: Hutchinson).

Ohmae, K. (1991), *The Borderless World: Power and Strategy in the Interlinked Economy* (New York: Harper Perennial).

Orloff, A. (1993), 'Gender and the Social Rights of Citizenship: The Comparative Analysis of Gender Relations and Welfare States', *American Sociological Review*, 58(3): 303–28.

Overbye, E. (1994), 'Convergence in Policy Outcomes: Social Security Systems in Perspective', *Journal of Public Policy*, 14(2): 147–74.

Palier, B. (2000), ' "Defrosting" the French Welfare State', *West European Politics*, 23(2): 113–36.

—— (2001), 'Beyond Retrenchment: Four Problems in Current Welfare State Research and One Suggestion How to Overcome Them'. In J. Clasen (ed.), *What Future for Social Security? Debates and Reforms in National and Cross-national Perspective* (The Hague: Kluwer Law International), pp. 105–20.

Palme, J. (1990), *Pension Rights in Welfare Capitalism* (Stockholm: Swedish Institute for Social Research).

—— et al. (2000), *Welfare at Crossroads: Summary of Interim Balance Sheet for Welfare in the 1990s*. (Stockholm: SOU), p. 3.

Pampel, F. and Williamson, J. (1989), *Age, Class, Politics, and the Welfare State* (Cambridge: Cambridge University Press).

Pfaller, A., Gough, I. and Therborn, G. (eds.) (1991), *Can the Welfare State Compete?* (London: Macmillan).

Pierson, P. (1994), *Dismantling the Welfare State?* (Cambridge: Cambridge University Press).

—— (1996), 'The New Politics of Welfare State', *World Politics*, 48(2): 143–79.

—— (1998), 'Irresistible Forces, Immovable Objects: Post-industrial Welfare States Confront Permanent Austerity', *Journal of European Public Policy*, 5(4): 539–60.

—— (2000), 'Increasing Returns, Path Dependence and the Study of Politics', *American Political Science Review*, 94(2). 251–67.

—— (ed.) (2001), *The New Politics of the Welfare State* (Oxford: Oxford University Press).

Pinder, J. (1968), 'Positive Integration and Negative Integration: Some Problems of Economic Union in the EEC', *The World Today*, 24(3): 88–110.

Powell, M. and Barrientos, A. (2004), 'Welfare Regimes and the Welfare Mix', *European Journal of Political Research*, 43(1): 83–105.

Przeworski, A. (1987), 'Methods of Cross-National Research, 1970–83: An Overview'. In M. Dierkes, H. Weiler, and A. Antal (eds.), *Comparative Policy Research* (Aldershot: Gower).

Rhodes, M. (1998), ' "Subversive Liberalism": Market Integration, Globalisation, and European Welfare States'. In W. Coleman, and G. Underhill (eds.), *Regionalism and Global Economic Integration: Europe, Asia and the Americas* (London: Routledge).

Rieger, E. and Leibfried, S. (2003), *Limits to Globalization: Welfare States and the World Economy* (Cambridge: Cambridge University Press).

Rimlinger, G. V. (1971), *Welfare Policy and Industrialization in Europe, America and Russia* (New York: John Wiley and Sons).

Rodrik, D. (1997), *Has Globalisation Gone Too Far?* (Washington, DC: Institute for International Economics).

Roseveare, D., Leibfritz, W., Fore, D., and Wurzel, E. (1996), *Ageing Populations, Pension Systems and Government Budgets: Simulations for 20 OECD Countries*. Economics Department Working Papers No. 168, Paris.

Ross, Fiona. (2000), ' "Beyond Left and Right": The New *Partisan* Politics of Welfare', *Governance* 13(2): 155–83.

Ruggie, J. (1982), 'International Regimes, Transactions and Change: Embedded Liberalism in the Postwar Economic Order', *International Organization*, 36(2): 379–415.

Sardon, J-P. (2002), 'Recent Demographic Trends in the Developed Countries', *Population* (English Edition), 57(1): 111–56.

Scharpf Y. Mény (1998), 'Positive and Negative Integration in the Political Economy of European Welfare States'. In M. Rhodes, and E. Mény (eds.), *The Future of European Welfare: A New Social Contract?* (London: Macmillan).

Scharpf, F. (2000), 'Economic Changes, Vulnerabilities, and Institutional Capabilities'. In F. Scharpf and V. Schmidt (eds.), *Welfare and Work in the Open Economy, Vol. I: From Vulnerability to Competitiveness* (Oxford: Oxford University Press), pp. 21–124.

Scharpf, F. W. and Schmidt, V. A. (eds.) (2000a), *Welfare and Work in the Open Economy, Vol. I: From Vulnerability to Competitiveness* (Oxford: Oxford University Press).

—— (eds.) (2000b), *Welfare and Work in the Open Economy, Vol. II: Diverse Responses to Common Challenges* (Oxford: Oxford University Press).

Schmidt, M. G. (1996), 'When Parties Matter: A Review of the Possibilities and Limits of Partisan Influence on Public Policy', *European Journal of Political Research*, 30(2): 155–83.

Schulz, J. (2002), 'The Evolving Concept of "Retirement": Looking Forward to the Year 2050', *International Social Security Review*, 55(1): 85–105.

Sen, A. (2001), 'Gender Equity and the Population Problem', *International Journal of Health Services*, 31(3): 469–74.

Shirer, P. (1996), 'The Myth of the Demographic Imperative'. In C. Steuerle and M. Kawai (eds.), *The New Fiscal World Order: Implications for Industrialized Nations* (Washington, DC: Urban Institute Press), pp. 61–84.

Siaroff, A. (1999), 'Corporatism in 24 Industrial Democracies: Meaning and Measurement', *European Journal of Political Research*, 36(2): 175–205.

Smeeding, T. (2002), 'Globalization, Inequality and the Rich Countries of the G-20: Evidence from the Luxembourg Income Study (LIS)', *Luxembourg Income Study Working Paper* No. 320, Luxembourg.

Sorrentino, C. (1990), 'The Changing Family in International Perspective', *Monthly Labor Review*, 113(3): 41–58.

Stephens, J. (1979), *The Transition From Capitalism to Socialism* (London: Macmillan).

Stephens, R. (1999), 'Economics and Social Policy'. In D. Milne and J. Savage (eds.), *Reporting Economics* (Wellington: Journalists Training Organisation), pp. 189–204.

Stimson, J. (1985), 'Regression in Space and Time: A Statistical Essay', *American Journal of Political Science*, 29(4): 914–47.

Strange, S. (1996), *The Retreat of the State: The Diffusion of Power in the World Economy* (Cambridge: Cambridge University Press).

Summers, R. and Heston, A. (1991), 'The Penn World Table (Mark 5)', *Quarterly Journal of Economics*, 106(2): 327–68.

Swank, D. (2001), 'Political Institutions and Welfare State Restructuring: The Impact of Institutions on Social Policy Change in Developed Democracies'. In P. Pierson (ed.), *The New Politics of the Welfare State* (Oxford: Oxford University Press).

—— (2002), *Global Capital, Political Institutions, and Policy Change in Developed Welfare States* (Cambridge: Cambridge University Press).

Teeple, G. (1995), *Globalisation and the Decline of Social Reform* (Toronto: Garamond).

Therborn, G. (1983), 'When, How and Why Does a Welfare State Become a Welfare State?' *ECPR Workshops*, Freiburg (March).

—— (1995), *European Modernity and Beyond: The Trajectory of European Societies, 1945–2000* (London: Sage Publications).

Thomson, D. (1994), *Selfish Generations? The Ageing of New Zealand's Welfare State* (Wellington: Bridget Williams Books).

Titmuss, R. M. (1974), *Social Policy: An Introduction* (London: George Allen and Unwin).

Tsebelis, G. (1995), 'Decision Making in Political Systems: Veto Players in Presidentialism, Parliamentarianism, Multicameralism and Multipartism', *British Journal of Political Science*, 25(3): 289–325.

—— (1999), 'Veto Players and Law Production in Parliamentary Democracies: An Empirical Analysis', *American Political Science Review*, 93(3): 591–608.

Tsoukalis, L. and Rhodes, M. (1997), 'Economic Integration and the Nation State'. In M. Rhodes, P. Heywood, and V. Wright (eds.), *Developments in Western European Politics* (London: Macmillan), pp. 19–36.

UNESCO (various years), *Unesco Statistical Yearbook*. Paris.

United Nations (1998), *World Population Prospects: The 1998 Revision* (New York: UN Population Division) [Available electronically].

—— (1999), *Classification of Expenditures According to Purpose*. Statistical Papers, Series M, No. 84, New York.

—— (2001), *Replacement Migration: Is it a Solution to Declining and Ageing Populations* (ST/ESA/SER.A/206). (New York: Department of Social and Economic Affairs, Population Division).

Van de Kaa, D. J. (1996), 'Anchored Narratives: The Story and Findings of Half a Century Research into the Determinants of Fertility', *Population Studies*, 50(3): 389–432.

Van Kersbergen, K. (1995), *Social Capitalism: A Study of Christian Democracy and the Welfare State* (London: Routledge).

Visser, J. and Hemerijck, A. (1997), *'A Dutch Miracle'* (Amsterdam: Amsterdam University Press).

Von Rhein-Kress, G. (1993), 'Coping with Economic Crisis: Labour Supply as a Policy Instrument'. In F. Castles (ed.), *Families of Nations: Patterns of Public Policy in Western Democracies* (Aldershot: Dartmouth), pp. 131–78.

Walker, A. (ed.) (1996), *The New Generational Conflict* (London: UCL Press).

Webb, M. (1995), *The Political Economy of Policy Coordination: Economic Adjustment Since 1945* (Ithaca, NY: Cornell University Press).

Whiteford, P. (1995), 'The Use of Replacement Rates in International Comparisons of Benefit Systems', *International Social Security Review*, 48(2): 3–30.

Wilensky, H. L. (1975), *The Welfare State and Equality* (Berkeley: University of California Press).

—— and Lebeaux, C. N. (1958), *Industrial Society and Social Welfare* (New York: Russell Sage Foundation).

World Bank (1994), *Averting the Old Age Crisis* (New York: Oxford University Press).

World Christian Encyclopedia (1982), 1st edn. (Nairobi: Oxford University Press).

—— (2001), 2nd edn. (New York: Oxford University Press).

World Health Organisation (1993), *World Health Statistics Annual* (Geneva).

Index

Note: t indicates a table